Simple Spreadsheets
for
Hard Decisions

Carol Jacoby

City Shore Press

Simple Spreadsheets for Hard Decisions
Published by
City Shore Press
3646 Long Beach Blvd., Suite 222
Long Beach, California 90807 USA

Microsoft is a registered trademark of Microsoft Corporation in the United States and/or other countries. Macintosh is a registered trademark of Apple Inc. Other product or company names mentioned herein may be the trademarks of their respective owners.

The example businesses, organizations, products, people, and events depicted herein are fictitious. No association with any real business, organization, product, person, or event is intended or should be inferred.

All items are provided "as is". The author and publisher make no representations or warranties, express or implied, for the applicability of the methods or examples contained herein. In no event shall the author or publisher be liable for any claim, damages or liability arising from, out of or in connection with the practice of any of the methods or use of any of the spreadsheets contained herein or in a related website. The author is not, and makes no claims to be, a professional financial advisor. Before making any major decisions, please consult with the appropriate professional.

ISBN-13: 978-0-9800958-0-7
ISBN-10:   0-9800958-0-8

To Jerry and Kristen

Acknowledgments

Many people helped to make this book a reality. Thanks especially to Kathey Schuster of WorldWideWords for the excellent editing of the book through multiple revisions. The book is much tighter and clearer than it ever would have been without her expertise. (Any errors you might find were subsequently introduced by the author.) Thanks to her as well for writing the back cover description, which, I think, gets to the heart of what I set out to do.

Brian Bottorff, Dean Davis, Matt Hanson, Larry Klein, Jim Lewis, Judy Lewis, and Tawny Nicolayson reviewed the book and gave me insightful and excellent suggestions that made the book much clearer and more useful. Tom McKendree and Bill Sutherland pointed me to excellent resource materials. Their recommended books are listed in Appendix E. Steve Schuster, Nancy Rantowich, Rob Jaffe, Kristen Jacoby, and Jerry Jacoby suggested spreadsheets based on their own decisions that inspired some of the examples in this book. Thanks, too, to my students in systems engineering and decision making for asking good questions and suggesting decisions.

I also want to thank all of the members of the lunch bunch (you know who you are) for their continuing support and encouragement, even Sandy, who thinks Excel isn't good for anything. I hope this book changes her mind.

I especially want to thank my family, Jerry Jacoby and Kristen Jacoby, for putting up with my disappearing for hours on end while writing this book. I particularly want to thank Jerry for encouraging me in what turned out to be a lengthy endeavor, and, especially, for telling me when to stop.

Contents

Introduction

You have decisions to make—decisions at home and decisions at work. Usually, the right choice depends on what might happen. This means that good decision-making benefits from visualizing outcomes in various situations.

Chances are that you already have a powerful tool for making decisions on your computer: Excel, part of the popular Microsoft Office package. *Simple Spreadsheets for Hard Decisions* teaches you how to harness this power to understand, explore, and decide. You can use its techniques without any prior experience with Excel, programming, statistics, or financial analysis.

I started using spreadsheet programs more than 25 years ago, back even before Excel appeared on the scene. I found Excel and its predecessors to be wonderful tools for making all sorts of decisions because: 1) all assumptions and results are visible, 2) the spreadsheets are easy to change, helping you explore alternatives or understand key issues, and 3) they easily expand to answer further questions. Visible intermediate calculations clarify what's going on and what's driving the outcome. Spreadsheets help you explore the problem, even before fully understanding it. They let you look at alternative outcomes and at the effect of one aspect of the decision on others. I soon started using Excel for my own personal and business decisions, many of which inspired the examples in this book.

Decisions from real life

The typical Excel book focuses on data analysis, the science of organizing and making sense out of large quantities of data. But, usually, the decisions most of us need to make have *small* amounts of data to support them. For example, a reader who is 30 years old and wants to retire at 55 might ask, "How much money should I save each year?" There are only two numbers here! You need something other than data analysis to make this decision. *Simple Spreadsheets for Hard Decisions* teaches both *how* and *why* to use Excel. Examples of decisions we all must make are the foundation for presenting powerful yet simple Excel techniques. You will use the techniques to develop spreadsheets that lead to decisions on increasingly complex sample life challenges in the many case studies. Screen shots accompany the examples to show each step, so you can work along with the book. In addition, you get all of the completed examples, which you may examine, apply, and modify for your own use. In this way, you will learn more than the mechanics of Excel—you will learn how to apply it to real problems.

Some decisions the book covers include:

> *Should I buy a house or rent?*
> *How much money can I spend?*
> *Which car should I buy?*
> *How much do I need to save to send my child to college?*
> *Which health insurance should I buy?*
> *Can I afford to retire?*
> *Should I change jobs?*
> *Can I handle the risks of aggressive investments?*

Even if you have questions other than these, working through the examples will empower you with decision and Excel techniques that you can immediately apply.

Consider the decisions you face. You probably need to make long-range financial decisions for your family. These decisions have become increasingly complex as businesses cut benefits and shift much of the responsibility for retirement and healthcare to the employee. There has been a gradual move away from company-sponsored pensions to self-managed 401(k) plans. There are expanded employee health care options, but generally these impose more limitations and employee cost. Trade-offs are complex and choices can have long-range impact. You need a way to understand and evaluate options (without taking courses in statistics or programming!).

You probably face yet another set of decisions at work. But, since these are usually industry-specific, they are beyond the scope of a single book. This book presents familiar personal decisions as a framework for understanding Excel and decision techniques you can use to customize spreadsheets for your individual business questions. Rather than wait for simulation or analysis staff to give you answers, you can use a spreadsheet to focus on key issues, uncover new avenues of investigation, demonstrate possible outcomes, and optimize results.

How to use this book

This book assumes only a basic knowledge of standard computer techniques, such as selecting from menus, using scrollbars, and saving files. If you've ever used any other program in the Microsoft Office suite, that's all you need. It's OK if you've never used Excel before. All of the techniques you'll need are explained in Appendix A for Excel 2007 and earlier, both Windows and Macintosh. If you want more details, go to Excel Help or any Excel book. This book focuses on those features and functions that best support decision-making, and discusses others that you can investigate if you wish.

You will alternate between learning techniques and applying these to real-world-decision case studies. Though the book builds on decision and Excel techniques learned in previous chapters, you may start with any case study that interests you. Once you have the basics of entering data and formulas, you can use Appendix A to acquire further techniques. The Toolkit list at the beginning of each case study tells you what you'll need.

Excel is not a spectator sport! You need to work along with the book and build your own spreadsheets. On the screen and in the illustrations are merely calculated numbers. To really understand what is going on, you must click on the cells to see the formulas behind the whole thing, which are doing all the work.

Even better, build your own spreadsheets. Surprisingly, formulas are easier to enter than to read. Start with a blank or partially completed spreadsheet and enter the data and formulas presented. Check your numbers with those in the corresponding illustration. For help, check the formulas in the completed example spreadsheets. Building formulas is no harder than examining the spreadsheets, and you'll be surprised how much more you learn by actually doing it.

Each case study starts with a question. Try building a spreadsheet to answer it before reading further. You'll have all the Excel tools you need as you progress. You can download all of the example spreadsheets from:

www.decisionspreadsheets.com/simplespreadsheets.html.

You may find that, as in real life, you initially lack some of the information you need to make the case study decision. The chapter will fill in those holes and show you a possible solution.

Special notation will help you distinguish formulas, FUNCTIONS, **commands**, **Excel files**, and *Excel techniques* described in Appendix A. See Appendix B for a complete description of this and other notation.

Simple spreadsheets

You will learn how to write a few simple formulas and grow them into a complete spreadsheet that you can use to analyze complex decisions. For long-term planning, watch how the future might play out. Change conditions (such as the rate of inflation or investment growth) and see what happens. Often you will get unexpected results that lead to new insights. You can do all of this with surprisingly simple formulas, yet achieve complex and insightful results. Excel has built-in functions to handle the *heavy* lifting. So, let's get started!

1

Hard decisions
Deciding with help from Excel

Excel is a great help in making decisions, especially if you use it interactively. Decision involves uncertainties. The power of Excel becomes apparent when you change assumptions about these uncertainties and see what happens: *What if my investments fail? What if I get too many orders? What if I get too few? What if inflation increases?*

You need more than a printout to answer questions like these. Besides, it's a lot easier to scroll and sort through a spreadsheet on the computer than a big stack of paper. Gather everyone around the computer. Try changing things. Look at the formulas to see what the spreadsheet is doing. Better yet, build your own spreadsheets. You'll find that formulas are easier to enter than to read.

You've probably used a calculator to help you make decisions. You may have found yourself asking, "Now, how did I get this answer?" The calculator can give you the answer, but it forgets how it arrived at this answer. Do the same calculations in Excel and the path to your answer is all there—to examine, modify, expand, or reuse.

Just forget that calculator and keep Excel open on your computer to explore everyday decisions. Many a useful spreadsheet started life as a quickie calculation to check options or possible outcomes.

What makes a decision hard?

Decisions should be easy; just look at the alternatives and choose the one that gives you the best outcome. What's so hard about that? Well, two things: first, outcomes usually depend on what happens in the future (Do we have a crystal ball?) and, second, there is usually more than one criterion that makes something "best." You generally have to trade off, say, price for features, aesthetics for practicality, or performance for risk.

The case studies give you examples of how to handle real-world decisions. Learn how to play "what-if" with the future (Case Studies 5, 6, and 11 through 18), how to balance many criteria (Case Studies 2, 8, 9 and 10), and how to assess risk (Case Study 19).

Defining the decision

What is it you want to decide? Without a destination, any road will do. Answers are easy. They are everywhere. The hard part is asking the right question, and then selecting the right answer from the choices. If you wish, use the questionnaire at the end of this chapter (questionnaire.doc) to help you think about your decision. See Appendix C for examples of this questionnaire filled out for some of the case studies in this book.

What are you trying to decide?

Start by writing a question you are trying to answer. Here are some examples that this book explores:

> *Should I buy a house or rent?*
> *Which car should I buy?*
> *How much do I need to save to send my child to college?*
> *Which health insurance should I buy?*
> *Can I afford to retire?*
> *Should I change jobs?*
> *Can I handle the risks of aggressive investments?*

Selection. Some of these, such as buying vs. renting or choosing a car, are selection decisions. You may have several alternatives or only two (Buy or rent? Change my job or stay?).

Use this book's techniques for making the decision. For example—especially if you have only two choices—list pros and cons (as in Case Study 2). If you find that some of the pros and cons are more important than others, Chapter 10 offers techniques for balancing preferences, followed by examples in Case Studies 8, 9, and 10.

Quantity. Some decisions ask for a quantity and start "How much...?" Usually the issue is money, but it may be another (*How much inventory do I need to keep? How many people should I hire?*) The idea here is to determine the quantity that meets your goal. The tricky part is predicting what will happen between now and then. Excel is good for doing these calculations as well as for building models of how things will or could play out.

Possibility. Similar models answer questions that ask "Can I...?" They help you visualize what could happen. These questions often evolve into "How much...?" questions. For example,

> *Can I afford to retire now? If not, **how much** longer must I work before I can?*

> *Can I handle the risks of aggressive investments at the level planned? If not, **how much** should I put into these investments?*

How will you measure success?

Ask yourself a few more questions to clarify your goal.

If I reach my goal, what will it look like?
Identify your measures of success. Often this is money but, even then, there are various ways to ask the question. For example, in a buy or rent decision, you might want to minimize:

- Average monthly cost over five years
- Total expenditures over five years
- Present value of total expenditures over five years
- Present value of total expenditures over twenty years

As you'll see, each of these may lead you to a different choice.

What am I trying to accomplish?
For example, if the question is how to invest during retirement, the following two goals lead you to very different investment strategies:

- Minimize the chance that I will outlive my money.
- Maximize the amount of money I leave my heirs.

Remember the subjective factors! It's easy to get caught up in the calculations and forget the important things that are hard to quantify. Go ahead and compute the expected long-term pay differences in the two jobs, but then ask yourself about the subjective considerations relative to the financial. For example, you might ask, "Is the increased job satisfaction worth giving up the pay difference?"

Usually there are multiple success criteria. You want a job close to home, with great facilities, interesting assignments, and high pay. Identify everything that's important to you and the relative importance of each. Though we want it all, we must make tradeoffs.

What are the alternatives?

Spend some time brainstorming and researching the alternatives. An analysis of several choices, no matter how thorough, is worthless if it leaves out the best option. In making any decision, always consider the alternative of leaving everything the way it is. See whether you can convince yourself that a change is better than what you are doing now.

You can eliminate some alternatives early on. For a complex decision, you may want to keep track of all of the alternatives you considered and why you rejected the ones you did.

What do you know?

Think about all of the factors that influence the outcome. Some are known and fixed. Some are under your control and others are outside of it. For example, suppose you are investing money for a future goal. You know for certain how much money you have to invest now and the amount you add to the investment in future years is under your control. Both certainties and uncertainties are inputs to your spreadsheet.

You may find that you need to do research to fill in inputs you need. Examples are your total assets, tax tables, or historical inflation rates. Make a note of these and then start digging.

You also know what your goal is, but you may change it, if your analysis tells you it will be too difficult. Vary the factors you can control and see whether you meet your goal, or determine which approach works the best. Your spreadsheet's output tells whether you meet your goal under various conditions. Later, discover even how to find the input that gets you to your goal.

What don't you know?

One of the reasons that decisions are hard is that the outcome depends on unknowns. *What will inflation be? What will the stock market do? How long will I live? How much medical care will I need? How long will I stay at the new job? How big will my future raises be?* Include these unknowns in your spreadsheet if they affect the outcome. Play "what-if" with them to visualize outcomes. Vary factors that are outside of your control and see what happens. What happens in a typical case? Can you handle the worst case? Do sensitivity analysis (see Case Study 16 or 18) to find out how much these factors matter. Do a Monte Carlo analysis (see Chapter 14) to see how likely various outcomes are.

Building a model

A model is a simplified representation. A map is a model of a city. A blueprint is a model of a building. A spreadsheet, which you can create, is a model of possible outcomes of your decision. It is easier to work with a model than with the real thing. It helps you visualize the future. As you'll learn, you can make decisions by quickly building useful models of what will or might happen, using only a few simple formulas.

Take your time. Start by focusing on the most essential question. Sometimes, this is all you need, but often the results raise other questions. Then, gather more data and expand the model. Some of the book's complex case studies (for example, Case Studies 11, 12, and 13) evolve in this way.

Using formulas

Formulas give Excel its power. Formulas can use common arithmetical operations, like addition or division, and anything from Excel's library of functions. The magic happens when you change any of the data. The formulas automatically and immediately recalculate everything. This is great for "what-if" analysis. This feature—being able to change any input and immediately see the output—inspired the name of the first computerized spreadsheet, VisiCalc, short for visible calculator.

Exploring the model

The model won't give you the answer. The answer comes from exploring the model, trying variations, and thinking about what you learn. Explore the model, as follows:

Make your best guess for unknowns and then look at the results.

Check that the results make sense and that your spreadsheet is working properly.

Examine the results.

> *Will I meet my goal?*
> *Which alternative looks better?*

Play "what-if" with the inputs. Change some of the things you control.

> *What if I saved more money each month?*
> *What if I chose a less expensive house?*

Change some of the unknowns.

> *What if inflation was higher?*
> *What if I had major medical expenses?*

These explorations often lead to other questions. For example, you may find that the result is very sensitive to the rate of inflation and you'll want to learn more about historical and predicted inflation rates. You may find that you want to expand the model to examine other questions. For example, you might ask whether increasing your savings rate a little each year achieves your goal. You'd need to add to the model to answer this. There's an example of this in Case Study 17.

On the next page is a questionnaire to help you think about your decision. You will find a copy of it in Word format at:

www.decisionspreadsheets.com/simplespreadsheets.html

where it is called questionnaire.doc. This website is where you go to get all the example spreadsheets used in this book.

Check Appendix C for examples of the completed questionnaire.

What are you trying to decide? Write a question you are trying to answer.

How will you measure success? List all of the criteria as quantitatively as possible, but remember the subjective considerations as well.

What are the alternatives? This might be a list of options or a quantity.

What do you know? List only items that affect your measure of success.

What don't you know, but can learn? You'll need to do some research.

What don't you know, but can control? Vary to see how they change success.

What don't you know and can't control? Vary to see how well you can adapt.

2

Simple spreadsheets
All you need to know about Excel

This chapter introduces Excel. If you've been using Excel for a while, you may skip ahead and start making decisions right away. (You can always return to this chapter or check *Appendix A - Excel Techniques* for a reminder.)

A first look at the Excel workbook

First some terminology. An Excel file is called a *workbook*. It consists of multiple *worksheets*, though most of the time you only need to use one. You enter text, data, and formulas into the blank worksheet to turn it into a *spreadsheet*, a worksheet that does something useful. The major spreadsheets that you create become *decision models*—models (simplified representations) of what will or might happen, used to make a decision.

You can build fairly sophisticated and interesting decision models using just a few basic Excel techniques. All of these techniques work for all Excel versions (except maybe some really ancient ones). There are slight differences between Windows and Macintosh versions, mostly in the keyboard. In those cases, the Macintosh steps are in [brackets]. Excel 2007 has a new interface. These instructions are in {braces}.

What goes in the cells?

Excel presents rows and columns of rectangular cells. The cells are where you enter your information, one cell at a time. You can fill cells in whatever order you wish. There are three basic types of information you can put in a cell: text, data, or formulas.

Text

Some very useful Excel spreadsheets contain only text. Examples are a list of your music CDs, a packing list for a trip, and an address list. The nice thing about using Excel for these types of lists is that Excel can ***sort them or filter them*** (see Appendix A). Even if you are building a numerical spreadsheet, you use text to label the rows and columns. You can put text comments in any empty cell in your spreadsheet. You can even use text in calculations. For example, one of your columns might ask a question and a related cell could give one result if the answer is "yes" or another if the answer is "no."

Data

Spreadsheets, before the age of computers, were large books of grid paper, full of numbers, used by bookkeepers or accountants. These were the models for Excel and other computerized spreadsheets. So, people use Excel spreadsheets mostly to keep track of numerical data. The data can be dates, times, currency, general numbers, or even text. Excel gives you general and specialized tools for working with data (for example, adding a column of numbers or computing the number of days between two dates).

Formulas

The power of Excel is in being able to perform calculations with your data. You can base a formula on the contents of cells anywhere in the spreadsheet, including other formulas. Formulas can use common arithmetical operations like addition or division. Furthermore, Excel includes a library of functions to use in the formulas. These include everything from simple calculations like the average of a column or the maximum of two numbers, to conditional formulas that give answers based on conditions, to complex calculations like mortgage payments or statistical analysis. The magic happens when you change any of the data. The formulas automatically and immediately recalculate everything. This is great for "what-if" analysis.

Fundamental Excel features

Excel has a lot of powerful features, but you can develop some very useful decision models using just a few of them. Appendix A tells you all you need. When later chapters and case studies use these techniques, they appear in ***bold italic***. If you're using a pre-2007 Excel version, be sure the Standard and Formatting Toolbars and the Formula Bar are visible. Bring them up using **View** and **View > Toolbars**, if you need to.

If you're new to Excel...

The basic techniques listed below are all you need to know to get started. Take time to explore and try each one. If you want to learn more, you can use the built-in Excel Help. Open it using the **Help** menu. There is a lot of good reference material in Excel Help. However, it can be difficult to find what you want. You can try the Search, Contents, or, possibly, Index.

You might also want to get one of the many books available on using Excel. Be sure to select one that is written for your version of Excel and that has an extensive discussion of formulas and functions. Before buying, look up some of these techniques to see whether the explanations are clear. Better yet, save your money and check the Web. For example, as of the writing of this book, www.ozgrid.com/Excel/ has a free tutorial.

If you've been using Excel for a while...

Glance through the list below. Review any that are unfamiliar. You can always come back to Appendix A to remind yourself how to do something. If you're familiar with Excel formulas and naming cells, you can skip Chapter 3 and Case Study 3.

Basic techniques

Be sure you know how to perform these basic Excel techniques:

- Open a worksheet
- Work with cells
    - Reference cells
    - Select cells
    - Enter information in cells
    - Edit the contents of cells
    - Clear an area of the spreadsheet
    - Undo

- AutoSum to add a column of numbers
- Format
  - Format cells (bold and italic, increase or decrease decimal, currency and percent, special formats for numbers)
  - Copy formats
  - Change column width
  - Wrap text within a cell
  - Hide rows or columns
  - Split the worksheet
- Rearrange the worksheet
  - Insert rows, columns, or cells
  - Copy a cell or a block of cells

Learning from case studies

The case studies give examples of using Excel to make decisions, and, at the same time, give you practice in using what you've learned. Start by opening a new blank worksheet or one of the examples that's partially filled out. Try to complete the worksheet yourself, and then check it against the examples. When you're finished, close the worksheet, but don't save your changes or you'll mess up the example. If you want to save what you've done, for example, you've entered your own checkbook or savings goals, save it under a different name.

Get your free example spreadsheets at:

www.decisionspreadsheets.com/simplespreadsheets.html

How much do I need to save for college?

Preview of coming spreadsheets

FOCUS: Seeing a finished spreadsheet, learning how it grew from defining the decision and how it is used to support the decision

TOOLKIT: Opening a workbook, entering data (both in Appendix A), decision steps (Chapter 1)

Here's an example you'll see later. It looks into the future to see whether a goal will be met.

? Brian and Jaci have a new baby, Zachary. They have already saved $10,000 toward Zachary's college education. The college they would like him to attend currently costs $140,000 for four years, including room and board. They are planning to put aside $15,000 a year in his college fund, which is expected to earn 8% per year. They expect college costs to go up at a rate of 9% per year. Will they have enough money saved for four years of college by the time he turns 18?

You'll build a spreadsheet for the decision in Case Study 17. Right now, take a sneak peek at it. *Open* the file, **college1.xls**, which you can download from:

> www.decisionspreadsheets.com/simplespreadsheets.html.

Start by thinking about the decision, following the steps described in Chapter 1.

<u>What are you trying to decide?</u> Here's the basic question: *Is $15,000 a year enough to get to the goal?* Implicit in this are possible follow-

up questions. *If not, how much is enough? Are there other strategies to reach the goal, such as more aggressive investments, increasing annual savings each year, or choosing a less expensive college?*

How will you measure success? Compare the expected future cost of college with the predicted amount saved. If the difference is 0 by the time he reaches 18, that's success!

What are the alternatives? The key choice is the amount put into college savings each year, but there are alternatives, such as investment strategies, college choices, or expecting Zachary to pay for college himself.

What do you know? The one quantity that is known and fixed is the initial $10,000 in savings. The inputs under your control are the amount added to the account each year and, to a lesser extent, the goal. All of these are inputs to the spreadsheet.

What don't you know? Investment growth and growth rate of college costs are unknown and outside your control, so it's beneficial to see the effect of various values. So, these are also inputs.

Now take a look at the spreadsheet. All of the inputs are in the first five rows, with names and text descriptions. Below them is a table that predicts progress toward the goal, year by year. Excel calculates all of this for each future year: Zachary's **Age**, the **Amount** in college savings, the **Cost of college**, and the **Shortfall** between the cost of college and the amount saved so far. Click on just about any of these cells and you'll see formulas appear in the formula bar.

All you really care about is the last row, when Zachary is old enough for college. The other rows just help you get there. You'll find that it's often easier to build up to an answer like this than to calculate it directly. You might notice that, except for the first, the formulas in any one column look similar. Later you'll learn how to build a column like this out of one simple "bucket brigade" formula.

	A	B	C	D	E
1	Start	$10,000	Initial amount in the savings fund		
2	Add	$15,000	Amount added to the fund at the beginning of each		
3	Inv growth	8%	Annual growth rate of the fund's investments		
4	Cost growth	9%	Annual increase in the cost of college		
5	Current goal	$ 140,000	Cost of 4 years of college		
6					
7	Age	Amount	Cost of college	Shortfall	
8	0	$ 10,000	$ 140,000	$ 130,000	
9	1	$ 25,800	$ 152,600	$ 126,800	
10	2	$ 42,864	$ 166,334	$ 123,470	
11	3	$ 61,293	$ 181,304	$ 120,011	
12	4	$ 81,197	$ 197,621	$ 116,425	
13	5	$ 102,692	$ 215,407	$ 112,715	
14	6	$ 125,908	$ 234,794	$ 108,886	
15	7	$ 150,980	$ 255,925	$ 104,945	
16	8	$ 178,059	$ 278,959	$ 100,900	
17	9	$ 207,303	$ 304,065	$ 96,762	
18	10	$ 238,888	$ 331,431	$ 92,543	
19	11	$ 272,999	$ 361,260	$ 88,261	
20	12	$ 309,839	$ 393,773	$ 83,934	
21	13	$ 349,626	$ 429,213	$ 79,587	
22	14	$ 392,596	$ 467,842	$ 75,246	
23	15	$ 439,003	$ 509,948	$ 70,944	
24	16	$ 489,124	$ 555,843	$ 66,719	
25	17	$ 543,254	$ 605,869	$ 62,615	
26	18	$ 601,714	$ 660,397	$ 58,683	

So there's your answer in the last row (cell D26). When Zachary is 18 there's a shortfall of $58,683. The savings will be insufficient. But, this is only the beginning of good decision-making.

TRY IT! What could this couple do to meet their goal? What if they invested $20,000 a year? Try it. **Enter** 20000 in cell B2.

Immediately the whole spreadsheet recalculates. The shortfall at 18 is now negative (as indicated by parentheses, or possibly red numbers). $20,000 will overshoot the goal. In fact, they'll reach the goal by the time he is only 12.

	A	B	C	D	E
1	Start	$10,000	Initial amount in the savings fund		
2	Add	$20,000	Amount added to the fund at the beginning of eac		
3	Inv growth	8%	Annual growth rate of the fund's investments		
4	Cost growth	9%	Annual increase in the cost of college		
5	Current goal	$ 140,000	Cost of 4 years of college		
6					
7	Age	Amount	Cost of college	Shortfall	
8	0	$ 10,000	$ 140,000	$ 130,000	
9	1	$ 30,800	$ 152,600	$ 121,800	
10	2	$ 53,264	$ 166,334	$ 113,070	
11	3	$ 77,525	$ 181,304	$ 103,779	
12	4	$ 103,727	$ 197,621	$ 93,894	
13	5	$ 132,025	$ 215,407	$ 83,382	
14	6	$ 162,587	$ 234,794	$ 72,207	
15	7	$ 195,594	$ 255,925	$ 60,331	
16	8	$ 231,242	$ 278,959	$ 47,717	
17	9	$ 269,741	$ 304,065	$ 34,324	
18	10	$ 311,320	$ 331,431	$ 20,110	
19	11	$ 356,226	$ 361,260	$ 5,034	
20	12	$ 404,724	$ 393,773	$ (10,951)	
21	13	$ 457,102	$ 429,213	$ (27,890)	
22	14	$ 513,670	$ 467,842	$ (45,829)	
23	15	$ 574,764	$ 509,948	$ (64,816)	
24	16	$ 640,745	$ 555,843	$ (84,902)	
25	17	$ 712,005	$ 605,869	$ (106,136)	
26	18	$ 788,965	$ 660,397	$ (128,568)	

TRY IT! Try other alternatives. What if you could get 9% on your money? What if you chose a less expensive college, at $120,000? Click on any input cells, change the value, and see what happens.

Case Study 17 first builds this spreadsheet and then expands it to look at a strategy for increasing savings each year.

Should I change jobs?
Pros and cons

FOCUS: Making a decision by weighing pros and cons, using basic Excel techniques

TOOLKIT: Change column widths, bold formatting, wrap text, AutoSum (all in Appendix A)

Sometimes, simple lists are all you need to make a decision. Whenever I talk to people about how they make personal decisions, there is one technique that is mentioned more than any other: make two columns and list the plusses and minuses of the choice being considered. The columns can be labeled "pros" and "cons," "positives" and "negatives," or "why" and "why not." This is a good way to start on any decision. It helps organize your thoughts and draw out issues. It can be done quickly on a piece of paper. Often, that's all you need. Sometimes, though, there are too many items on each side to tell which is best. Put the lists in Excel and rate them.

? Jenna has been working at a small company near her home for several years. She has just been offered a job with a large company downtown for more pay. Should she take it?

Listing pros and cons

Jenna thinks about the two jobs. The current job is familiar and close to home. She has been treated well there and made many friends, but she has advanced about as far as she can and is starting to get bored. The new job comes with a raise, a promotion, and potential for career growth. The building has childcare, a fitness center, and several good restaurants. But she will have a longer commute and will need to travel occasionally for business, which she does not enjoy.

Jenna made two columns, one each for the positive and negative aspects of the new job relative to the old one, labeled **Pros** and **Cons**. She left an empty column between them for later use. They are listed in the file called **jobs1.xls**.

She *changed the column widths* of A and C to make them wider and *wrapped the text* to keep the cells from getting too wide. She made the headers in row 1 *bold* to distinguish them. You can try it yourself.

	A	B	C	D
1	**Pros**		**Cons**	
2	Higher salary		Transportation costs	
3	More prestigious		Cost of parking	
4	Change		Change	
5	Better lunches		Less casual	
6	On-site child care		Leave friends	
7	On-site fitness center		Away from home longer	
8	Promotion opportunities		Business travel	
9			Loyalty to current company	

Rating the pros and cons

Notice that Jenna put "change" in both columns. She sees change as a positive—the excitement of a new environment and new challenges, as well as a negative—leaving behind the familiarity of a job and company that she knows well. How can she balance these?

She sees there are more "cons" than "pros." So far, this seems to tell her that she should stay with her current job. Even so, she has a feeling that the pros are stronger and may outweigh the cons. So, she adds a rating for each item in the lists. She rates them from 1 to 5, 5 being the most important to her. Here is the result, in **jobs2.xls**. Go ahead and open it:

	A	B	C	D
	Pros	**Rating of Pro**	**Cons**	**Rating of Con**
1				
2	Higher salary	5	Transportation costs	1
3	More prestigious	2	Cost of parking	1
4	Change	4	Change	2
5	Better lunches	1	Less casual	2
6	On-site child care	1	Leave friends	2
7	On-site fitness center	1	Away from home longer	3
8	Promotion opportunities	5	Business travel	1
9			Loyalty to current company	3

Higher salary and promotion opportunities are most important to her. She rates lunches, childcare, and fitness center low, since she figures she will make little use of these. Business travel is a minor inconvenience, since the trips will be short and infrequent. Added transportation and parking costs are small compared to the increased salary. She also rates the positive aspects of change higher than the negative ones, since she's getting bored and seeking a new environment.

Adding the ratings

Jenna sees that her top three reasons for taking the job outweigh even the best reasons not to take it. She is leaning toward taking the job, but she wants to try one more thing. She adds up the points for the pros and cons.

TRY IT! Add the ratings in columns B and D using *AutoSum* in B10 and D10. Here's what it looks like. This is called **jobs.xls:**

	A	B	C	D
1	**Pros**	**Rating of Pro**	**Cons**	**Rating of Con**
2	Higher salary	5	Away from home longer	3
3	More prestigious	2	Loyalty to current company	3
4	Change	4	Change	2
5	Better lunches	1	Less casual	2
6	On-site child care	1	Leave friends	2
7	On-site fitness center	1	Transportation costs	1
8	Promotion opportunities	5	Cost of parking	1
9			Business travel	1
10	Totals	**19**		**15**

Taking a look at the results

Now Jenna sees that she has given more points to the choice of taking the job. What do these points represent? They are just an aid in understanding your preferences. They might be thrown off if one of the lists were to contain many more minor items. Chapter 10 explores more precise ways to consider the relative importance of various factors in a decision.

In making your decisions, be especially careful about overlapping or redundant issues. For example "Leave friends" and "Miss the camaraderie" would be double counting.

Here's the real value in doing these totals. When you're done, ask yourself something like, "This says I should take the new job. How do I feel about that?" Are you disappointed? Did you find yourself rooting for one outcome or the other? Are there other pros or cons that should be added? Are the ratings reasonable? Decisions like this are subjective and the challenge is to get at the goals, needs, and desires under the surface.

Jenna takes a look at the results. The cons are all too weak to keep her. There are many important reasons to change. She realizes that she was disappointed when the list showed more reasons to stay than to go and she was hoping that the pros would win. Jenna decides to take the new job.

3

The magic formula
Formulas for a simple spreadsheet

The formula is the workhorse of Excel and you'll learn how to write simple, useful formulas as you work through the case studies. In Case Study 1, as you changed input values in the college spreadsheet, the entire table changed. That's because the table is full of formulas, which are calculation instructions. When you clicked on cells in column B of the **college1.xls** spreadsheet, you saw something like this:

=B8*(1+Inv_growth) + Add

Don't worry if you don't understand this yet. You will.

This is how formulas look; they always start with an equal sign. That tells Excel that you are entering a formula. Usually, there are also references to cells, such as B8 in this example and to named cells, such as Inv_growth and Add. You can also type numbers, parentheses, function names, spaces (which Excel ignores), and the following arithmetical operators:

+   add
-   subtract
*   multiply
/   divide
^   raise to a power (exponent)

Here's how Excel follows the instructions given in this formula. It starts inside the parentheses, adding 1 to whatever number is in the cell named Inv_growth. Then, it works in this order: ^, * and /, + and -. So, next, it multiplies that answer by the contents of cell B8. Finally, it adds the contents of the cell named Add.

Excel provides a library of functions that you can use in your formulas. Chapters 7 and 8 introduce some of the most useful functions and show you how to explore and use the entire function library. Case studies throughout this book take advantage of many of these functions. But, you don't need functions for the example that follows.

Starting a spreadsheet with inputs

Now you're ready to build your first decision spreadsheet. Jerry is thinking about buying some computer equipment, but he is not sure how much he can afford to buy. He has $1,400 to spend. You'll make a spreadsheet to help him figure it out. He's made a list of everything he wants and the prices.

CPU	$500
Big monitor	$800
Ext disk drive	$300
MS Office	$300

? What is the total cost of all of the items on the list, including 8.25% sales tax? Is it less than $1,400?

Open a new workbook. Start by putting everything that you will need in the spreadsheet. You need the sales tax rate, so start with that. Enter the label **Tax rate** in A1 and **8.25%** in B1. When you enter the sales tax rate include the %. Excel understands what you mean and formats and uses it properly.

	A	B
1	Tax rate	8.25%

Naming names

As you saw in the example formula above, you can give names to cells to which you often refer, such as those that contain inputs or constants. Names for frequently used cells, such as B1 above, make formulas easier to read. You can then copy the formulas and they always refer to the same cells. This technique is best for cells with adjacent labels.

How to create names for cells:

1. Enter names in cells next to the cells you want to name.

   Usually you already have labels that you can use for names.

2. *Select* the area that includes the names and the cells.

3. From the **Insert** menu, select **Name**. Then, select **Create** from the submenu {**Formulas > Defined Name > Create from Selection**}.

   The **Create Names** dialog box asks you where the names are relative to the cells.

4. Select the location of the names or leave it as-is, if Excel guessed right (which it usually does). Then, click **OK**.

TRY IT! Create a name for the tax rate. This will give cell B1 the name Tax_Rate. Notice that the created name automatically uses an underscore in place of the space. Follow the steps above and then check yourself against the steps below.

1. You've already entered the name Tax rate.

2. The name is in column A and the cell in column B, so select both A1 and B1.

3. Choose **Insert > Name > Create** {**Formulas > Defined Name > Create from Selection**}.

4. Excel correctly guesses that the name is to the left, so click **OK**.

Click on B1. The name Tax_Rate appears in the name box in the Formula Bar, showing that you were successful.

Entering the rest of the information

Next skip a row and enter everything on his list on page 26. Include the $ when you type in the prices. After the first three, Excel gets the hang of it and puts a $ in front of the rest of the prices, even if you don't.

Here's what it might look like. The spreadsheet on the website is called **cost0.xls**. By the way, you may find that column A is not wide enough for the descriptions and they will be cut off. Don't worry

	A	B
1	Tax rate	8.25%
2		
3	CPU	$500
4	Big monitor	$800
5	Ext disk drive	$300
6	MS Office	$300

about it. The information is not lost; click on it to see. *Change the column width* if you want to.

Using AutoSum

You wish to put the total of the items below them, say in cell B8. Enter the label Total next to it in cell A8. Select A8 and B8 and *create a name* for the cell.

Select B8. Now get the total by clicking on the *AutoSum* button. Excel makes its best guess as to what you want to sum and writes a formula for you. Here's what you should have:

=SUM(B3:B7)

This means, sum B3 through B7. That works since it adds the blank in B7 as a 0. Press **Enter**.

	A	B
1	Tax rate	8.25%
2		
3	CPU	$500
4	Big monitor	$800
5	Ext disk drive	$300
6	MS Office	$300
7		
8	Total	$1,900

AutoSum is just a quick way to write a formula using one very common function. There are lots of other built-in functions and, later, you will learn about and use them. The SUM function is just the most used one and, so, gets its own handy button.

Writing a formula

The formula gives Excel its power. You're ready for your first one: the formula that calculates the sales tax.

Writing a formula is just thinking about which numbers you would use from your spreadsheet to get an answer and how you'd combine them to get that answer.

How to write a formula:

1. Click on the cell where you want the formula result to appear.

2. Type =

   The equal sign tells Excel that you are entering a formula. Until you **Enter** the formula, you are in the formula entry mode and everything you do goes into the formula. When you click on cells they become part of your formula. Clicking cells is actually the easiest way to enter formulas. But first...

3. Think about what you want the formula to do with the numbers it uses.

   You may find it helpful to write a ***descriptive formula***. You'll learn about this in Chapter 5 and Case Study 4.

4. Input the formula by clicking on the desired cells and typing arithmetical operators. Remember to click on the numbers themselves, rather than on the labels.

   Use spaces in your formulas if you want; Excel ignores them.

5. Press **Enter** to accept the formula.

   The computed value appears in the cell. Verify that it shows the answer you expected.

TRY IT! Write a formula in cell B9 to calculate taxes. Remember that you calculate a percentage of something by multiplying. First *enter* the label **Sales tax** in cell A9.

1. Put the tax calculation right below the total. Click on B9.

2. Always start with =.

3. All you need to do is multiply the tax rate and the total. Think, "tax rate, multiply, total."

4. Click on the tax rate, type * (multiply), and finally click on the total amount. Remember to click on the numbers, not their labels. You should get:

=Tax_rate*Total

It uses the names you created and gives you a nice readable formula.

5. Press **Enter**.

=Tax_rate*Total

	A	B
1	Tax rate	8.25%
2		
3	CPU	$500
4	Big monitor	$800
5	Ext disk drive	$300
6	MS Office	$300
7		
8	Total	$1,900
9	Sales tax	156.75

Entering the total cost formula

The final step is to add the total of the items and the tax on those items. Label it **Total cost** in A10.

TRY IT! Enter the formula in B10 by clicking and typing. Here is what you should get:

=Total + B9

	A	B
1	Tax rate	8.25%
2		
3	CPU	$500
4	Big monitor	$800
5	Ext disk drive	$300
6	MS Office	$300
7		
8	Total	$1,900
9	Sales tax	156.75
10	Total cost	2056.75

If you had given the tax amount a name, it would have shown up here instead of the cell identifier B9. The answer, $2,056.75, looks reasonable. Give B3 through B10 the *currency format*.

Using the spreadsheet

So now Jerry has a spreadsheet (**cost.xls**) that tells him the cost of his wish list. But what it's really good for is playing "what-if." This is more than he wanted to pay. What if he bought a smaller, less expensive monitor for $400? Enter a new label and price for the monitor. Just select each cell and type the new entry. See how that changes the total. Notice that the sales tax changes.

	A	B
1	Tax rate	8.25%
2		
3	CPU	$ 500.00
4	Small monitor	$ 400.00
5	Ext disk drive	$ 300.00
6	MS Office	$ 300.00
7		
8	Total	$ 1,500.00
9	Sales tax	$ 123.75
10	Total cost	$ 1,623.75

Still not low enough. He needs to buy Microsoft Office (so he can use Excel, of course!), but what if he didn't buy the external disk drive?

TRY IT! *Clear the cells* with the name and amount (A5 and B5). Excel ignores blanks in a sum, so the calculations still work.

	A	B
1	Tax rate	8.25%
2		
3	CPU	$ 500.00
4	Small monitor	$ 400.00
5		
6	MS Office	$ 300.00
7		
8	Total	$ 1,200.00
9	Sales tax	$ 99.00
10	Total cost	$ 1,299.00

That looks a lot more affordable. That's what he'll buy.

Now, what if he bought it all in the next county, where the sales tax is only 7.75%?

TRY IT! Enter 7.75% as the tax rate in B1.

	A	B
1	Tax rate	7.75%
2		
3	CPU	$ 500.00
4	Small monitor	$ 400.00
5		
6	MS Office	$ 300.00
7		
8	Total	$ 1,200.00
9	Sales tax	$ 93.00
10	Total cost	$ 1,293.00

It's not worth the trip—he'd save only $6.

Taking a look at your spreadsheet

Here is the spreadsheet with all of the formulas displayed. You named cells B1 and B8, which made the formulas more readable.

	A	B
1	Tax rate	8.25%
2		
3	CPU	$ 500.00
4	Small monitor	$ 400.00
5		
6	MS Office	$ 300.00
7		
8	Total	=SUM(B3:B7)
9	Sales tax	=Tax_rate*Total
10	Total cost	=Total+B9

4

Send in the clones
Using AutoFill

You've seen that useful spreadsheets, like **college1.xls**, can become fairly large. You may be concerned about how long it takes to enter something like that. The secret weapon here is called AutoFill. It's a way of telling Excel "and so on."

How to AutoFill:

1. Enter whatever you want to start things going, if it isn't already there.

2. Select one or more cells that you would like to clone.

   This could be data or formulas.

3. Move your cursor, without clicking, to the lower right corner of the block of cells until you see a fill handle.

   It looks like one of these:

4. Click and hold the fill handle and drag it down the column(s) or across the row(s) as far as you want to fill.

   As you drag data, a Screen Tip may show what will appear in each newly filled cell.

5. When you get to the last cell that you want to fill, release the mouse button and the whole thing fills.

AutoFilling data

Decision makers often want to use row or column labels that are in a sequence, such as 1, 2, 3, 4, ... or January, February, March, ... AutoFill can fill in the rest of the sequence once you get it started. You can also fill in multiple cells with the same number.

TRY IT! *Open* a new workbook and use AutoFill to put several 1s in the first column.

1. **Enter** 1 in A1 to get it started.

2. Click on A1.

3. Find the fill handle in the lower right corner of A1.

4. Click the fill handle and drag it down the column as far as you want.

5. Release.

You've now filled several cells with the same number.

Next fill a sequence by giving Excel the first *two* entries.

TRY IT! Use AutoFill to fill the first column with 1, 2, 3, 4, and so on up to 12.

You already have 1 in A1. **Enter** 2 in A2 and select *both* A1 and A2. Click the fill handle in the lower right corner of A2 and drag it down the column. Excel fills in all the numbers.

	A
1	1
2	2
3	3
4	4
5	5
6	6
7	7
8	8
9	9
10	10
11	11
12	12

You can use AutoFill to fill even less obvious sequences, such as times, days of the week, dates, and text-number mixes, such as 1st Phase, 2nd Phase, ... or Topic1, Topic2, ... by giving it the first two items, selecting them both, and dragging the fill handle.

Excel makes its best guess as to what you want. It sometimes makes mistakes from just one entry, even if you want them to be identical, so it's best to enter the first two by hand, to make it clear what you want.

Cloning formulas with AutoFill

The real power of AutoFill is in cloning formulas. Write a nice formula once and then clone it everywhere else. The spreadsheets in this book actually contain very few *distinct* formulas.

Open **autofill0.xls**. This is a list of sales orders, yet to be filled out:

	A	B	C	D	E
1	Tax rate	7.50%			
2					
3	Order number	Price	Shipping	Tax	Total
4	101	$ 436.19	$ 6.73	$ 32.71	$ 475.63
5	102	$ 380.17	$ 9.55		
6		$ 261.17	$ 5.60		
7		$ 104.84	$ 7.25		
8		$ 249.98	$ 8.82		
9		$ 196.32	$ 9.27		
10		$ 199.52	$ 2.42		
11		$ 108.38	$ 6.63		
12		$ 55.97	$ 3.60		
13		$ 360.04	$ 4.17		
14		$ 82.23	$ 3.89		
15		$ 191.96	$ 6.25		

First you see that the order numbers haven't been completed. You can fill them in using AutoFill as above. (**TRY IT!**)

You'd also like to complete the Tax and Total columns. Cells D4 and E4 contain formulas to calculate the tax and total cost for the first order. Take a look at them. First click on D4. The formula reads:

=B4*Tax_rate

Notice that the author had already ***created*** a ***name*** for the tax rate, which displays in the Name box when you click on B1. This formula multiplies the amount of the order (Price) by the tax rate to get the amount of the sales tax.

Now click on E4. You see this formula that adds the price, shipping, and tax to get the total cost for the first order:

=B4+C4+D4

You'd like to use formulas like these to compute the tax and total for *each* order. AutoFill to tell Excel, "Do the same thing" for the rest of the orders:

TRY IT! Use *AutoFill* to apply these same formulas to all the orders. Follow the steps above.

1. You already have formulas in D4 and E4 to clone.

2. Select the cells you want to clone, D4 and E4. You can clone multiple formulas at once.

3. Locate the fill handle in E4.

4. Drag it down the column as far as you want to go (to row 15).

5. Release

Ta Da! Computed amounts instantly appear as soon as you release the button (**autofill.xls**). Do they look reasonable?

You can even take it past the end of what you've entered so far, so that it's there as you get more orders. Or, you can always do this again later to extend it as you add rows.

	A	B	C	D	E
1	Tax rate	7.5%			
2					
3	Order number	Price	Shipping	Tax	Total
4	101	$ 436.19	$ 6.73	$ 32.71	$ 475.63
5	102	$ 380.17	$ 9.55	$ 28.51	$ 418.23
6	103	$ 261.17	$ 5.60	$ 19.59	$ 286.36
7	104	$ 104.84	$ 7.25	$ 7.86	$ 119.95
8	105	$ 249.98	$ 8.82	$ 18.75	$ 277.55
9	106	$ 196.32	$ 9.27	$ 14.72	$ 220.31
10	107	$ 199.52	$ 2.42	$ 14.96	$ 216.90
11	108	$ 108.38	$ 6.63	$ 8.13	$ 123.14
12	109	$ 55.97	$ 3.60	$ 4.20	$ 63.77
13	110	$ 360.04	$ 4.17	$ 27.00	$ 391.21
14	111	$ 82.23	$ 3.89	$ 6.17	$ 92.29
15	112	$ 191.96	$ 6.25	$ 14.40	$ 212.61

How formulas change as they're cloned

Click on the newly cloned cells and see how the formulas differ from the originals. Do they do what you want?

Named cells stay the same

Click on D5. Here's its formula:

=B5*Tax_rate

Compare it with the formula in D4 that you cloned. Excel took the original formula and changed the references relative to the new position. Now it multiplies the tax rate by the cost of the second order, which is exactly what you want it to do. The key thing to notice is that it still refers to the tax rate (B1), not the empty cell below it, since the author had given it a name.

This is a powerful, yet simple, technique to make sure your cloned formulas always refer to the right cells. Create names for any cells that you will refer to from various places. Usually, you'll want to create names for your inputs for this reason. You'll see that most of the case studies do just that.

Unnamed cells change relatively

You saw in D5 that the B4 (price of the first order) reference from the original formula became B5 (the price of the second order). This new formula is looking at the second order, just as you wanted.

Now look at E5:

=B5+C5+D5

It adds the three amounts for the second order and gives you the total for that order...just what you want it to do. Click on some of the other cells in column E to see that they are all adding the amounts from their own row.

But what if I don't want to adjust everything?

In this example, you want every unnamed cell in the formula to change as you copy it down the column. However, you can tell Excel how to copy a formula depending on how you write it. Using $ in front of the row or column in the cell reference keeps it fixed, so that it refers to that same row or column wherever the formula goes. This is called an *absolute reference*.

TRY IT! Type =D4 in some empty column and *AutoFill* it down the column. (Remember the = sign.)

Every cell has the same $32.71 from D4. If you AutoFill or copy and paste the cell with this formula, it still refers to cell D4. If you want, you can tie down just the row or just the column. $D4, for example, always refers to column D, even when it is copied, while D$4 always refers to row 4.

So D4, $D4, D$4, and D4 are four different ways to refer to the same cell. The difference shows up when they are copied. You may see this notation with the two dollar signs in some of the Excel dialog boxes.

You also saw that naming a cell makes it stay put when it's copied. Cell B1 is named Tax_rate and this name shows up in the formula for computing the tax. When that formula is cloned down the column, it keeps Tax_rate, fixing the reference so that it always refers to the proper cell (B1).

AutoFill examples and tips

The case studies that follow are chock full of examples of using AutoFill. In fact, it's used in every case study from here on out. AutoFill is the secret to simple spreadsheets to solve hard problems.

Here are a few tips for AutoFilling:

- If you overshoot when you're dragging the fill handle, just drag it back.

- You can always make the area with the cloned formulas bigger. Just select the last row or two, grab the fill handle in the lower right and drag. You could expand it to more columns similarly.

- You can AutoFill across a row or down a column. You can even drag it backwards to fill cells above or to the left.

- Create names for inputs or anything else that will be used from various places in your spreadsheet. Then they will automatically keep proper references when you AutoFill.

- If you're AutoFilling down a column, check the rows of the cells in your formula. If you always want to use the same row, give an *absolute reference* with a $ in front of the row number. Similarly, if you're AutoFilling across a row, check the columns and put a $ in front of the column letter whenever you want it to stay put. It's easiest to construct the formula first by clicking on cells, and then edit it to insert the $s.

- Sometimes, if you're really lucky, you have a formula that applies to a whole table. Write it once, check it, and then clone it across and then down to fill the whole area. You'll use this technique in Case Study 9.

   Here's how:

1. Select the cell you want to clone.

2. *AutoFill* it across to as many columns as you want.

3. While you still have the first filled row selected, drag the fill handle in the last cell of the selection down as many rows as you wish.

Do I need to cut back on spending?

Building a spreadsheet from a single formula

FOCUS Using AutoFill to build a spreadsheet from one formula

TOOLKIT Formulas (Chapter 3), AutoFill (Chapter 4), formatting and other basic techniques (Appendix A)

Steph is self-employed, so her income varies. She wants to be sure that her spending is in line with her income.

? Steph's income and expenditures appear in the table below and in **spending0.xls**. What is her net income (the amount by which income exceeds expenses) each month? How often do expenses exceed her income? Does she need to cut back on spending?

This is a simple example that shows the use of *AutoFill*. **TRY IT!**

Building the Spreadsheet

1. *Open* her spreadsheet, **spending0.xls**.

   She has already given the month in A2 a *special format* for month and year and columns B, C and D the *currency format*.

	A	B	C	D
1	Month	Income	Expenses	Net
2	Jan-07	$ 5,541.35	$ 3,498.46	
3		$ 8,924.11	$ 4,040.40	
4		$ 8,909.56	$ 2,053.00	
5		$ 8,174.60	$ 3,406.47	
6		$ 4,857.94	$ 2,053.00	
7		$ 4,621.38	$ 6,068.00	
8		$ 6,141.50	$ 5,459.85	
9		$ 3,779.56	$ 2,053.00	
10		$ 3,012.00	$ 4,430.32	

2. Click on A2 and *AutoFill* down the column to fill in the rest of the months:

	A	B	C	D
1	Month	Income	Expenses	Net
2	Jan-07	$ 5,541.35	$ 3,498.46	
3	Feb-07	$ 8,924.11	$ 4,040.40	
4	Mar-07	$ 8,909.56	$ 2,053.00	
5	Apr-07	$ 8,174.60	$ 3,406.47	
6	May-07	$ 4,857.94	$ 2,053.00	
7	Jun-07	$ 4,621.38	$ 6,068.00	

3. On paper, write a formula to compute the net difference between income and expenses.

First think about what it would do. Does it look like this?

Net = Income - Expenses

4. Click on D2.

5. Write the formula for the first month's difference by following the descriptive formula in step 3 and clicking on the cells. Remember to start with "=." Did you get the following formula?

=B2 - C2

Did you get $2,042.88 as the result?

6. Check that this formula works for all rows if copied down.

   Since you're copying down, the B and C column references stay the same and the 2s for the rows change to 3s, 4s, and so on. This is exactly what you want it to do.

7. *AutoFill* down column D:

	A	B	C	D
1	Month	Income	Expenses	Net
2	Jan-07	$ 5,541.35	$ 3,498.46	$ 2,042.88
3	Feb-07	$ 8,924.11	$ 4,040.40	$ 4,883.71
4	Mar-07	$ 8,909.56	$ 2,053.00	$ 6,856.56
5	Apr-07	$ 8,174.60	$ 3,406.47	$ 4,768.13
6	May-07	$ 4,857.94	$ 2,053.00	$ 2,804.94
7	Jun-07	$ 4,621.38	$ 6,068.00	$ (1,446.62)
8	Jul-07	$ 6,141.50	$ 5,459.85	$ 681.65
9	Aug-07	$ 3,779.56	$ 2,053.00	$ 1,726.56
10	Sep-07	$ 3,012.00	$ 4,430.32	$ (1,418.32)
11	Oct-07	$ 9,519.37	$ 2,053.00	$ 7,466.37
12	Nov-07	$ 3,012.00	$ 2,223.97	$ 788.03
13	Dec-07	$ 4,450.99	$ 3,699.30	$ 751.69
14	Jan-08	$ 3,228.67	$ 2,053.00	$ 1,175.67
15	Feb-08	$ 6,339.25	$ 6,910.11	$ (570.86)
16	Mar-08	$ 3,012.00	$ 4,764.87	$ (1,752.87)
17	Apr-08	$ 3,297.33	$ 3,607.10	$ (309.78)
18	May-08	$ 9,772.98	$ 2,053.00	$ 7,719.98
19	Jun-08	$ 3,012.00	$ 2,633.27	$ 378.73
20	Jul-08	$ 6,824.46	$ 3,566.39	$ 3,258.06
21	Aug-08	$ 8,579.03	$ 4,748.52	$ 3,830.51
22	Sep-08	$ 3,854.11	$ 2,303.13	$ 1,550.98
23	Oct-08	$ 4,997.83	$ 4,030.78	$ 967.05
24	Nov-08	$ 3,957.92	$ 2,053.00	$ 1,904.92
25	Dec-08	$ 7,001.46	$ 2,447.82	$ 4,553.65

Excel fills in the difference formula for the rest of the column.

8. Click on one of the cells in the **Net** column to check that you get the formula you want. This is **spending1.xls**.

Using the spreadsheet

That completes the spreadsheet. So, what about Steph and her spending? She sees that she is ahead financially most months. In fact, the first five months give her enough excess to cover all five months that have a shortfall (indicated by parentheses). Her spending level is quite comfortable if her income continues like this. Yes, there will be down months and unpredictable fluctuations, but by now it appears that she has built up enough of a reserve to ride it out.

She'd like to know exactly how much of a reserve she had each month and how much she has built up by now. That reserve is the total of the excess funds shown in the **Difference** column for all months up to now. It turns out that you can view a running total like this by using two simple formulas, as you'll see in the next chapter. Leave this spreadsheet open.

5

Call in the bucket brigade
Complex calculation
by cloning simple formulas

In the last case study, Steph wanted to figure out how much she had netted total by the month. This is called a running total or cumulative result. You can grind this out for her in a new Running Total column E in your spending spreadsheet or **spending1.xls**.

The first month, the total is simply what she had left the first month:

E2: =D2

The second month is the total of the net (the difference) for each of the first two months:

E3: =D2 + D3

And so on:

E4: =D2 + D3 + D4
E5: =D2 + D3 + D4 + D5

Well, this certainly is tedious! Fortunately, there's a much easier way, as it turns out.

TRY IT! Is there a way to use AutoFill to complete the column in just a few steps?

First see what you want to keep that you already have. Running total in E1 is OK as a column header, so leave it alone. Click E2.

The simple formula for the running total for the first month works, just as before:

=D2

The next row is where things get interesting. Working carefully, you can write a single formula to put in E3 that works for every month following, and then clone it down the rest of the column.

TRY IT! Find a new, clone-able formula for E3. **Hint:** Take full advantage of any calculations that were done in the row above.

Take a look at the formulas above. Each answer, after the first, is just the previous with one more **Net** number added, like so:

Running total: =*Running total* previous + *Net*

This is a **descriptive formula** that you can use as instructions on entering the formula you want. Case Study 4 walks you through building and using a descriptive formula. Click on E3. **Enter** the formula above by clicking on the appropriate cells, as follows:

1. Type =
2. Click on the number for Running total in the previous row (E2)
3. Type +
4. Click on the number for Net in this row (D3)

This is the formula that now displays for E3:

=E2+D3

TRY IT! Convince yourself that this will still work if you clone it down to the other cells. Then do it.

AutoFill from E3 down the rest of the column.

Check that you got the same answers that you got the more tedious way. (*Change column width* if you see cells filled with #s.) Check the other cells by clicking on them to see the formulas. These have the same general form.

The completed example is **spending.xls**:

	A	B	C	D	E
1	Month	Income	Expenses	Net	Running total
2	Jan-07	$ 5,541.35	$ 3,498.46	$ 2,042.88	$ 2,042.88
3	Feb-07	$ 8,924.11	$ 4,040.40	$ 4,883.71	$ 6,926.59
4	Mar-07	$ 8,909.56	$ 2,053.00	$ 6,856.56	$ 13,783.15
5	Apr-07	$ 8,174.60	$ 3,406.47	$ 4,768.13	$ 18,551.29
6	May-07	$ 4,857.94	$ 2,053.00	$ 2,804.94	$ 21,356.22
7	Jun-07	$ 4,621.38	$ 6,068.00	$ (1,446.62)	$ 19,909.60
8	Jul-07	$ 6,141.50	$ 5,459.85	$ 681.65	$ 20,591.26
9	Aug-07	$ 3,779.56	$ 2,053.00	$ 1,726.56	$ 22,317.81
10	Sep-07	$ 3,012.00	$ 4,430.32	$ (1,418.32)	$ 20,899.49
11	Oct-07	$ 9,519.37	$ 2,053.00	$ 7,466.37	$ 28,365.86
12	Nov-07	$ 3,012.00	$ 2,223.97	$ 788.03	$ 29,153.89
13	Dec-07	$ 4,450.99	$ 3,699.30	$ 751.69	$ 29,905.58
14	Jan-08	$ 3,228.67	$ 2,053.00	$ 1,175.67	$ 31,081.25
15	Feb-08	$ 6,339.25	$ 6,910.11	$ (570.86)	$ 30,510.39
16	Mar-08	$ 3,012.00	$ 4,764.87	$ (1,752.87)	$ 28,757.51
17	Apr-08	$ 3,297.33	$ 3,607.10	$ (309.78)	$ 28,447.74
18	May-08	$ 9,772.98	$ 2,053.00	$ 7,719.98	$ 36,167.72
19	Jun-08	$ 3,012.00	$ 2,633.27	$ 378.73	$ 36,546.45
20	Jul-08	$ 6,824.46	$ 3,566.39	$ 3,258.06	$ 39,804.52
21	Aug-08	$ 8,579.03	$ 4,748.52	$ 3,830.51	$ 43,635.03
22	Sep-08	$ 3,854.11	$ 2,303.13	$ 1,550.98	$ 45,186.01
23	Oct-08	$ 4,997.83	$ 4,030.78	$ 967.05	$ 46,153.05
24	Nov-08	$ 3,957.92	$ 2,053.00	$ 1,904.92	$ 48,057.98
25	Dec-08	$ 7,001.46	$ 2,447.82	$ 4,553.65	$ 52,611.62

Bucket brigade formulas

You've just used a basic Excel technique here: keeping a running account. Even if you're interested in only the last number (the current balance), have Excel compute and display all the intermediate values. As later examples illustrate, this is a way of building up some fairly complex calculations from simple ones. Like a bucket brigade, each row does some simple calculation on the numbers passed to it, and then passes the result on to the next row. The final answer takes into account all the rows and can represent surprisingly complex relationships. If you come up with a formula that works for all subsequent rows, as you did here, you can build a complicated calculation using just one simple formula. Write the formula once and use *AutoFill* to clone it to all rows.

There are several advantages of this "bucket brigade" approach:

- Formulas are simpler to write and easier to understand than those that give you the answer in one step.

- Seeing intermediate values helps you to check that your spreadsheet is working properly.

- The spreadsheet is easy to modify, since you are using only a single, simple formula that you can change and re-clone.

- Many complex problems can be solved only in this way.

The computer may be doing a lot of work, but that's OK if it makes things easier for *you*.

How to write a bucket brigade formula

There are two things you need to make this work: A starting row and a formula that works for all other rows by using the calculations on the row above. This way you can fill in the whole column using only two formulas. Sometimes you don't even need a distinct starting row.

Starting at the starting line

In the running total, the formula for the first line was different from the others. You needed a "starting line" to get things going. Many spreadsheets use an initialization line like this. Use the first row to let the spreadsheet know the initial values, such as current bank balance.

Bucket brigade formula

Use the other rows to predict or keep track of what happens in the future using a bucket brigade formula. Take full advantage of the calculations done in the row above.

How to write and use a bucket brigade formula:

1. Fill in the first row (the "starting line") of the table using data and/or formulas.

2. Think about what you want the formula to do with the numbers it uses. Think especially about how you could use the numbers calculated in the row above to calculate the result you want.

3. Write a *descriptive formula* that indicates how to do the calculation.

4. Convince yourself that the formula will work for all rows.

5. Enter the descriptive formula in the second row of your table by typing and clicking the appropriate cells. Edit to use *absolute references*, if necessary.

6. *AutoFill* the formula down the rest of the column.

7. Check that you got the formulas and answers you expected.

Examples

Here are examples of some useful bucket brigade formulas. You'll find them in **examples.xls**. The case studies further use and describe these techniques.

Each example uses *descriptive formulas*. The actual formula you see looks different from this. Here's how descriptive formulas work. Identify each cell by its column header, possibly followed by "previous." This tells you whether the cell is in this row or the previous one. Use this to guide you when you enter the formula by clicking on cells. Here, names in italics represent the column header you want to use. All of these show the first row as a formula, but it could be a number, as in the Investment, Inflation, and Present value examples.

Ditto

This is the simplest example. Each cell is the same as the one above it all the way down the column. For example, if you have a fixed mortgage, you can calculate the payment once and make it the same for all subsequent months.

First row:
> =*initial value*

Rest of the rows:
> =*value* previous

Counting or incrementing

This is the next simplest example. Start with some number and increase it by one each row. For example, say you want to make a table to plan for retirement, with each row representing a year in the future. You want one column with the year and another with your age that year. Here's how to make a table of *value* starting with *initial value* and increasing by 1 each row.

First row:
> =*initial value*

Rest of the rows:
> =*value* previous + 1

Running total

The running total, as you saw at the beginning of this chapter, keeps track of or predicts the total amount to date. If you have a column that keeps track of an *amount*, here's how to get its *running total*.

First row:
> =*amount*

Rest of the rows:
> =*running total* previous + *amount*

Income and expenditures

If you have both *inflows* and *outflows*, you can still keep a *running total*, including any *initial amount* that you have when you start.

First row:
    =*initial amount*

Rest of the rows:
    =*running total* previous + *inflow* - *outflow*

The next case study uses this technique to construct a checkbook record.

Inflation

What will you have to pay for rent 10 years from now? What will college cost by the time your child gets there? How much income will you need when you retire?

These questions all depend on the inflation rate. Here's how to make a table of the future *cost* of some *initial amount* at some *inflation rate*.

First, find a place to put the *inflation rate* input and **create a name** for it. Then all of your formulas refer to the same cell to get this number.

First row (representing the current year):
    =*initial amount*

Rest of the rows (representing future years):
    =*cost* previous * (1 + *inflation rate*)

Investment growth

You have $10,000 invested at 6%. How much will you have in 20 years? Just as with inflation, you have some *amount* that is growing at some *growth rate*, which is a named input.

Here's how to make a table of the *amount* for each year, starting with an *initial amount*. It's the same as for inflation.

First row (current year):

    =initial amount

Rest of the rows (future years):

    =amount previous * (1 + *growth rate*)

Present value

Because money can be invested and grow, future money is worth less than present money. In fact, if you assume some growth *rate*, a dollar next year will be worth only as much as 1/(1+*rate*) dollars now. So, for example, with a growth rate of 6%, a dollar next year is worth only about 94 cents. This is called its present value. Present value is useful, for example, if you're trying to decide whether to invest money now for future gains.

Here's how to make a table of the *present value* of some *amount* in each year in the future. An input is the growth *rate*. **Create a name** for it, as in the previous two examples.

First row (current year):

    = *amount*

Rest of the rows (future years):

    =present value previous / (1 + *rate*)

Tip: If the *amount* in the first row is $1.00 you get a table of the present value of a dollar in the future. You can then use this as a multiplier to calculate the present value of any future amount or income stream (see Case Studies 14 and 15).

Copy

Copy a *column* to *another column* somewhere else in the spreadsheet. For example, copy the row headers to a related table. Then any changes to the original headers automatically carry over to the related table. This may also be used to copy rows by AutoFilling across. See examples in Case Studies 8, 9, 16 and 18.

All rows in *another column*:

    = *column*

6

Decision taming

From a vague question to a spreadsheet answer

At this point, you have most of the techniques you need to build and use decision spreadsheets. But, you'll find that many important decisions are vaguely stated, at least at first. The issues or options may be ill defined. You'll find that many of your decisions are even less clearly delineated than are the case studies in this book and that even these often lack information or require multiple versions to arrive at an answer.

It turns out that Excel is a good tool, both for making decisions and for clarifying them. Here are steps (and their descriptions) to take you from a vague question to a decision spreadsheet to a solid decision:

How to design, build and use a decision spreadsheet:

1. Expand the question.

2. Plan the spreadsheet.

3. Build the spreadsheet.

4. Use the spreadsheet.

Expanding the question

Spend some time thinking about the decision you need to make to be sure the spreadsheet you build addresses the right issues.

Remember that your goal is a decisive answer, rather than an elegant spreadsheet.

How to expand the question:

1. Define the decision.

   Ask yourself about your decision, as described in Chapter 1:

   What am I trying to decide?
   How will I measure success?
   What are the alternatives?
   What do I know?
   What don't I know?

   You may want to use the questionnaire (questionnaire.doc, see Chapter 1 and Appendix C).

2. Decide what you want the spreadsheet to do to help you make your decision.

You may find it helpful during this step to "doodle" in Excel. Do some trial calculations or organize your data. The goal is to help you think rather than to develop an analytical tool. If your doodles happen to grow into a full and useful spreadsheet, that's a bonus.

Planning the spreadsheet

A useful spreadsheet usually contains a lot of data and requires organization. Excel works best if you organize the data into a rectangular table of rows and columns. So, the first thing to do is to decide what the rows and columns are to be. This gives you a structure on which to build. It saves time to get the structure right from the start. But, you can always add rows or columns as you think of things you forgot.

You may also have inputs that you want to be able to use from various places in the table. Here's how to plan such a spreadsheet:

How to plan a spreadsheet:

1. Decide what the rows should represent.

   Generally these are items you're tracking, predicting, or evaluating, such as months, years, orders, checks, employees, purchases, or criteria. Since you can see more rows than columns on the screen, it makes sense to use rows for these. But, sometimes, it works out better to use columns (for example, Case Study 18).

2. Decide what the columns should represent.

   Think about what you'll need to know for each of the rows. Each of these quantities or descriptions is a column.

3. Identify the inputs.

   This is everything that might affect your chance of success. Use your lists of what you know and what you don't know. Include the unknowns and plan to vary them to see the impact.

4. Decide which inputs are general and should be clustered at the top.

   This includes anything that multiple cells use or any value that you want to vary.

5. Make sure the output you care about shows up somewhere in the spreadsheet.

Recall the example of Case Study 1, **college1.xls**:

	A	B	C	D	E	F
1	Start	$ 10,000	Initial amount in the savings fund			
2	Add	$ 15,000	Amount added to the fund at the beginning of each year			
3	Inv growth	8%	Annual growth rate of the fund's investments			
4	Cost growth	9%	Annual increase in the cost of college			
5	Current goal	$ 140,000	Cost of 4 years of college			
6						
7	Age	Amount	Cost of college	Shortfall		
8	0	$ 10,000	$ 140,000	$ 130,000		
9	1	$ 25,800	$ 152,600	$ 126,800		
10	2	$ 42,864	$ 166,334	$ 123,470		
11	3	$ 61,293	$ 181,304	$ 120,011		

These steps could give you a spreadsheet like this for the college savings question. Each row represents a year in the future. Many of the case studies you'll encounter use the rows to represent years. The columns are quantities that you need to track each year. Here, the columns hold the child's age, the amount saved so far, the future cost of college, and the anticipated shortfall. Rows 1 through 5 hold the inputs that the table below them uses. Change any of these numbers and see what happens. The table proper has a header in row 7, a starting line in row 8, and bucket brigade formulas for the rest. The output you care about shows up in the shortfall at age 18.

The technique above works for most of the decision spreadsheets you'll build. Later you'll see some that use additional or different techniques. For example, Case Study 18 uses a spreadsheet laid out by columns instead of rows, though the steps are the same. You'll also see some with more than one table (such as in Case Study 9).

Building the spreadsheet

Now you're ready to build your spreadsheet. Enter the inputs first. Try to include everything you need. But, if you forget something, it's easy enough to *insert a row* to add it later.

Fill as much of the table as possible with data before writing formulas. It's always easier to check your formulas if you have reasonable numbers for them to use. Look for simple formulas to fill in the rest. Try to build from the previous row with bucket brigade formulas.

How to build a spreadsheet:

1. Put the general inputs together at the top of the spreadsheet. *Create names* for them so that cloned formulas use them properly.

2. *Enter* the column headers and the row headers (if any) for the main table.

3. Fill in the starting row.

   Enter data or write *formulas* that use the inputs or other cells in the first row of the table.

4. If you've already entered all your inputs, go to step 5.

   Otherwise, *Enter* any other inputs in the body of the table.

   You'll usually do this step if you have inputs that are already in table form. Be sure all the information you gathered goes somewhere in the spreadsheet.

5. Find *bucket brigade formulas* to get from one row to the next.

   Often the first row formula works.

   Think or write it as a *descriptive formula*. Then enter it in the second row of your table by clicking on the cells.

6. Check that all these formulas will work when cloned to the other rows.

   If not, edit to insert $s for absolute references.

7. *AutoFill* to complete the table.

You may find it easier to do steps 3 through 7 for each column in turn. See, for example, Case Studies 11 through 13. This lets you concentrate on one quantity at a time.

Using the spreadsheet

Now your spreadsheet is ready to help you make the decision. It gives you a first cut at the answer. To find the final answer, try various alternatives and situations and think about the outcome and how you would respond.

How to use a decision spreadsheet:

1. Check that the spreadsheet is working.

    Did you get the results you expected? Try different inputs. Use zero or other values for which the correct output is obvious. Make corrections as necessary.

2. Examine the results and explore the model.

    Play "what-if" with the inputs. Look at the worst case. Try alternatives. Think about how you would react to the outcomes.

3. Expand the model.

    Exploration often suggests other questions. Extend the model to address them.

Case studies that follow provide many examples of using and expanding decision spreadsheets.

How much can I afford to spend?
Building a check register

Focus: Using a bucket brigade formula to build a useful checkbook spreadsheet

Toolkit: Formulas (Chapter 3), AutoFill (Chapter 4), bucket brigade formulas and descriptive formulas (Chapter 5), building a decision spreadsheet (Chapter 6), some Excel basics (Appendix A)

Now you can build a useful spreadsheet: a checking account log. If you are one of the many people who buy a computer to balance their checkbooks, here's an Excel spreadsheet that does just that. This is primarily a record-keeping application–the sort of task at which Excel, well, *excels*.

? You have a record of all the checks and deposits you have made. How much do you currently have available in your checking account?

The spreadsheet combines text and dollar entries with some simple calculations. Follow the steps from Chapter 6. The completed spreadsheet is **bank2.xls**.

Expanding the question

First, think about what you would like the spreadsheet to do:

- List all checks with the date, check number, recipient, and a description of its purpose.

- List all deposits, with the date, source, and description.

- Keep a running account of the balance so you know how much you can spend.

- Keep a record of which checks have cleared.

- Compute the bank balance (counting only checks and deposits that have cleared) to compare with the bank statement and balance your checkbook.

The first three are the usual manual tasks in your check register. Start with these. Add the bank balance later in Case Study 7. Excel's flexibility makes it easy to grow the spreadsheet a little bit at a time.

Planning the spreadsheet

You probably have a lot of checks and deposits, so this spreadsheet must be well organized and easy to interpret. It should let you add checks and deposits in the future.

Deciding what the rows should represent

TRY IT! What should the rows represent? Should there be one table for checks and another for deposits? Think about it before going on.

There are a lot of checks and deposits, so these are the rows. In general, in deciding what should be in the rows and what should be in the columns, you want to have more rows than columns since you can see more rows on the screen. Besides, in this case, this is how it looks in your checkbook register. It helps if the spreadsheet looks familiar.

So should the checks and deposits be separate or interspersed? If you separate them in different areas of the spreadsheet or on different worksheets, you can make specialized formulas for each. But, in this case, there is a lot of commonality in the information that you record for each (date, purpose, etc.). The calculations are similar as well, except that you add deposits and subtract checks. This commonality tells you that it is easier to intersperse checks and deposits; any row could be one or the other. However, you treat the amounts differently, which indicates that you want to put check amounts and deposit amounts in different columns.

Deciding what the columns should represent

TRY IT! What columns do you want to use to keep track of each check or deposit? Think about it before going on. List the column headings on a piece of paper. Remember that you'll want to distinguish check amounts from deposit amounts.

Column headings label whatever you want to track for the checks and deposits. Here are some possible column headings:

Number	Date	To/From	Description	Check	Deposit	Balance

You could cheat and get similar headings out of your own checkbook. But keep them short, since they are labels. For example, use "Check," rather than "Payment/Debit."

Building the spreadsheet

Open a new workbook. There aren't any general inputs, so the table starts at the top. Enter the column headings in row 1. Use the **Tab** key to move from one column to the next:

	A	B	C	D	E	F	G
1	Number	Date	To/from	Description	Check	Deposit	Balance

Make this row *bold*. *Change column width* to make the columns wide enough. Make the To/from and Description columns plenty wide, since they contain names and descriptions. But try to keep them narrow enough that you can see all the columns on the screen at once, or *wrap text*. Now you're ready to fill in the rows.

Starting at the starting line

Use the first row for initialization, to let the spreadsheet know how much you have in your account to start. Enter the starting date and starting amount, with a description. Leave the rest of the cells blank in this row since they don't apply.

	A	B	C	D	E	F	G
1	Number	Date	To/from	Description	Check	Deposit	Balance
2		1/9		Starting balance			220.17

This starting line is a common Excel technique. Many spreadsheets feature an initialization row like this to set the starting conditions for bucket brigade formulas. Cell values in the initialization row may derive from formulas that are different from those of cells in the other rows.

Entering the check and deposit data

Now you're ready to start entering your checks and deposits. Use your actual checkbook or the example below. It helps to enter at least a few rows of data before you write formulas, so that you can see immediately whether your formulas do what you expect. Until you have real data, make up something reasonable. Just remember to overwrite it with good numbers before you start drawing conclusions from it!

Click on a cell and start typing. Press **Tab** or **Enter** to save the data and go to the next cell. Leave the cells under Balance blank for now.

Tip: Use **Tab** to enter data for each check or deposit and move across through the cells. You can also move through cells by using the arrow keys unless you're entering a formula. Here's what the check register might look like:

	A	B	C	D	E	F	G
1	**Number**	**Date**	**To/from**	**Description**	**Check**	**Deposit**	**Balance**
2		1/9		Starting balance			220.17
3	117	1/12	Von's	Groceries	103.56		
4	118	1/13	Footlocker	Shoes	54.11		
5		1/16	Megacorp	Pay check		591.22	
6	119	1/16	Visa	Credit card	275.14		
7	120	1/17	Ralphs	Groceries	87.63		
8		1/19	ATM	Cash	100		

This is **bank1.xls**. Open it if you want to use it for the example, rather than typing it all.

Note: Your dates may be in a format that's different from the above. Use *special formats* to change it if you wish.

Using a bucket brigade formula for the balance

Now you are ready to develop formulas to compute the balances. Chapter 5 showed how to come up with a bucket brigade formula that you can use for the whole column. Follow the steps given there.

TRY IT! Enter a formula in G3 to compute the balance. Think about how you can use the previous balance in calculating the current one.

1. The first row is already done.

2. Think about what you want the formula to do with the numbers it uses.

   Although G3 has only a check, think ahead to rows with deposits. Your formula should handle either case.

   You want to compute the balance by subtracting the check or adding the deposit to the previous balance. So you want the formula to start with the previous balance, subtract the check (if any) and add the deposit (if any). Notice that adding or subtracting a blank cell doesn't change anything, since Excel sees it as zero. So it's OK to subtract the check *and* add the deposit every time.

3. Think up a ***descriptive formula*** for the calculation.

   You start with the previous balance, subtract the check, and add the deposit. So, here is the descriptive formula:

   = Balance previous *- Check + Deposit*

   This tells you that, no matter which row you put the formula in, it uses the Check and Deposit numbers from that same row and the Balance from the previous row (the row just above it). This is a bucket brigade formula, since it uses the Balance computed in the previous line. Notice that this works when the check or deposit amount is blank, because Excel adds blanks as zeros.

4. Enter the formula by following the descriptive formula.

Start with =. Click on the indicated cells (even if they're empty). Type the arithmetical operators between them.

$$= \textit{Balance} \text{ previous} \quad - \quad \textit{Check} \quad + \quad \textit{Deposit}$$

Click!   Click!   Click!

$$= \text{G2} \quad - \quad \text{E3} \quad + \quad \text{F3}$$

The formula in G3 now reads:

=G2 - E3 + F3.

5. Press **Enter** to accept the formula.

	A	B	C	D	E	F	G
				=G2-E3+F3			
1	Number	Date	To/from	Description	Check	Deposit	Balance
2		1/9		Starting balance			220.17
3	117	1/12	Von's	Groceries	103.56		116.61
4	118	1/13	Footlocker	Shoes	54.11		
5		1/16	Megacorp	Pay check		591.22	
6	119	1/16	Visa	Credit card	275.14		
7	120	1/17	Ralphs	Groceries	87.63		
8		1/19	ATM	Cash	100		

The computed value appears in the cell. Verify that it gives the answer you expected.

Cloning the formula using AutoFill

Check the *descriptive formula* that you just wrote. Convince yourself that you have a good general formula that works just as well for the other rows, whether they contain checks or deposits. *AutoFill* from G3 down the rest of the column.

Take a look at the result. Click on one of the newly filled cells. Note that Excel both copied the formula and adjusted it for each particular row. For example, G4 has the formula:

=G3 – E4 + F4.

Check that the calculations make sense. You now have a basic check register:

	A	B	C	D	E	F	G
				=G3-E4+F4			
1	Number	Date	To/from	Description	Check	Deposit	Balance
2		1/9		Starting balance			220.17
3	117	1/12	Von's	Groceries	103.56		116.61
4	118	1/13	Footlocker	Shoes	54.11		62.5
5		1/16	Megacorp	Pay check		591.22	653.72
6	119	1/16	Visa	Credit card	275.14		378.58
7	120	1/17	Ralphs	Groceries	87.63		290.95
8		1/19	ATM	Cash	100		190.95

Formatting the spreadsheet

This looks like a pretty good check register, except for one thing—the decimal points for the amounts do not line up. Select columns E, F, and G and give them the *currency format.*

This completes the basic checkbook spreadsheet. It is called **bank2.xls.**

Taking a look at what you've done

Step back for a moment and review what you did to create this spreadsheet. Spreadsheets use these techniques again and again.

You wrote a single formula for checks and deposits

You may have wondered why you bothered to include the deposit amount in the G3 formula when there isn't a deposit on that line. It would seem that you could have one simple formula that subtracts the check for those lines that have a check and another formula that adds the deposit for lines that have a deposit. After all, that is certainly how you do it when balancing your checkbook by hand.

The reason is that one of the most powerful features of Excel is its ability to take a formula that you have entered and checked out in one cell and copy it to many other cells. You can even copy it to all the other cells in the column or row. It's surprising how many otherwise sophisticated Excel users laboriously enter formulas in all the cells rather than take advantage of this technique. This copying technique lets you enter formulas for the first or second line, then use them to *AutoFill* in the entire spreadsheet. The secret is in writing good formulas that work for *all* data. You don't want to type in all those formulas, and you certainly don't want to change them if you put a deposit in a line where you had expected to have a check.

But why waste time in empty cells?

You may object, noting that there is a lot of unnecessary work going on. In every line that uses this formula the computer wastes time adding deposits that aren't there or subtracting nonexistent checks.

The answer is based on a key guideline for developing spreadsheets: *It is better to have the computer do some unnecessary calculations if it saves you work.* Remember that, once you have a formula that works, it is easy to copy it throughout the spreadsheet. So, if you can write one formula that works for all rows, you can skip typing them all in. So what if the computer is wasting its time looking in empty cells and adding and subtracting zeroes? It takes no noticeable time for *you*.

Another reason to have a single formula that works for all lines is that *you can change data without changing formulas.* Later, examples of "what-if" analysis enable you to see how changing data in the spreadsheet affects the outcome. For this example, you know that, if you copy your formula down to the next entry, it works, whether that entry is a check or a deposit.

You used a "bucket brigade" formula

You wrote a single formula that builds on the Balance from the previous row. It also works for either checks or deposits. If you clone it to another row, it works there just as well. This allows you to build the whole spreadsheet using only one formula.

You wrote and used a descriptive formula

Take a look at how you got this spreadsheet to do what you wanted. You came up with a nifty formula for computing the balance. It worked for both checks and deposits and it still worked when you copied it to the other rows. That formula is:

=G2 - E3 + F3

But this looks meaningless! To make sense of it, first you need to know that this formula is in cell G3. Then you need to know what the cells G2, E3, and F3 represent. It is meaningful only in the context of the current spreadsheet. Writing it in another spreadsheet or a report without context would be nonsensical. Even if you have the spreadsheet in front of you, it takes a moment (let's see now…G2 is the previous balance…) to figure out what it is doing.

It helps that Excel highlights the cells for you as you edit the formula, but it still requires some thought to see how the formula is getting its answer and what it represents.

	A	B	C	D	E	F	G	H
1	Number	Date	To/from	Description	Check	Deposit	Balance	Cleared?
2		1/9		Starting balance			$ 220.17	
3	117	1/12	Von's	Groceries	$ 103.56		=G2-E3+F3	yes
4	118	1/13	Footlocker	Shoes	$ 54.11		$ 62.50	yes
5		1/16	Megacorp	Pay check		$ 591.22	$ 653.72	yes
6	119	1/16	Visa	Credit card	$ 275.14		$ 378.58	
7	120	1/17	Ralphs	Groceries	$ 87.63		$ 290.95	yes
8		1/19	ATM	Cash	$ 100.00		$ 190.95	

The ***descriptive formula*** is much easier to understand:

Balance: = *Balance* previous - *Check* + *Deposit*

Even if it *were* possible to type it into Excel this way, the fastest way to enter a formula is by clicking on the cells. This formula description is a roadmap that guides you to click on the right cells to enter the formula. It's just as quick to enter a formula from this form as from the standard form with G2, E3, and F3—maybe even quicker. When you're building a spreadsheet, you can usually do descriptive formulas in your head, but you might want to write them out to document or communicate what you did.

This book presents descriptive formulas for two reasons:

• You can use the description to enter the formula anywhere.

- It is immediately clear what the formula is doing, making it easier to interpret the model.

Now close the spreadsheet. Use **File > Save As...** to save it with a new name if you entered your own checkbook information. Case Study 7 re-visits this.

Marry a millionaire!
Predicting future finances

FOCUS: Building a spreadsheet with inputs and a table, using bucket brigade formulas to predict future financial situations, playing "what-if" to answer a question

TOOLKIT: Bucket brigade formulas, inflation formula, investment growth formula, and descriptive formulas (all in Chapter 5), AutoFill (Chapter 4), some basic Excel techniques (Appendix A), techniques for building a spreadsheet (Chapter 6)

Tiffany, age 22, has just had a marriage proposal from her boyfriend. She doesn't love him, but he has a million dollars, well protected in conservative investments. She's imagining her life of luxury—every year filled with extravagance and ease. Can you help her picture it?

? Tiffany's boyfriend has $1,000,000 invested at an effective annual interest rate of 4%. They are planning to live off it at the moderate rate of $100,000 per year, plus 3% annual inflation. Tiffany is 22 now and has a life expectancy of 86. Will this plan keep her comfortable for the rest of her life?

TRY IT! Follow the steps from Chapter 6 to plan a spreadsheet for this decision. Check your solution against the one that follows.

Expanding the question

Tiffany wants to know how much money they will have available each year in the future. Since spending increases each year, she'll need to predict that. She'll also need to track the annual state of their investments.

Planning the spreadsheet

Goals of the spreadsheet determine what its rows and columns represent and the inputs that drive the outcome.

Rows

You want a table to keep track of their financial situation each year in the future. This suggests that the rows should represent years. This table will let you see how much money they will have left each year and whether it expires before Tiffany does.

Columns

Think about what is of interest each year. At the beginning of the year, they take out the money they will spend that year and put it in a checking account that does not pay interest. The rest of their funds are left to grow in the investments.

You'll want to keep track of each of the following:

Age   Tiffany's age that year
Spending Amount they will spend that year
Funds   Amount left invested at the beginning of the year

Inputs

All of the inputs are stated in the question. There does not seem to be anything else that is needed to proceed. So, the next step is to decide which of these inputs to group at the top. There is no harm in putting them all at the top, but take a look at them one by one.

The growth rates for inflation and investments will have an impact every year. This suggests that they need to be named inputs at the top of the spreadsheet. You also know Tiffany's age, the initial amount of money, and the initial spending rate. All of these are initial values, and so could go directly in the starting line of the table. They could just as well be inputs at the top, referenced by the starting line. This is a judgment call. As a general rule, anything that might change should go at the top to make it easier to play "what-if." This example puts the initial amount and the initial annual spending at the top for that reason. Tiffany's age goes in the starting line since it's not under her control. If the spreadsheet you built does it differently, that's no problem. There are several "right" spreadsheets.

Building the spreadsheet

Enter data, headings, and formulas, then analyze the results, as follows.

General inputs

Enter the inputs in a new worksheet. *Create names* for them using A1 through B4 or, if you want to save typing, just open **millionaire0.xls**:

	A	B	C	D
1	Start	$1,000,000	Initial amount of money	
2	Annual	$100,000	Annual spending the first year	
3	Inv growth	4%	Annual growth rate of investments	
4	Inflation	3%	Annual inflation rate	

Row and column headers

Enter the chosen column headings—Age, Spending, and Funds— in row 6. Her age works perfectly well as a row header; so you already have one.

The starting row

Row 7 is the first row of the table proper and it represents the current year.

TRY IT! Fill it out:

A7 (Age):   22
Tiffany is 22 in the starting year.

B7 (Spending):   =Annual
This is the annual spending this first year.

C7 (Funds):   =Start - B7
or if you prefer: =Start - Annual
This is what they started with minus what they took out to spend that year.

	A	B	C	D
1	Start	$ 1,000,000	Initial amount of money	
2	Annual	$ 100,000	Annual spending the first year	
3	Inv growth	4%	Annual growth rate of investments	
4	Inflation	3%	Annual inflation rate	
5				
6	Age	Spending	Funds	
7	22	$ 100,000	$ 900,000	

Bucket brigade formulas for the first future row

Row 8 is the first row to represent a year in the future. Write *bucket brigade formulas* beginning here, so you can finish it all with *AutoFill*.

TRY IT! Look for ways you can use the previous row to calculate this one. Write *descriptive formulas* and then enter them.

Age
A8:   =*Age* previous +1
She will be one year older.

Spending
B8:   =*Spending* previous * (1 + Inflation)
Spending increases by *the inflation rate*, which is the same as multiplying by (1 + *the inflation rate*).

Funds
Build the formula for C8 in steps. First, the funds they started with the previous year will grow at the investment growth rate:

=*Funds* previous * (1 + Inv_growth)

Then, they will take away the spending money for the year. So, here's the full formula:

C8:   =*Funds* previous * (1 + Inv_growth) - *Spending*

Summary of the formulas
Enter these by clicking on the appropriate cells, and you get:

A8:   =A7 + 1
B8:   =B7*(1+Inflation)
C8:   =C7*(1+Inv_growth) - B8

6	Age	Spending	Funds
7	22	$ 100,000	$ 900,000
8	23	$ 103,000	$ 833,000

Checking and AutoFilling the rest of the rows

The answers look reasonable. Now take a look at these formulas.
They reference only their own row, the previous row, and named
inputs. These are *bucket brigade formulas*. You can clone them
to the rest of the rows. Select A8 through C8, grab the fill handle at
the lower right corner of C8, and *AutoFill* all these formulas down
to row 71. That completes the rest of the table. *Change column
width*, if necessary, to see the big numbers. This is
millionaire.xls.

	A	B	C	D
1	Start	$ 1,000,000	Initial amount of money	
2	Annual	$ 100,000	Annual spending the first year	
3	Inv growth	4%	Annual growth rate of investments	
4	Inflation	3%	Annual inflation rate	
5				
6	Age	Spending	Funds	
7	22	$ 100,000	$ 900,000	
8	23	$ 103,000	$ 833,000	
9	24	$ 106,090	$ 760,230	
10	25	$ 109,273	$ 681,367	
11	26	$ 112,551	$ 596,070	
12	27	$ 115,927	$ 503,986	
13	28	$ 119,405	$ 404,740	
14	29	$ 122,987	$ 297,942	
15	30	$ 126,677	$ 183,183	
16	31	$ 130,477	$ 60,033	
17	32	$ 134,392	$ (71,958)	

Taking a look at the results

The funds become negative in row 17.

Surprise, Tiffany! You will run out of money before you're 32.

TRY IT! So, how much *can* they spend? Try different amounts for annual spending (B2). It turns out that an initial annual spending rate of $20,618 will just keep her going until age 86.

Tiffany breaks up with her boyfriend and gets a job waiting tables.

TRY IT! Exercise for the reader: How much money should her next boyfriend have?

7

Learning to function
Using Excel's built-in functions

In Case Study 2 you added a column of numbers using *AutoSum*.
This gave you a formula that uses the built-in SUM function. SUM
is the most often used function. That's why it gets its own button on
a toolbar. But there are many other useful functions.

Excel provides a powerful library of functions that can be part of a
formula. They generate random numbers, make calculations that
depend on conditions, or compute the maximum, the average, loan
payments, complex statistics, and much more.

You must tell the function what to use. The SUM function, for
example, needs to know what you want it to sum. These items of
information that you provide are called the *arguments* of the
function. Every function name is followed by its arguments in
parentheses and separated by commas. A function uses your
arguments to compute its result. An argument could be a number, a
cell, a range of cells, some text (enclosed in double quotes), or
another function, among others. It could be some formula-looking
expression that combines some of these (but without the = sign).
The number, type, and interpretation of the arguments vary from
function to function.

The simplest way to use a function is to write a formula like this:

=*function name* (*arguments*)

Remember the equal sign. It tells Excel that this is a formula you
want it to calculate. The function name can be upper or lower case;
Excel is not case-sensitive.

SUM takes up to 30 arguments. Each can be a single value or a range of cells. For example, =SUM(1,2,5) produces the answer 8. SUM, in its most common form, has a single argument that is a range of cells. For example, to add the numbers stored in cells B1 through B6, write either

=SUM(B1:B6)
or
=SUM(B1, B2, B3, B4, B5, B6)

Just as you click on cells to include them in a formula, you can enter a range like this by selecting it while you're writing the formula.

TRY IT! Open **cost0.xls**. Write a formula in B8 using the SUM function (not the AutoSum button) to total the four items for this example from Chapter 3. Drag over the numbers you want to sum. Be sure to remember the = and both parentheses.

Your formula should now read:

=SUM(B3:B6)

Here is what it might look like:

=SUM(B3:B6)	
	A	B
1	Tax rate	8.25%
2		
3	CPU	$500
4	Big monitor	$800
5	Ext disk drive	$300
6	MS Office	$300
7		
8	Total	$1,900

This is the technique you use to make formulas from functions. But how do you know what functions are available and what their arguments are?

Browsing the function library

Say you'd like to pay your credit card balance of $2,000 down to $500 over the next year and you want to know what your monthly payment should be. The interest rate is 1.5% per month. You can find a function that figures this for you. Browsing the function library gives you a list and descriptions of all of the functions available, and helps you select the right one and its arguments.

How to browse the function library:

1. Select the cell where you want the function to calculate.

2. Click on the Insert Function *fx* button on the formula bar [standard toolbar].

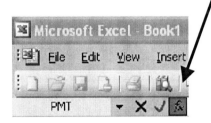

3. Select a category and then a function from the list.

4. Read the description at the bottom to see what it does. Click **OK** if it does what you want.

   Another window opens, telling you exactly what information (arguments) you need to give the function. Drag it to the side, if you need to, so you can see your inputs.

5. Fill in the arguments one by one by clicking on cells you want to use and tabbing through the arguments. Use the description of each argument that appears below the argument fields to help you. Click **OK** when you're done.

TRY IT! Open **credit0.xls**. This already includes inputs and *created names* for them. Follow the steps above to compute the credit card payments.

1. Select B7.

2. Click on the Insert Function button.

3. Select the category **Financial**, then click on the function **PMT** and read the description.

4. The description tells you that it does just what you want, so go ahead and click **OK**.

   A window opens. Click the top of it and drag it out of the way of your inputs if you need to.

5. Fill in the arguments one by one by clicking on cells you want to use. The descriptions should lead you to select these arguments:

For this argument field	Click on the cell named	Cell reference
Rate	Interest_rate	B4
Nper	Loan_length	B3
Pv	Amount	B2
Fv	Remaining	B5
Type		

   The present value (Pv) is what you owe now ($2,000) and the future value (Fv) is what you hope to owe in the future ($500). The type is 0, since you pay at the end of the month, so you can leave it out. Click **OK**.

Now, your formula looks like this:

=PMT(Interest_rate, Loan_length, Amount, Remaining)

The result (**credit.xls**) tells you that you must pay $221.70 each month to get down to $500 in 12 months, assuming you don't add any new charges:

	A	B	C
1	Inputs		
2	Amount	$2,000	
3	Loan length	12	months
4	Interest rate	1.5%	per month
5	Remaining	$500	
6			
7	Payment	($221.70)	

The parentheses (and possibly a red number) indicate a negative number, which represents an outflow or expenditure.

Case Study 6 provides a closer look at this and related functions.

This formula gives you an example of what Excel functions look like—the function name followed by the arguments in parentheses and separated by commas. You could have entered it directly like this and you probably will for functions that you use repeatedly. Looking at the function library is useful for finding new functions or recalling the order of the arguments for functions you know. Recent versions of Excel show you the arguments as soon as you enter the function name and first parenthesis.

As you'll see, you can do operations on the arguments. For example, if you had an *annual* interest rate, you'd have to divide it by 12 to make it a monthly rate, so your first argument would be Interest_rate/12. You can even use functions in the arguments, nesting functions within each other.

You can also do operations on the function itself. For example, this result shows a negative answer, as indicated by the parentheses around it. If you want to make it positive you can change its sign by editing the formula to put a - in front of it.

```
=-PMT(Interest_rate, Loan_length, Amount, Remaining)
```

Here are some examples from later in the book just to let you see how functions can combine with operations and other functions to do sophisticated calculations. You probably won't understand these, and you don't need to. Just notice where the functions (all caps followed by a parenthesis) show up, and how complex the arguments can become.

=-PMT(Interest_rate/12, Loan_length, Amount)

=IF(AND(Cash > 1000, Owing = 0), "buy", "don't buy")

=F13+12*PPMT(Interest_rate/12,A14*12-6,Term*12,Loan)

=IF(Age < 62, Pre_62, IF(Age > Life_exp, 0, Post_62))

=MIN((Expenses-B10) * (1-C2), D2)

=IF(RAND( ) < .60, "rain", "clear")

=E30*(1+$B20+($C20-$B20)*RAND( ))

=COUNTIF(Outcome, "win") / 100

Formulas with functions can become quite complex. The major challenge is keeping them understandable.

8

Useful functions
Introducing some handy functions

Now for a brief introduction to the most useful functions for decision-making...

You'll get plenty of practice applying these functions in later case studies. So it's OK if you don't understand them just yet. For now, get a flavor of the functions available to you. Try them out in a scratch workbook to see what they do. These are all the functions you need for the rest of the book. You'll learn more about each of them as you go along.

In all of these forms the italics indicate what each of the arguments represents. These are to be replaced by numbers, cell references, or expressions that look like formulas without the = sign.

SUM, AVERAGE, MIN, MAX

You've already used the SUM function to add a column of numbers. It accepts up to 30 arguments, which may be individual values or ranges. The other functions in this group accept the same arguments. You can get all of these by opening the menu on the *AutoSum* button.

SUM	Totals the values in the arguments
AVERAGE	Computes the arithmetic mean of the arguments
MIN	Finds the smallest value among the arguments
MAX	Finds the largest value among the arguments

Here are some examples:

=SUM(1,5,6,3) gives 15

=SUM(C4, 3, 5) adds 3 and 5 to the contents of cell C4.
=AVERAGE(1,5,6,3) gives 3.75
=MIN(1,5,6,3) gives 1
=MAX(1,5,6,3) gives 6

Total everything in column B: =SUM(B:B)

Find the average grade of the student whose test scores are in C17 through R17: =AVERAGE(C17:R17)

Find the profit, if any: =MAX(income-expenses, 0)

Find the loss, if any: =MIN(income-expenses, 0)

IF, SUMIF, and COUNTIF

These conditional functions give answers that depend on conditions anywhere in the spreadsheet. IF tests a condition and gives different results depending on whether the condition is true or false. Here is its form:

> IF(*logical test, value if true, value if false*)

For example:

=IF(D3 > 10000, "no", "buy")

The logical test is whether the number in cell D3 is larger than 10,000. This formula displays "no" if the cost stored in D3 is more than 10,000. Otherwise, it displays "buy." If D3 changes, the cell with this formula may change as well.

SUMIF checks a range of cells against a condition and adds only the entries that correspond to the cells that meet the condition.

COUNTIF searches through a range of cells and counts all nonblank values that satisfy some condition.

> SUMIF(*range to test, criteria, sum range*)
> COUNTIF(*range, criteria*)

For the next examples, here's a portion of a record of sales that goes to row 1000:

	A	B	C
1	Date	Amount	Salesperson
2	1/3	$ 2,692.45	Smith
3	1/3	$ 1,548.87	Lopez
4	1/3	$ 4,769.21	Brown
5	1/4	$ 1,997.25	Chung
6	1/4	$ 3,235.49	Smith

=SUMIF(C2:C1000, "Smith", B2:B1000) gives you Smith's total sales in dollars. Notice that text in arguments is enclosed in quotes.

=COUNTIF(C2:C1000, "Smith") counts the number of sales Smith made.

Chapter 9 explores how to write logical tests and criteria and it provides more examples of the use of these powerful functions.

SUMPRODUCT

SUMPRODUCT multiplies associated items together and sums these products. This is good for weighted averages.

SUMPRODUCT(*array1*, *array2*)

Here *array1*, *array2* are ranges of the same size. As an example, SUMPRODUCT(A1:A3, B1:B3) is the same as
A1*B1 + A2*B2 + A3*B3

Here's a portion of a professor's grade book. Each test counts toward some portion of the grade, with the final exam counting the most: 40% of the grade for the class.

	A	B	C	D	E	F	G
1		Test 1	Test 2	Midterm	Test 3	Test 4	Final
2	Test weight	10%	10%	20%	10%	10%	40%
3	Student 1	87	75	89	93	78	86

=SUMPRODUCT(B2:G2, B3:G3) calculates the grade for the semester for Student 1.

Financial functions

Excel has several financial functions, such as depreciation and internal rate of return, which you can explore. One that's especially handy is PMT, which computes loan payments, as you saw in the last chapter. IPMT and PPMT give you interest and principal payments. See the following case study for details.

Here's the typical use, to find the monthly payment on a fixed loan of some *amount* that goes for *loan length* years at some annual *interest rate*:

=-PMT(*interest rate*/12, *loan length**12, *amount*)

RANK

Compare alternatives. Which is number one? RANK assigns a ranking to each alternative, with 1 being the best. Ties are assigned the same rank. You need to tell it whether more is better (order = 0) or less is better (order = 1). See Chapter 10 and Case Study 8 for more details and an example. Here is the form:

=RANK(*score, range of scores of all alternatives, order*)

RAND

This is a random number generator. There may be parts of your decision that you can't know, such as stock market growth over the next 20 years. This function lets you look at random possible outcomes. RAND has no arguments, but you still need the parentheses: RAND( ). Learn more in Chapter 14.

RAND gives you a random number between 0 and 1. Every time you change anything in the spreadsheet you get a new random number, so you can see multiple possible outcomes. Here's a formula to give random outcomes according to a probability:

=IF(RAND( ) < *probability, outcome if it happens, outcome if it doesn't*)

Can I afford this car?

Loan payments

FOCUS: Example of a spreadsheet built using functions, preparation for later loan case studies, example of a sanity check

TOOLKIT: Functions PMT, PPMT, and IPMT (Chapter 8), AutoFill (Chapter 4), bucket brigade formulas (Chapter 5), browsing the function library (Chapter 7), descriptive formulas (Chapter 5 and Case Study 4)

Margie is considering buying and financing a car, keeping it for a year, and then selling it. She needs to understand what she will owe each month and when she sells.

? Margie wants to finance a $20,000 car loan at 6% annually, paid over three years (36 months). What will the monthly payments be? How much will she owe if she sells the car after a year?

You saw in Chapter 7 that a single formula using PMT answers the first question. While that payment is the same every month, it goes into two different pots, principal and interest, which vary. She needs to use the principal to figure out what she'll owe in a year. Figuring all this out is complicated. Fortunately, Excel has the functions PPMT and IPMT to do it for you.

Part of payment	Description	Excel function
Principal	Amount that goes toward paying off the loan. *Each month part of your payment goes to decreasing the amount you owe.*	PPMT
Interest	Amount you pay the bank for use of the money. *The bank recalculates this each month based on the remaining principal.*	IPMT

Expanding the question

There are actually two questions here—the monthly payment and the amount owing at month 12. The first needs but a single formula and is the same each month. The second, though, depends on all of the principal payments made the previous 11 months. This suggests a table of principal payments and loan amounts remaining for all 12 months. Once again, it's easier to use bucket brigade formulas to calculate each step than it is to find the last value.

While you're at it, include calculations for the portion that goes to interest. You don't need this to answer the question, but it helps you see what's going on. And, just for kicks, run it out the full 36 months of the loan.

Planning the loan payment spreadsheet

TRY IT! Make a new spreadsheet to look at the following each month:

- The number of the month (for reference)
- Payment
- Amount of the payment credited to principal
- Amount of the payment that goes to interest
- Loan amount remaining

Check your spreadsheet against the following steps.

You're interested in monthly payments, so the rows will represent months. The list above gives you the columns.

The inputs are the amount borrowed, the length of the loan, and the interest rate. These are general inputs that go at the top of the spreadsheet.

Building the spreadsheet

Open a new workbook. Collect the inputs and group them at the top with their labels, as shown below. *Create names* for them. Add text clarification in column C. Or just open **loan0.xls**.

Next, build the structure of the table proper. Label columns for the month and the four values to compute. Enter numbers for the 36 months. **(Hint:** Enter 1 and 2, select both, and then *AutoFill*.)

	A	B	C	D	E
1	Inputs				
2	Amount	$ 20,000			
3	Loan length	36	months		
4	Interest rate	6%			
5					
6	Month	Payment	Principal	Interest	Remaining
7	1				
8	2				
9	3				
10	4				

Now complete the formulas for the table. This is easiest to keep straight if you take it one column at a time and follow the steps: starting row, bucket brigade formula, check, and *AutoFill*.

Building a loan payment function

Start in the Payment cell for the first month (B7). You want a formula for the payment for the first month (which, incidentally, is the same all the other months because it's a fixed loan).

Browse the function library to find the financial function PMT and the arguments that it needs. Move the window, if necessary, to see your inputs. Enter values by clicking on cells and typing the rest. Press **Tab** to go to the next argument.

TRY IT! Write a formula for the monthly payment. Notice that the interest rate is for a year, not a month.

Argument	Description	Enter this value
Rate	*Interest rate per period of the loan.* The period is a month, since you make payments every month. So, the rate here is not the 6%, which is for the whole year, but 1/12 of that. Click and type.	Interest_rate/12
Nper	*The number of pay periods* (months). Click on the 36 in cell B3 to enter this.	Loan_length
Pv	*The worth of the stream of payments.* This is exactly the amount of the loan. Click on the $20,000 in cell B2 to enter it.	Amount
Fv	*Future value* (optional). This is the balance left after all the payments. It'll be paid off at that point, so this is 0, which is the default.	
Type	*Type* (optional). This can be omitted, since payments are at the end of the month.	

When you're done, click **OK**. Your formula appears in the formula bar:

=PMT(Interest_rate/12, Loan_length, Amount)

Now you have the formula for the loan payment in the first month Payment cell. It tells you that your loan payment is -$608.44.

(Depending on formatting, the negative may be shown by parentheses and/or red text rather than the negative sign.) Why negative? Because you are paying it out rather than receiving it. You want to show it in the cell without the negative sign. You can always change the sign of a formula with a "-." *Edit* the formula in B7, inserting a - right after the =. You'll get:

`=-PMT(Interest_rate/12, Loan_length, Amount)`

	A	B	C	D	E
			=-PMT(Interest_rate/12, Loan_length, Amount)		
1	Inputs				
2	Amount	$20,000			
3	Loan length	36	months		
4	Interest rate	6%			
5					
6	Month	Payment	Principal	Interest	Remaining
7	1	$608.44			

This answers the first question. Margie decides she can afford the $608.44 per month for this car. Now she wants to go ahead and finish the spreadsheet to see how much she will owe if she sells the car before it's paid off.

Completing the payment column

Enter the Payment formula for month 2 (B8).

Since this is a fixed loan, all of the payments are exactly the same. So, enter a formula that makes this cell the same as the one above:

=*Payment* previous

So, in B8 you have:

=B7

By the way, you could have just copied the month 1 formula down the column, but that would make the spreadsheet look a lot more complicated than it really is.

AutoFill this formula for month 2 down the rest of the column.

Computing the principal payments

Next is the Principal column, starting in month1 (cell C7).

TRY IT! Write a formula to compute principal payments each month. Use PPMT.

1. *Browse the function library* to look through Excel's financial functions to find PPMT and let it walk you through the arguments.

    Most of these look familiar from PMT. Fill them in as before. There is one new argument called **Per**, the number of the period. The periods are months, so this is just the month number that appears in the Month column. Enter this one by clicking.

2. Insert a negative sign in front of the function to switch the number to positive as before.

    Here is the completed *descriptive formula*:

    =-PPMT(Interest_rate/12, *Month*, Loan_length, Amount)

    Here's what you get in C7:

    =-PPMT(Interest_rate/12, A7, Loan_length, Amount)

3. Convince yourself that this formula works for all the rows.

4. *AutoFill* the formula down the column.

Computing the interest payments

TRY IT! Write a formula for the interest payments using IPMT. Hint: IPMT has the exact same form as PPMT.

Here's what you should get in D7:

=-IPMT(Interest_rate/12, A7, Loan_length, Amount)

Again, this formula works for all months. *AutoFill* this down the whole Interest column.

That takes care of principal and interest. A single formula was all you needed to complete each of these columns!

=-IPMT(Interest_rate/12, A7, Loan_length, Amount)			
	A	B	C	D
1	Inputs			
2	Amount	$20,000		
3	Loan length	36	months	
4	Interest rate	6%		
5				
6	Month	Payment	Principal	Interest
7	1	$608.44	$508.44	$100.00
8	2	$608.44	$510.98	$97.46
9	3	$608.44	$513.54	$94.90
10	4	$608.44	$516.10	$92.34
11	5	$608.44	$518.68	$89.75
12	6	$608.44	$521.28	$87.16

Computing the amount remaining on the loan

Now you can use the Principal column to figure out what's left owing. Each month the principal helps you pay off a little more of the loan. Start with the first month.

TRY IT! Enter a formula for the amount Remaining in month 1 (E7).

This is the original amount owing, reduced by the principal from that first payment. So Remaining for month 1 is the amount of the loan minus that first principal payment. The *descriptive formula* looks like:

=Amount - *Principal*

E7:   =Amount - C7

Did you get $19,491.56?

TRY IT! Now fill in the formula for month 2.

This is just what remained the previous month minus the new principal payment or, as a descriptive formula:

=*Remaining* previous - *Principal*

E8:   =E7 - C8

AutoFill the month 2 formula (E8) down to the rest of the column.

Caution: Use month 2, rather than month 1 since the first month is a special case.

	A	B	C	D	E
1	Inputs				
2	Amount	$20,000			
3	Loan length	36	months		
4	Interest rate	6%			
5					
6	Month	Payment	Principal	Interest	Remaining
7	1	$608.44	$508.44	$100.00	$19,491.56
8	2	$608.44	$510.98	$97.46	$18,980.58
9	3	$608.44	$513.54	$94.90	$18,467.04
10	4	$608.44	$516.10	$92.34	$17,950.94

Taking a look at the spreadsheet

Here is a summary of the *descriptive formulas* used:

For the first month:
Payment: =-PMT(Interest_rate/12, Loan_length, Amount)
Principal: =-PPMT(Interest_rate/12, *Month*, Loan_length, Amount)
Interest: =-IPMT(Interest_rate/12, *Month*, Loan_length, Amount)
Remaining: =Amount - *Principal*

For all other months:
Payment: =Payment previous
Principal: =-PPMT(Interest_rate/12, *Month*, Loan_length, Amount)
Interest: =-IPMT(Interest_rate/12, *Month*, Loan_length, Amount)
Remaining: =*Remaining* previous - *Principal*

Here is what your finished loan spreadsheet looks like (using a *split worksheet* to show the top and bottom). It is **loan.xls**.

	A	B	C	D	E
1	**Inputs**				
2	Amount	$20,000.00			
3	Loan length	$36.00	months		
4	Interest rate	$0.06			
5					
6	Month	Payment	Principal	Interest	Remaining
7	1	$608.44	$508.44	$100.00	$19,491.56
8	2	$608.44	$510.98	$97.46	$18,980.58
9	3	$608.44	$513.54	$94.90	$18,467.04
10	4	$608.44	$516.10	$92.34	$17,950.94
11	5	$608.44	$518.68	$89.75	$17,432.26
34	28	$608.44	$581.73	$26.71	$4,759.79
35	29	$608.44	$584.64	$23.80	$4,175.15
36	30	$608.44	$587.56	$20.88	$3,587.59
37	31	$608.44	$590.50	$17.94	$2,997.09
38	32	$608.44	$593.45	$14.99	$2,403.63
39	33	$608.44	$596.42	$12.02	$1,807.21
40	34	$608.44	$599.40	$9.04	$1,207.81
41	35	$608.44	$602.40	$6.04	$605.41
42	36	$608.44	$605.41	$3.03	($0.00)

Sanity check

Before you use this table, make sure you believe it. Always do a "sanity check" on any spreadsheet to convince yourself that it is doing what you expect it to do. Ask yourself:

- Are the answers what you would expect?
- Are the computed quantities related as they should be?

Did you pay off the car in 36 months?

This is a 36-month loan, so you would expect it to be paid off by then. In fact it is; the amount remaining after the last payment is 0. But why the parentheses? How can 0 be negative? Because of tiny round-off errors in the calculations, the result did not come out to exactly 0, but some fraction of a cent short. Close enough.

Do principal and interest add up to the payment?

Let Excel do the work. Take a look at **loancheck.xls**. This includes a new column F, called P&I (for principal and interest), which simply adds the two.

=*Principle* + *Interest*

You see that all these sums are the same as the payment. So that works as it should.

Is the interest applied properly?

You used the interest function in the interest column, but you could just as well have computed the monthly interest payments by applying the monthly interest percentage to the amount of the loan remaining. The Computed interest column (G) in **loancheck.xls** computes this for you.

=*Remaining* previous * Interest_rate/12

This is the same as column D, as you'd expect.

	A	B	C	D	E	F	G
1	Inputs						
2	Amount	$20,000					
3	Loan length	36	months				
4	Interest rate	6%					
5							
6	Month	Payment	Principal	Interest	Remaining	P&I	Computed interest
7	1	$608.44	$508.44	$100.00	$19,491.56	$608.44	$100.00
8	2	$608.44	$510.98	$97.46	$18,980.58	$608.44	$97.46
9	3	$608.44	$513.54	$94.90	$18,467.04	$608.44	$94.90
10	4	$608.44	$516.10	$92.34	$17,950.94	$608.44	$92.34
11	5	$608.44	$518.68	$89.75	$17,432.26	$608.44	$89.75

Using the spreadsheet

You can use this spreadsheet, **loan.xls**, for any loan. Try changing the loan length, interest rate, or amount, and see what happens. You can add more rows by selecting the filled cells of the last two rows and using *AutoFill*.

Margie sees that she will still owe more than $13,000 after a year (12 months). She decides to buy the car, but plans on keeping it at least a couple of years.

9

It depends
Using conditionals

Remember the bank account example from Case Study 4? It computed your balance based on all the checks you'd written and deposits you'd made, whether or not they'd cleared the bank. The bank balance, that number you use to balance your checkbook, depends on which checks and deposits have cleared. Just about any complex decision has these types of dependencies and Excel can handle them using the conditional function, IF. Try writing formulas using IF and SUMIF and see what they do when you change things.

Paying attention to what's going on

Complex decisions depend on the context, the current conditions under which the decision is made. Excel's most powerful function, IF, checks conditions and adjusts its answer accordingly. It allows you to make your formulas act differently based on conditions anywhere else in the spreadsheet. Facility with the IF function allows you to develop some very sophisticated models. Many spreadsheets developed in later chapters use IF. This function can be part of a larger formula, even inside another IF.

The function IF

This function has two possible outcomes, depending on the results of a test. Here's the basic form for the IF function:

=IF(*Logical test, Value if true, Value if false*)

Argument	Description
Logical test	The condition (a statement that's either true or false at any given time) that determines what the function IF is going to do
Value if true	What the function produces if the condition holds
Value if false	What the function produces if the condition does not hold

The *Value if true* and the *Value if false* are expressions that could contain numbers, text, functions, and so on. In fact they often look just like formulas, but without the =. If you want more than two possible outcomes you can nest IF functions. See, for example, Case Study 14.

What are "logical tests?"

Logical tests can evaluate TRUE or FALSE, depending on current values in the spreadsheet. Examples of logical expressions that could be conditions in an IF function are SUM(A1,A2,A3)=0, C2>C1+3, and E5=TRUE. If you know the values in the referenced cells, you can say whether each of these is true or false. The status may change if a referenced cell changes, but at a given time it is either true or false. You can build some fairly complex logical expressions and later examples explore these.

A typical logical expression is two expressions of the same type (e.g., both numbers), separated by one of the following operators:

=	is equal to
>	is greater than
<	is less than
>=	is greater than or equal to
<=	is less than or equal to
<>	is not equal to

Complex logical expressions

If you want to get fancy, there are functions that combine logical expressions:

=AND(*logical1, logical2,...*) is true if all of the arguments are true.

=OR(*logical1, logical2,...*) is true if at least one is true.

=NOT(*logical*) is true if its argument is false.

So for example,

=IF(AND(Cash > 1000, Owing = 0), "buy", "don't buy")

tells you "buy" only when you have more than $1,000 in cash and no balance owing on your credit card. If either of these conditions is false, it says, "don't buy."

The function SUMIF

Use this function to total only those items that meet some criteria. Here are its arguments:

Argument	Description
Range	The range of cells you want to check against the criteria
Criteria	The condition that defines which cells to add See below.
Sum_range	The potential cells to sum You may omit this, in which case SUMIF uses the cells in *Range*.

Here's the form:

=SUMIF(*Range, Criteria, Sum_range*)

Typically *Criteria* is a number or cell reference. SUMIF then adds all the cells in *Sum_range* that correspond to cells in *Range* with value equal to the number or to the contents of the referenced cell. However, *Criteria* could also be text, such as "yes" or "no." In that case, enclose it in quotes to tell Excel that it is text.

Here's a portion of a record of sales that goes to row 1000:

	A	B	C
1	Date	Amount	Salesperson
2	1/3	$ 2,692.45	Smith
3	1/3	$ 1,548.87	Lopez
4	1/3	$ 4,769.21	Brown
5	1/4	$ 1,997.25	Chung
6	1/4	$ 3,235.49	Smith

This formula totals all sales for the date 1/3:

=SUMIF(A2:A1000, A2, B2:B1000)

But, what if you need to do something more than look for exact matches? Say you want to count all sales over $3,000? That's where expressions come in. You can precede the number, cell reference or text by one of the comparison operators you saw above, >, <, >=, <=, or <>. The trick is to put the expression in quotes:

=COUNTIF(B2:B1000, ">3000")

These are the most complex *criteria* either of these functions accepts. So if, say, you wanted to sum everything in a column that's greater than MAX(D1:D5)-E1, you'd need to put that expression as a formula in some cell and then have **SUMIF** reference the cell.

Now what about *Range* and *Sum_range*? These can be rectangular areas of any size. In fact, **SUMIF** goes merrily about its business even if they differ in size, so you need to be careful. Usually, they're corresponding parts of two rows or two columns.

Other conditionals

In addition, Excel has logical functions to check all sorts of things, such as ISBLANK or ISTEXT. If you're interested, you can *browse the function library* to explore these functions.

Does my checking account balance?

Extending the checkbook spreadsheet

FOCUS: Adding to a spreadsheet, conditional calculations

TOOLKIT: IF function (Chapter 9), AutoFill (Chapter 4), descriptive formulas (Chapter 5)

Back in Case Study 4, you developed the spreadsheet **bank2.xls** to keep track of checks and deposits. Now you can use the IF function to expand it for bank balances to use in balancing your checkbook.

? You have a record of all of your checks and deposits and which have cleared the bank. Do your records agree with the balance shown by the bank?

Open the spreadsheet **bank2.xls** or your own checkbook spreadsheet. You'll expand it to consider what has cleared so far and what balance the bank reports.

Add two more columns to keep track of what has cleared the bank and the bank balance. Enter a yes under the Cleared? column (H) for checks or deposits that the bank reports cleared, as shown below. In this example it turns out that all previous checks and deposits have cleared, so the initial Bank Balance is the same as the initial Balance.

	A	B	C	D	E	F	G	H	I
1	**Number**	**Date**	**To/from**	**Description**	**Check**	**Deposit**	**Balance**	**Cleared?**	**Bank Balance**
2		1/9		Starting balance			$220.17		$220.17
3	117	1/12	Von's	Groceries	$103.56		$116.61	yes	
4	118	1/13	Footlocker	Shoes	$54.11		$62.50	yes	
5		1/16	Megacorp	Pay check		$591.22	$653.72	yes	
6	119	1/16	Visa	Credit card	$275.14		$378.58		
7	120	1/17	Ralphs	Groceries	$87.63		$290.95	yes	
8		1/19	ATM	Cash	$100.00		$190.95		

If you're using your own checkbook spreadsheet, add similar columns to it.

Now you're ready to complete the table with a formula to compute the bank balance.

A formula for the bank balance

The bank balance is the amount of money that the bank thinks you have, based on what they have cleared so far. It matches the current balance shown on your bank statement if you and your bank are correct.

The calculation is similar to what you did for the **Balance**, except that you *only* consider checks and deposits that have cleared the bank. This indicates that you want to use **IF** to compute the bank balance and that it depends on the value of **Cleared?**.

TRY IT! Take another look at the IF function. Think about what you will use for each argument.

The first argument is *Logical test*.

Logical test

The condition of interest is whether **Cleared?** says "**yes**," written:

Cleared? = "yes"

Note that you enclose the word in double quotation marks. This is to let Excel know that it is text.

The formula if it is "true"

The next argument is *Value if true*, what you want the formula to give you if the condition is true, i.e., if **Cleared?** is **yes**. If the condition is true, the check or deposit has cleared the bank; you want to subtract it from or add it to the previous balance. So, just as you did before, you have:

Bank Balance previous - *Check* + *Deposit*

Note that there is no = here since this is only part of a formula.

The formula if it is "false"

The final argument, *Value if false*, is the value you want the formula to give you if the condition is false. "False" means that the check or deposit has not cleared; as far as the bank is concerned nothing has changed. You have just the previous balance:

Bank Balance previous.

Taking a look at the formula you built

Put it all together. Here is the final formula:

=IF(*Cleared?* = "yes", *Bank Balance* previous - *Check* + *Deposit*, *Bank Balance* previous)

Enter this in I3 by clicking on the cells, and it should read,

=IF(H3="yes", I2 - E3 + F3, I2).

Do you get the answer you expected?

By the way, you can use **IF** functions (or any other functions for that matter) as part of a larger formula. For example, you could have just as well written this formula as:

= *Bank Balance* previous + IF(*Cleared* = "yes", *Deposit - Check*, 0)

Take a moment to convince yourself that this gives you the same answer as the other form.

Now *AutoFill* your formula down to the rest of the rows. Take a look at the computed bank balances. Did Excel add or subtract whatever had cleared? Did it leave the **Bank Balance** alone if the transaction hadn't cleared? The bottom value for **Bank Balance** is the only one to use when balancing your checkbook. This should match the balance that the bank shows in the statement.

		=IF(H3="yes", I2 - E3 + F3, I2)							
	A	B	C	D	E	F	G	H	I
1	**Number**	**Date**	**To/from**	**Description**	**Check**	**Deposit**	**Balance**	**Cleared?**	**Bank Balance**
2		1/9		Starting balance			$220.17		$220.17
3	117	1/12	Von's	Groceries	$103.56		$116.61	yes	$116.61
4	118	1/13	Footlocker	Shoes	$54.11		$62.50	yes	$62.50
5		1/16	Megacorp	Pay check		$591.22	$653.72	yes	$653.72
6	119	1/16	Visa	Credit card	$275.14		$378.58		$653.72
7	120	1/17	Ralphs	Groceries	$87.63		$290.95	yes	$566.09
8		1/19	ATM	Cash	$100.00		$190.95		$566.09

As more checks clear, put more **yes**es in column H. Excel automatically recalculates your bank balance for you. That's a great feature of IF: It responds as things change.

TRY IT! Put **yes** in H6. See how that changes your bank balance.

Did you get $290.95?

It may seem that there is a lot of excess calculation, computing all these intermediate bank balances. However, it is easier for you (if not for the computer) to build up answers step by step. The formulas are simpler and you can more easily see what is going on.

If you used **bank2.xls**, you can check your work against the **bank.xls** spreadsheet. Close it when you're done. If you used your own information, use **Save As...** to save it under a new name.

10

Comparing apples and oranges
Decisions with multiple objectives

What makes a decision hard? You would think you could just pick your measure of "goodness" (lowest cost, best performance, highest return) and then choose the alternative with the best score. What's so hard about that? Well, two things. One is assessing future performance or return. Later chapters present many examples of this. The other problem is that there is seldom just one measure of goodness. There are always tradeoffs—performance vs. price or returns vs. risk. You want a big house with low maintenance, in a good neighborhood and at a low price. Sounds great. Does it exist? No. You have to make tradeoffs.

For example, here's a list that compares some makes of car. Which is best?

	A	B	C	D	E
1	**Factor**	**Kumquat**	**Excrutia**	**Pretensio**	**Dingo**
2	Price	$13,680	$13,625	$13,915	$14,660
3	Warranty	4	3	3	3
4	Consumer rating	9.2	9.5	9	9.3
5	Crash test	Good	Average	Excellent	Excellent
6	Engine displacement	2	2.2	2	1.7
7	Seating capacity	5	5	5	5
8	4-wheel disc brakes	yes	no	no	no
9	Luggage capacity	11.4	13.9	14.8	12.9
10	Highway mileage	35	34	35	38

The Excrutia is best in price, the Kumquat is best in warranty, the Pretensio has the most luggage capacity, and the Dingo has the best gas mileage. No clear winner here. How can you even compare all these considerations? They are all expressed in different terms—dollars, years, subjective ratings, words, liters, people, yes/no, cubic feet, and miles per gallon. Not only that, but sometimes more is better (luggage capacity) while other times less is better (price).

Case Study 9 works this decision out. Here are some ways of thinking about decisions like this and the Excel techniques that support them.

Rank order

It's easier to compare scores for each factor if you convert them to ranks. For each factor, give each alternative a rank representing how it compares with the others—1 if it's the best, 2 for second best, and so on. Excel has a built-in function RANK that does this for you. Here is the form:

=RANK(*score, range of scores of all alternatives, order*)

Here *order* tells Excel whether less is better (order = 1) or more is better (order = 0). RANK gives the same number to alternatives in the case of a tie. So, for example, four choices may be ranked 1, 2, 2, and 4.

RANK only works with numbers. It doesn't know that Excellent is better than Good. So, before you do this, give everything a numerical score, such as Excellent = 5, Good = 4, and so on. Usually, 1 is yes and 0 is no. It turns out that this 0-1 coding can make some formulas simpler; the 0 score makes everything irrelevant go away.

Once you rank everything, here are some simple techniques to help you make a decision:

- Count how many times each alternative is ranked number 1. Do it by hand or use COUNTIF. The higher the count the better.

- Add up the rankings for each alternative. The lower the better.

Normalized scores

One problem with ranks is that they treat big, important differences and insignificant differences the same. Normalizing gives you scores that show the big differences. Best of all, you can compare them factor-to-factor.

The idea is to come up with a score for each factor that represents how close to ideal it is. The best score that you could imagine for an alternative you'd consider gets a normalized score of 1.0. The worst gets 0. Everything else gets a decimal fraction score somewhere in between. This works even if less is better. Here's the formula to convert from arbitrary scores to normalized scores:

$$=(score - worst)/(best - worst)$$

Now you can compare normalized scores across factors. If all factors are equally important, add them up for each alternative. More is better.

Weighted totals

The problem is that usually not all factors are equally important. You can give each factor its own score representing its importance. This is completely subjective. It's a way of representing which of the considerations are of most value to you. You've probably seen weighting used in assigning grades in classes you've taken. The ordinary tests may count toward 10% of your grade, while the final may be 40%. This indicates that the final is far more important. The weights always add up to 100%. You multiply each score by its weight and add them all together to get the overall score (provided that more is better). SUMPRODUCT does this for you.

You could assign weighting numbers to each factor, adjusting them until they add up to 100%. But there's an easier way. Give each factor a preference score. It doesn't matter how you do this, just so that you give proportionately higher scores to the most important factors. Then SUM them all. Here's the weighting for each factor:

$$=weight/\text{SUM}(weights\ of\ all\ factors)$$

Case Studies 9 and 10 use weighted normalized scores.

Even Swaps

Often when you make a decision, you tell yourself things like, "I'd be willing to give up a little gas mileage for a more powerful engine." Hammond, Keeney and Raiffa, in their excellent book,

Smart Choices: A Practical Guide to Making Better Life Decisions, present a technique for turning these mental tradeoffs into a complete decision process, called the Even Swap Method. It turns out that you can build an Excel spreadsheet to support this method. See Case Study 8.

The idea is to imagine each of your alternatives modified in some way, using an even swap to make it easier to compare to the others. Imagine that you could give the Dingo a 2-liter engine, but you had to give up gas mileage. How many miles per gallon would you give up as an even swap? Once you do that you can imagine a Dingo variant that you rate equal to the original, but that is easier to compare with the other 2-liter-engine alternatives. Compare the new alternatives. Is any one of them better than some other in all categories? If so, you can eliminate the poorer one. Keep doing this until you have one alternative that's better in all respects than the others that remain.

This is a good technique, since it gets around the problems of relative importance of the various factors and of "apples and oranges" comparison. It even works if an improvement in something is more important in some cases than others. For example, an extra 0.1 liter in engine size is worth more if the car is underpowered. In selecting an apartment, a pool for exercise may be less valuable if the complex has a fitness center. Most importantly, this technique forces you to think. What are you trying to achieve? What really matters and why?

Which apartment should I choose?

Even swaps

FOCUS: Even Swap, building a spreadsheet with multiple tables

TOOLKIT: RANK function and the Even Swap method (Chapter 10), AutoFill and absolute reference (Chapter 4), Copy bucket brigade formula (Chapter 5)

Most decisions have multiple goals. Kathy wants to rent an apartment that has plenty of room, amenities, and a low cost. If she can find one that's best in all aspects, great. But, this is rare. More often, we need to trade, for example, space for cost.

? Kathy wants to rent an apartment. She's narrowed it down to three alternatives. She wants a bedroom, a guest room, an office and a place to exercise in the complex—either a fitness center or, preferably, a pool. She wants it as big as possible and as inexpensive as possible. Which should she choose?

Here are her choices (**aptchoose1.xls**):

	A	B	C	D
1		**Vista de Nada**	**Clark Gables**	**Stilted Manor**
2	Rent	$1,350	$1,250	$1,300
3	Pool?	1	1	0
4	Fitness Center?	1	0	1
5	Bedrooms	2	3	3
6	Dens	1	0	0
7	Sq. feet	1200	1000	1050

In this table, as is frequent, "yes" is coded as 1 and "no" as 0.

There are other factors, such as number of bathrooms and proximity to work, that she considered previously in narrowing down her choices. This table omits them, because these final choices are nearly the same on those factors.

As in many such decisions, she's comparing apples and oranges. Usually, more is better; but for rent, less is better. Some items have quantities, but there are also counts and yes/no codes. Furthermore, some of these considerations are more important than others. This is a good candidate for the Even Swap Method of Hammond, Keeney and Raiffa.

Introducing a spreadsheet to make trades

Open **aptchoose2.xls**. This is a spreadsheet built to use the even swap method. Use it for this decision to see how it works. This spreadsheet works for any even swap. **Insert rows** or **columns** to expand it for other decisions if you need to.

In a departure from other spreadsheets you've done so far, this has multiple related tables. Look at them one by one.

Original matrix

The first one (A1:E7) is just the original input comparison matrix:

	A	B	C	D	E
1		Vista de Nada	Clark Gables	Stilted Manor	less is better?
2	Rent	1350	1250	1300	1
3	Pool?	1	1	0	0
4	Fitness Center?	1	0	1	0
5	Bedrooms	2	3	3	0
6	Dens	1	0	0	0
7	Sq. feet	1200	1000	1050	0

It needs one more column so that you can rank the choices. Column E tells whether less is better. As usual, 1 means "yes" and 0 is "no." No formulas here. This is all input.

Trades

The next one (A9: D15) has the same row headers, but is otherwise blank so far.

9	Trades			
10	Rent			
11	Pool?			
12	Fitness Center?			
13	Bedrooms			
14	Dens			
15	Sq. feet			

There are no formulas here either; this is another input area. This is where you record the even swaps that Kathy would be willing to make as she compares her alternatives.

The row headers for all of these tables use the Copy *bucket brigade formula* to label the rows the same as on the original table. You can change the row labels in the top table and they all change. Click on one of these labels, say A10, to see this.

Comparing after trades

Below that is a table that looks like the original one, at least so far:

17	Compare after trades			
18	Rent	1350	1250	1300
19	Pool?	1	1	0
20	Fitness Center?	1	0	1
21	Bedrooms	2	3	3
22	Dens	1	0	0
23	Sq. feet	1200	1000	1050

The difference is that there are formulas here that change these numbers when you enter swaps. So, this is where you show the results of those swaps. These are the imagined alternatives. This table adds the trades to the original matrix, so it changes automatically as you swap. Each cell is the original plus the swap. For example, B18 is

=B2 + B10

You can *AutoFill* such a table from this single formula. *AutoFill* across the row first from B to D, then with B18 through D18 still selected, *AutoFill* it down, completing the table. (This has already been done for you.)

Ranking after trades

The final table ranks alternatives relative to each factor, with 1 being best. Take a look at the ranks. You see some factors, such as Bedrooms, with more than one in first place. Even so, you lack a choice that ranks first in everything and, therefore, you lack a clear winner. Furthermore, no choice is worse than some other overall, leaving all alternatives still in the running at this point.

25	Rank after trades			
26	Rent	3	1	2
27	Pool?	1	1	3
28	Fitness Center?	1	3	1
29	Bedrooms	3	1	1
30	Dens	1	2	2
31	Sq. feet	1	3	2

Now look inside this table to see how it works. This table uses the RANK function. Recall its form:

=RANK(*score, range of scores of all alternatives, order*)

Notice that column E in the original matrix gives you exactly what you need in the last argument to tell the ranking the *order*. In both cases, 0 means more is better and 1 means less is better. So, you can write a formula to rank this score relative to the other scores in the row. For example, here's B26:

=RANK(B18, $B18:$D18, $E2)

Convince yourself that this gives you the rank of Vista de Nada relative to the others, in terms of rent.

Note the use of the $ (*absolute reference*) to keep columns fixed so that it copies properly. It always finds the ranking within columns B through D, and always finds the order in column E. So, you can *AutoFill* it both across and down to complete the table.

Notice that this formula reaches back up into the first table to get the order from E2. Even when it's cloned, it pulls the right number from the first table. This works because the two tables are laid out the same; the formula in the second row of this table gets what it needs from the second row of the top table, and so on.

What would you trade?

Kathy thinks about what she would trade. Either a den or bedroom could be an office. So, if you could add a bedroom and take away a den in Vista de Nada you'd get an alternative that is just as good.

TRY IT! Enter her trades in the Trades table under the Vista de Nada column:
- Put 1 in B13 to indicate an added bedroom.
- Put -1 in B14 to show trading away the den.

	A	B	C	D	E
1		Vista de Nada	Clark Gables	Stilted Manor	less is better?
2	Rent	1350	1250	1300	1
3	Pool?	1	1	0	0
4	Fitness Center?	1	0	1	0
5	Bedrooms	2	3	3	0
6	Dens	1	0	0	0
7	Sq. feet	1200	1000	1050	0
8					
9	**Trades**				
10	Rent				
11	Pool?				
12	Fitness Center?				
13	Bedrooms	1			
14	Dens	-1			
15	Sq. feet				
16					
17	**Compare after trades**				
18	Rent	1350	1250	1300	
19	Pool?	1	1	0	
20	Fitness Center?	1	0	1	
21	Bedrooms	3	3	3	
22	Dens	0	0	0	
23	Sq. feet	1200	1000	1050	
24					
25	**Rank after trades**				
26	Rent	3	1	2	
27	Pool?	1	1	3	
28	Fitness Center?	1	3	1	
29	Bedrooms	1	1	1	
30	Dens	1	1	1	
31	Sq. feet	1	3	2	

Now what you see in **Compare after trades** (B18:B23) is an imagined apartment of equal value to Vista de Nada, but easier to compare to the others, since it also has 3 bedrooms and no den.

The ranks changed, but you still can neither choose nor eliminate an alternative. Still, the choices are now all equal for bedrooms and dens. You've eliminated two criteria, thus making the problem a little easier.

Next, she thinks about the exercise facilities. She would prefer a pool. In fact, she'd pay an extra $40 a month to get a pool instead of a fitness center. She imagines swapping $40 in additional rent to add a pool and take away the fitness center at Stilted Manor.

TRY IT! Add $40 in rent for Stilted Manor (40 in D10), add a pool (1 in D11) and take away the fitness center (-1 in D12). Check the rankings. A clear winner has yet to emerge.

Next, she thinks about Vista de Nada, with both a pool and fitness center. She'd hardly ever use the fitness center, so would be willing to pay only about $10 a month extra for it. Notice how this trade depends on other conditions. If there were no pool, she would be willing to pay more for a fitness center. This is a key feature of the Even Swap method. It acknowledges that the worth of a feature makes sense only in context. She swaps lowering the rent at Vista de Nada by $10 for removing the fitness center. Add these trades to the table.

Now the rankings say Vista de Nada is the same or better than Stilted Manor in all considerations. You still don't know which of the three choices is best, but you know it won't be Stilted Manor. So eliminate it. Cross it out by selecting column D and choosing **Format > Cells > Font > Effects > Strikethrough {Home > Cells > Format > Format Cells** and so on, similarly}.

	A	B	C	D	AN
1		**Vista de Nada**	**Clark Gables**	**~~Stilted Manor~~**	**less is better?**
2	Rent	1350	1250	~~1300~~	1
3	Pool?	1	1	~~0~~	0
4	Fitness Center?	1	0	~~1~~	0
5	Bedrooms	2	3	~~3~~	0
6	Dens	1	0	~~0~~	0
7	Sq. feet	1200	1000	~~1050~~	0
8					
9	**Trades**				
10	Rent	-10		~~40~~	
11	Pool?			~~1~~	
12	Fitness Center?	-1		~~-1~~	
13	Bedrooms	1			
14	Dens	-1			
15	Sq. feet				
16					
17	**Compare after trades**				
18	Rent	1340	1250	~~1340~~	
19	Pool?	1	1	~~1~~	
20	Fitness Center?	0	0	~~0~~	
21	Bedrooms	3	3	~~3~~	
22	Dens	0	0	~~0~~	
23	Sq. feet	1200	1000	~~1050~~	
24					
25	**Rank after trades**				
26	Rent	2	1	~~2~~	
27	Pool?	1	1	~~1~~	
28	Fitness Center?	1	1	~~1~~	
29	Bedrooms	1	1	~~1~~	
30	Dens	1	1	~~1~~	
31	Sq. feet	1	3	~~2~~	

Now it's a choice between Vista de Nada and Clark Gables. The swaps have made them comparable in everything but square footage and rent. Vista de Nada has an extra 200 square feet. Kathy figures the extra space is worth $50 a month.

TRY IT! Enter this swap on Clark Gables:

	A	B	C	D	E
1		**Vista de Nada**	**Clark Gables**	~~**Stilted Manor**~~	**less is better?**
2	Rent	1350	1250	~~1300~~	1
3	Pool?	1	1	~~0~~	0
4	Fitness Center?	1	0	~~1~~	0
5	Bedrooms	2	3	~~3~~	0
6	Dens	1	0	~~0~~	0
7	Sq. feet	1200	1000	~~1050~~	0
8					
9	**Trades**				
10	Rent	-10	50	~~40~~	
11	Pool?			~~1~~	
12	Fitness Center?	-1		~~-1~~	
13	Bedrooms	1			
14	Dens	-1			
15	Sq. feet		200		
16					
17	**Compare after trades**				
18	Rent	1340	1300	~~1340~~	
19	Pool?	1	1	~~1~~	
20	Fitness Center?	0	0	~~0~~	
21	Bedrooms	3	3	~~3~~	
22	Dens	0	0	~~0~~	
23	Sq. feet	1200	1200	~~1050~~	
24					
25	**Rank after trades**				
26	Rent	2	1	~~2~~	
27	Pool?	1	1	~~1~~	
28	Fitness Center?	1	1	~~1~~	
29	Bedrooms	1	1	~~1~~	
30	Dens	1	1	~~1~~	
31	Sq. feet	1	1	~~3~~	

We have a winner! Now the imagined Vista de Nada and Clark Gables are comparable in all but rent, with Clark Gables being better. Notice that it now ranks first in everything. This is **aptchoose.xls**.

Notice that all of the choices were completely subjective. If *you* were choosing among these apartments you might make a different choice. Either answer is a good decision, since it represents your individual preferences. This is an excellent technique to help you make and keep track of subjective tradeoffs in a realistic context.

Which car should I buy?

Balancing multiple objectives

FOCUS: Subjective considerations, balancing multiple criteria, adding considerations to a decision, weighted normal technique

TOOLKIT: Normalized scores and weighted totals (Chapter 10), AutoFill and absolute references (Chapter 4), IF, MIN, MAX, SUM, and SUMPRODUCT functions (Chapter 8)

Sometimes there are so many goals in a decision that it is difficult to make trades. You can approach a decision like this by normalizing and weighting the various factors.

Here's a decision that most of us need to make every few years—choosing a car to buy.

? Woody wants to buy a new car. He wants a reliable new sedan for under $20,000. He finds four cars that meet his basic requirements—the Kumquat, Excrutia, Pretensio, and Dingo. They each have plusses and minuses. Which one should he buy?

He starts by making a list of all of the considerations that are important to him. Then he fills in a table with information he finds on the Internet. His table is **car1.xls:**

	A	B	C	D	E
1	Factor	Kumquat	Excrutia	Pretensio	Dingo
2	Price	$ 13,680	$ 13,625	$ 13,915	$ 14,660
3	Warranty	4	3	3	3
4	Consumer rating	9.2	9.5	9	9.3
5	Crash test	Good	Average	Excellent	Excellent
6	Engine displacement	2	2.2	2	1.7
7	Seating capacity	5	5	5	5
8	4-wheel disc brakes	yes	no	no	no
9	Luggage capacity	11.4	13.9	14.8	12.9
10	Highway mileage	35	34	35	38

Comparing apples and oranges?

No clear winner here. How can you even compare all these considerations? Can you compare dollars, miles per gallon and subjective ratings? More is better for most of these, but less is better for price.

Well, one simple approach is to ask which car is best relative to each factor. Woody makes a spreadsheet, **car2.xls**, designed to look for winners. Here it is:

	A	B	C	D	E
1	Factor	Kumquat	Excrutia	Pretensio	Dingo
2	Price	$ 13,680	$ 13,625	$ 13,915	$ 14,660
3	Warranty	4	3	3	3
4	Consumer rating	9.2	9.5	9	9.3
5	Crash test	Good	Average	Excellent	Excellent
6	Engine displacement	2	2.2	2	1.7
7	Seating capacity	5	5	5	5
8	4-wheel disc brakes	yes	no	no	no
9	Luggage capacity	11.4	13.9	14.8	12.9
10	Highway mileage	35	34	35	38
11					
12					
13	Factor	Kumquat	Excrutia	Pretensio	Dingo
14	Price	0	1	0	0
15	Warranty	1	0	0	0
16	Consumer rating	0	1	0	0
17	Crash test	0	0	1	1
18	Engine displacement	0	1	0	0
19	Seating capacity	1	1	1	1
20	4-wheel disc brakes	1	0	0	0
21	Luggage capacity	0	0	1	0
22	Highway mileage	0	0	0	1
23					
24	Total	3	4	3	3

Each car earns a 1 if it is the best option for a factor. So, the Excrutia is best for price and the Kumquat is best for warranty. This is a quick-and-dirty technique. Count the number of factors in which each car is the "winner." You could do this by hand or, as in **car2.xls**, have Excel use the IF, MIN and MAX functions to check each car against each factor and see where it's best. Click on cells to see the formulas. They are different for various rows. Then use SUM to count the number of times each car wins.

It looks like the Excrutia is the best choice. But, is it? There are shortcomings to this quick-and-dirty analysis.

- Some differences that make a winner are very small.

  For example, the Excrutia costs only $55 less than the Kumquat.

- There's no accounting for differences among non-winners, which might be significant.

  For example, the Kumquat should get credit for its "good" crash test rating relative to the Excrutia's "average."

- All factors are given equal weight when, in fact, some are more important than others.

Soon, you'll use another technique that gets around these concerns. But, Woody is really bothered by the results. He considers the Excrutia the clunkiest, least responsive car he has ever driven. Something very important has been left out of the analysis—his subjective preferences.

Subjective considerations

Your subjective preferences are an important part of any decision, especially one as personal as choosing a car. Go with them. No need to justify or explain them. Just go ahead and incorporate them into the comparison.

The easiest way is to rate them on a scale of 1 to 5, with 5 being best. Think of them as poor, fair, average, good, and excellent. Woody adds two more considerations to his list, Driving enjoyment and Appearance, and rates each choice. This is in **car3.xls**.

	A	B	C	D	E
1	Factor	Kumquat	Excrutia	Pretensio	Dingo
2	Price	$ 13,680	$ 13,625	$ 13,915	$ 14,660
3	Warranty	4	3	3	3
4	Consumer rating	9.2	9.5	9	9.3
5	Crash test	Good	Average	Excellent	Excellent
6	Engine displacement	2	2.2	2	1.7
7	Seating capacity	5	5	5	5
8	4-wheel disc brakes	yes	no	no	no
9	Luggage capacity	11.4	13.9	14.8	12.9
10	Highway mileage	35	34	35	38
11	Driving	4	2	3	3
12	Appearance	5	4	1	3

Making the scores comparable

This list now includes all the important considerations. But it's still hard to work with. Some scores are words (good, average, excellent, yes, no) and others are numbers. The first step to fix this is to make the table all numerical.

	A	B	C	D	E
1	Factor	Kumquat	Excrutia	Pretensio	Dingo
2	Price	$ 13,680	$ 13,625	$ 13,915	$ 14,660
3	Warranty	4	3	3	3
4	Consumer rating	9.2	9.5	9	9.3
5	Crash test	Good	Average	Excellent	Excellent
6	Engine displacement	2	2.2	2	1.7
7	Seating capacity	5	5	5	5
8	4-wheel disc brakes	yes	no	no	no
9	Luggage capacity	11.4	13.9	14.8	12.9
10	Highway mileage	35	34	35	38
11	Driving	4	2	3	3
12	Appearance	5	4	1	3
13					
14	Numerical scores				
15	Factor	Kumquat	Excrutia	Pretensio	Dingo
16	Price	$ 13,680	$ 13,625	$ 13,915	$ 14,660
17	Warranty	4	3	3	3
18	Consumer rating	9.2	9.5	9	9.3
19	Crash test	4	3	5	5
20	Engine displacement	2	2.2	2	1.7
21	Seating capacity	5	5	5	5
22	4-wheel disc brakes	1	0	0	0
23	Luggage capacity	11.4	13.9	14.8	12.9
24	Highway mileage	35	34	35	38
25	Driving	4	2	3	3
26	Appearance	5	4	1	3

TRY IT! Make a *copy* of the table below itself in A15, so you can look at it as you work. Change the descriptive words into corresponding numbers. For example, the crash test results happen to be based on the same scale of poor through excellent that we used for the subjective considerations. So, make average 3, good 4, and excellent 5. As before, replace "yes" with 1 and "no" with 0. Enter these numbers (in rows 19 and 22 for this case study) in place of the words.

How close to perfect is it?

Now it's all numbers, but you still can't combine them in any meaningful way. For example, the average is dominated by price. Worse yet, sometimes more is better and other times less is better. The solution is to normalize (see Chapter 10) to get rid of units and convert everything into a number that represents how close to perfect that aspect of the car is.

All of these numbers make sense only when you compare them with something. So ask yourself, *what is the best it could be? What is the worst it could be?* Then you can assign each score a number that tells how far along it is from worst to best. The best is 1. The worst is 0. Halfway in between is 0.5. Something that's almost the best might be 0.9. Once you've done this for all of the considerations they will all be rated on a scale of 0 to 1, so you can compare them.

This is pretty easy to do for some of the considerations. Take the subjective ones. Best is 5, worst is 1, and 3 is halfway in the middle. So the normalized subjective scores will be 0, .25, .5, .75 and 1.

But the others are not so clear. What about the cost of the car? Is the best price 0? Or maybe they pay you to take it? The worst case gets even crazier. Some fancy sports cars cost as much as a house. Here's how to handle it. *Choose the best and worst of the ones you might reasonably consider.*

Woody figures that he could afford no more than $20,000 for a car, so he chooses that as the worst case. Even the most basic new car is at least $9,000, so he chooses that as the best case. As you'll see in a moment, it's important to visualize yourself in the best and worst situations. Woody fills in the best and worst case values for each consideration in new columns F and G in **car4.xls**:

14	**Numerical scores**						
15	Factor	Kumquat	Excrutia	Pretensio	Dingo	Worst	Best
16	Price	$ 13,680	$ 13,625	$ 13,915	$ 14,660	20000	9000
17	Warranty	4	3	3	3	3	6
18	Consumer rating	9.2	9.5	9	9.3	1	10
19	Crash test	4	3	5	5	1	5
20	Engine displacement	2	2.2	2	1.7	1.4	3
21	Seating capacity	5	5	5	5	2	5
22	4-wheel disc brakes	1	0	0	0	0	1
23	Luggage capacity	11.4	13.9	14.8	12.9	9	25
24	Highway mileage	35	34	35	38	10	45
25	Driving	4	2	3	3	1	5
26	Appearance	5	4	1	3	1	5

You also want to choose in such a way that every unit step from worst to best is about equally valuable. For example, Woody will keep the car a maximum of 6 years. So, even if he could get a 7-year warranty, it would be no more valuable than a 6-year warranty. Each year of the warranty is about equally valuable up through 6 years, which is consistent with calling 6 years the best.

Copying the headers to create a new table

Now you can build a table for normalized scores.

TRY IT! Start with **car4.xls** and lay out a new table called Normalized Scores (A28) to hold the normalized scores. Repeat the row and car name column headers from the table above. (**Hint:** Use the Copy *bucket brigade* formula. Put =A15 in A29. *AutoFill* it to the right through column E, and then click again on A29 and *AutoFill* it down to A40.)

=A15					
	A	B	C	D	E
24	Highway mileage	35	34	35	38
25	Driving	4	2	3	3
26	Appearance	5	4	1	3
27					
28	**Normalized scores**				
29	Factor	Kumquat	Excrutia	Pretensio	Dingo
30	Price				
31	Warranty				
32	Consumer rating				
33	Crash test				
34	Engine displacement				
35	Seating capacity				
36	4-wheel disc brakes				
37	Luggage capacity				
38	Highway mileage				
39	Driving				
40	Appearance				

This gives you headers for a new table, laid out just like the original one. The bonus of this layout is that you can copy formulas that refer back to the original table and they still work anywhere else in the new table, since everything is in the same relative positions.

Normalizing

Normalizing (Chapter 10) is a way to come up with a number between 0 and 1 that represents how close to perfect something is. Here's the form that does it:

(This value - worst) / (best - worst)

For example, here's how you'd calculate the normalized score for the price of the Kumquat:

=(13680 - 20000) / (9000 - 20000)

14	**Numerical scores**						
15	Factor	Kumquat	Excrutia	Pretensio	Dingo	Worst	Best
16	Price	**$ 13,680**	$ 13,625	$ 13,915	$ 14,660	**$ 20,000**	$ 9,000
17	Warranty	4	3	3	3	3	6

This works out to about 0.57. This means that the price is a little better (cheaper) than one halfway between best and worst. Notice that this makes sense even though, in this case, less is better.

This gives you a formula to put in B30, for the normalized price score for the Kumquat.

TRY IT! Enter the formula in B30 by clicking on the cells that you used above. Here's what you should have:

=(B16-F16)/(G16-F16)

This is a nice, simple formula that works equally well in all the other cells in this table. You could go ahead and copy it down the Kumquat column. But wait! The fill handle also works filling from left to right. It would be even better to be able to fill the whole table. Before you do, take a look at the formula. If you copy it as-is to the Excrutia column, it stops using the F and G columns that hold the best and worst values. Be sure that any formula pulls the best and worst out of columns F and G, rather than someplace else. So *edit* the formula to use *absolute references*:

=(B16-$F16)/($G16-$F16)

Now, you can copy it across the row. The fill handle works just as well if you drag it to the right, so grab the fill handle on B30 and drag it over to E30. Now take a look at C30. Sure enough, it gives you just what you want:

=(C16-$F16)/($G16-$F16)

Now you can fill the whole thing. Select the cells you just filled (B30 through E30), grab the fill handle at the lower right corner of E30, and drag it down to row 40. You've now completed this whole table with a single good formula.

Take a look at the normalized scores (after using *Decrease Decimal* if you need to make the formats consistent and easier to interpret):

28	**Normalized scores**				
29	Factor	Kumquat	Excrutia	Pretensio	Dingo
30	Price	0.575	0.580	0.553	0.485
31	Warranty	0.333	0.000	0.000	0.000
32	Consumer rating	0.911	0.944	0.889	0.922
33	Crash test	0.750	0.500	1.000	1.000
34	Engine displacement	0.375	0.500	0.375	0.188
35	Seating capacity	1.000	1.000	1.000	1.000
36	4-wheel disc brakes	1.000	0.000	0.000	0.000
37	Luggage capacity	0.150	0.306	0.363	0.244
38	Highway mileage	0.714	0.686	0.714	0.800
39	Driving	0.750	0.250	0.500	0.500
40	Appearance	1.000	0.750	0.000	0.500

Now you have scores you can compare. If something is the best it can be, it gets a 1. If it's the worst, it's 0. Everything else is somewhere in between. If values are close together relative to the range of possibilities, such as price or consumer rating, the normalized values are similar. You see that these choices differ greatly in appearance but hardly at all in consumer rating. Normalizing is a good way to put relative values in context. Forget worrying about units or whether more is better. If these things were all equally important to you, you could just add them up for each car and get numbers to compare.

What's most important?

But of course these considerations are not equally important. The next step is to give an importance rating to each consideration. However you do this, you'll normalize these too. You could start with a hundred imaginary points and allocate them to the various considerations. If price happens to be twice as important as trunk space it should get twice as many points.

Remember that everything is relative to best and worst. So ask yourself, *how much is it worth to you to move from the worst to the best?* For example, how many points is it worth to you to change the price from $20,000 to $9,000, everything else being equal? How much is it worth to get a 6-year warranty rather than a 3-year one? These points don't represent anything. They're just a way to help you think about relative importance. Here's what Woody entered when he did that (**car5.xls**):

28	**Normalized scores**					
29	Factor	Kumquat	Excrutia	Pretensio	Dingo	Preference
30	Price	0.575	0.580	0.553	0.485	50
31	Warranty	0.333	0.000	0.000	0.000	10
32	Consumer rating	0.911	0.944	0.889	0.922	10
33	Crash test	0.750	0.500	1.000	1.000	30
34	Engine displacement	0.375	0.500	0.375	0.188	20
35	Seating capacity	1.000	1.000	1.000	1.000	20
36	4-wheel disc brakes	1.000	0.000	0.000	0.000	10
37	Luggage capacity	0.150	0.306	0.363	0.244	20
38	Highway mileage	0.714	0.686	0.714	0.800	20
39	Driving	0.750	0.250	0.500	0.500	40
40	Appearance	1.000	0.750	0.000	0.500	30

The total of his preference scores is 260. Not very close to 100, but that's OK. (Usually when you do this you end up with more than 100, since everything is important.) The relative values are what matter. Price is 5 times as important to him as the length of the warranty. The driving experience is twice as important as highway mileage. If *you* were choosing among these cars your preference numbers would probably be different. This part is entirely subjective, as it should be. Check your relative preference scores to be sure you believe them before going on to the next step.

Weighting each consideration

Now you can use the preferences to get a *weighted average* of the scores for each car. First you need to scale back the weightings so that they add up to 1.0.

TRY IT! Use the preference scores to get a weighting. All you need to do is divide each preference score by the total of all of the preference scores, as follows:

1. Total the preferences in F42:

    =SUM(F30:F40)

2. Add a new column in G for the weightings.

3. Write a formula to divide the preference by the sum to get the weighting. Here's what it looks like in G30:

    =F30/F$42

    Remember to include the $ so that when it's copied down the column it always refers to the sum in row 42, rather than some blank cell below it (which would give you a "divide by zero" error).

4. *AutoFill* to copy this formula down the column.

5. Check the results:

28	**Normalized scores**						
29	Factor	Kumquat	Excrutia	Pretensio	Dingo	Preference	Weighting
30	Price	0.575	0.580	0.553	0.485	50	0.192
31	Warranty	0.333	0.000	0.000	0.000	10	0.038
32	Consumer rating	0.911	0.944	0.889	0.922	10	0.038
33	Crash test	0.750	0.500	1.000	1.000	30	0.115
34	Engine displacement	0.375	0.500	0.375	0.188	20	0.077
35	Seating capacity	1.000	1.000	1.000	1.000	20	0.077
36	4-wheel disc brakes	1.000	0.000	0.000	0.000	10	0.038
37	Luggage capacity	0.150	0.306	0.363	0.244	20	0.077
38	Highway mileage	0.714	0.686	0.714	0.800	20	0.077
39	Driving	0.750	0.250	0.500	0.500	40	0.154
40	Appearance	1.000	0.750	0.000	0.500	30	0.115
41							
42						260	1.000

Do the most important items have the largest weightings?
Compute the sum of all the weightings in G42 to verify that they
really do all add up to 1.

Getting a "desirability" number for each car

Now you're ready to finally get that weighted average of the scores
for each car that indicates the best choice. Excel has a built-in
function that's perfect for weighted averaging: SUMPRODUCT:

= SUMPRODUCT(*array1, array2*)

Typically, each of these arrays is part of a column and the same
length as the other. They may also be parts of rows. SUMPRODUCT
multiplies the first number in *array1* by the first number in *array2*,
and then it does the same thing for the second numbers, and so on.
Finally, it adds the products.

TRY IT! Apply this function to get a weighted average for the
Kumquat scores by dragging across the numbers you want to use:

1. Put the SUMPRODUCT of the scores and the weights in B42.
    Drag over the scores and weights to enter the formula:

    = SUMPRODUCT(B30:B40,G30:G40)

2. Make sure that it always uses the weighting column G, rather
    than some other column, so you can copy your weighted average
    formula across to the other cars. *Edit* it into a copy-able form
    that leaves the Gs alone:

    =SUMPRODUCT(B30:B40,$G30:$G40)

3. *AutoFill* it to the right to fill in the rest of the weighted
    averages.

Here it is after formatting the cells with decimal numbers using the
Decrease Decimal button if necessary.

28	Normalized scores						
29	Factor	Kumquat	Excrutia	Pretensio	Dingo	Preference	Weighting
30	Price	0.575	0.580	0.553	0.485	50	0.192
31	Warranty	0.333	0.000	0.000	0.000	10	0.038
32	Consumer rating	0.911	0.944	0.889	0.922	10	0.038
33	Crash test	0.750	0.500	1.000	1.000	30	0.115
34	Engine displacement	0.375	0.500	0.375	0.188	20	0.077
35	Seating capacity	1.000	1.000	1.000	1.000	20	0.077
36	4-wheel disc brakes	1.000	0.000	0.000	0.000	10	0.038
37	Luggage capacity	0.150	0.306	0.363	0.244	20	0.077
38	Highway mileage	0.714	0.686	0.714	0.800	20	0.077
39	Driving	0.750	0.250	0.500	0.500	40	0.154
40	Appearance	1.000	0.750	0.000	0.500	30	0.115
41							
42		0.686	0.522	0.521	0.550	260	1.000

Taking a look at the answer

Now each car has a "desirability" score, a number between 0 and 1 that represents how close to perfect the car is. It emphasizes issues that are most important. It looks like the Kumquat is the winner, at 0.686. This is **car6.xls**.

How do you feel about the answer?

Before you run out and buy the winner, ask yourself how you feel about the result. Were you surprised? Disappointed? Take another look at the ratings and weightings and ask whether you still believe them. Remember that the preference numbers are the value to you of moving from the worst to the best for that factor.

Changing the weightings

Woody is concerned about the small trunk on the Kumquat. He's thinking it's just as important as driving enjoyment. He changes the preference number for luggage capacity to 40:

28	Normalized scores						
29	Factor	Kumquat	Excrutia	Pretensio	Dingo	Preference	Weighting
30	Price	0.575	0.580	0.553	0.485	50	0.179
31	Warranty	0.333	0.000	0.000	0.000	10	0.036
32	Consumer rating	0.911	0.944	0.889	0.922	10	0.036
33	Crash test	0.750	0.500	1.000	1.000	30	0.107
34	Engine displacement	0.375	0.500	0.375	0.188	20	0.071
35	Seating capacity	1.000	1.000	1.000	1.000	20	0.071
36	4-wheel disc brakes	1.000	0.000	0.000	0.000	10	0.036
37	Luggage capacity	0.150	0.306	0.363	0.244	40	0.143
38	Highway mileage	0.714	0.686	0.714	0.800	20	0.071
39	Driving	0.750	0.250	0.500	0.500	40	0.143
40	Appearance	1.000	0.750	0.000	0.500	30	0.107
41							
42		0.648	0.507	0.510	0.529	280	1.000

TRY IT! Change F37 to 40. Notice that you don't have to change anything else. The weightings all rebalance themselves. The Kumquat still looks the best.

Adding other considerations

Woody has another consideration that he would like to add: acceleration (seconds to go from 0 to 60). Here's how to add another one to the spreadsheet. (**Tip:** Add any new rows before the last one, and then you don't need to redo the sum formulas; they'll fix themselves.)

1. *Insert Rows* in each of the three tables by selecting each of the Appearance rows.

2. Fill in the first new blank row by typing the entries for seconds to go from 0 to 60 mph.

12	Acceleration		15	13	13	20

3. Fill in the new row in the second table by copying from the first or typing numbers, and typing in the Worst and Best numbers, 25 and 10.

4. *AutoFill* B42 through E42 and G42 in the third table from the row above it and then fill in the word Acceleration and the preference score of 20 for the new consideration.

This is **car.xls**. You can see what it looks like on the next page.

The Kumquat still looks the best. Woody buys it.

	A	B	C	D	E	F	G
1	Factor	Kumquat	Excrutia	Pretensio	Dingo		
2	Price	13680	13625	13915	14660		
3	Warranty	4	3	3	3		
4	Consumer rating	9.2	9.5	9	9.3		
5	Crash test	Good	Average	Excellent	Excellent		
6	Engine displacement	2	2.2	2	1.7		
7	Seating capacity	5	5	5	5		
8	4-wheel disc brakes	yes	no	no	no		
9	Luggage capacity	11.4	13.9	14.8	12.9		
10	Highway mileage	35	34	35	38		
11	Driving	4	2	3	3		
12	Acceleration	15	13	13	20		
13	Appearance	5	4	1	3		
14							
15	**Numerical scores**						
16	Factor	Kumquat	Excrutia	Pretensio	Dingo	Worst	Best
17	Price	13680	13625	13915	14660	20000	9000
18	Warranty	4	3	3	3	3	6
19	Consumer rating	9.2	9.5	9	9.3	1	10
20	Crash test	4	3	5	5	1	5
21	Engine displacement	2	2.2	2	1.7	1.4	3
22	Seating capacity	5	5	5	5	2	5
23	4-wheel disc brakes	1	0	0	0	0	1
24	Luggage capacity	11.4	13.9	14.8	12.9	9	25
25	Highway mileage	35	34	35	38	10	45
26	Driving	4	2	3	3	1	5
27	Acceleration	15	13	13	20	25	10
28	Appearance	5	4	1	3	1	5
29							
30	**Normalized scores relative to worst**						
31	Factor	Kumquat	Excrutia	Pretensio	Dingo	Preference	Weighting
32	Price	0.575	0.580	0.553	0.485	50	0.167
33	Warranty	0.333	0.000	0.000	0.000	10	0.033
34	Consumer rating	0.911	0.944	0.889	0.922	10	0.033
35	Crash test	0.750	0.500	1.000	1.000	30	0.100
36	Engine displacement	0.375	0.500	0.375	0.188	20	0.067
37	Seating capacity	1.000	1.000	1.000	1.000	20	0.067
38	4-wheel disc brakes	1.000	0.000	0.000	0.000	10	0.033
39	Luggage capacity	0.150	0.306	0.363	0.244	40	0.133
40	Highway mileage	0.714	0.686	0.714	0.800	20	0.067
41	Driving	0.750	0.250	0.500	0.500	40	0.133
42	Acceleration	0.667	0.800	0.800	0.333	20	0.067
43	Appearance	1.000	0.750	0.000	0.500	30	0.100
44							
45		0.649	0.526	0.529	0.516	300	1.000

11

Chart your course
Visualizing data with charts

Charts give a nice visual view of data. A picture paints a thousand numbers! You can chart data that is arranged in rows or columns.

Excel gives you several choices of chart type. The first few are best for most cases:

This chart type	Is best for	Because
Column, bar, or line	Labeled data	It takes text as labels and plots any numbers.
Pie	Showing relative size	It uses labels, but converts numbers to percentages.
XY or scatter	Showing the relationships of quantities: sensitivity analysis and cost benefit comparison	It uses numbers, rather than labels. It puts the first column of numbers along the horizontal (X) axis and spaces them properly (the only type that does so).

There are many other chart types. You'll be able to explore these if you wish. Some are special purpose, but most of them just look cool, for those people who don't want their audience to know they are presenting dull, meaningless, or suspect results.

A basic chart

You can make a reasonably good chart easily by choosing the defaults for the chart features and formats. Excel 2007 does this for you automatically. Earlier versions step you through customization options, but allow you to skip ahead to the end.

How to make a basic chart, pre-2007 versions of Excel:

1. *Select* the data, and any associated labels, that you want to plot.

2. Click on the Chart Wizard, which walks you through building of the chart. It's on the Standard Toolbar and looks like a little column chart, such as:

  or

3. Select a **Chart type** and then a **Chart sub-type** and click **Finish**.

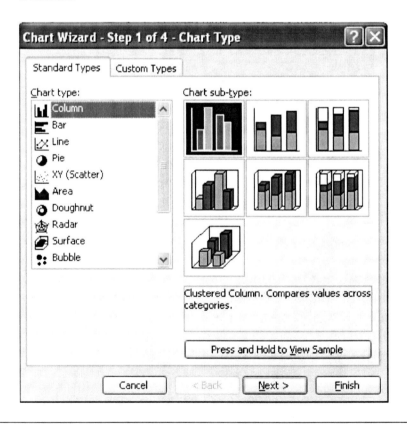

How to make a basic chart, Excel 2007:

The Wizard has been replaced by enhanced chart capabilities in the ribbon.

1. *Select* the data, and any associated labels, that you want to plot.

2. Under **Insert > Charts** click on a chart type icon.

3. Click on a chart sub-type.

A chart appears, floating on top of your spreadsheet. You may also get a Chart toolbar that lets you change your chart. Move it or close it if it's in your way.

Put your cursor in the white area around the chart itself. Drag the chart to some empty area of your spreadsheet. If the numbers or labels on the bottom are scrunched up, grab a handle on an edge and drag it to make the chart wider.

Customizing your chart

You can customize your chart with titles, legends, custom grid lines, and other features. The way you do this depends on which version of Excel you use.

In Excel 2007, you get **Chart Tools** as soon as you make a chart. If you don't see it, click on the chart and you'll see it at the top, with tabs labeled **Design**, **Layout**, and **Format** in the ribbon. Select the desired tab to customize your chart. For example, **Layout > Labels** lets you add or control titles and legends. Click on the desired icon, such as **Chart Title** and make a selection from the menu. Then type the desired title and **Enter**. Chart Tools replaces the Chart Wizard and is more intuitive to use. Explore these tabs to see what else you can do to customize your chart.

The Chart Wizard (pre-2007) lets you customize your charts as you build them. There are many features. Explore the Chart Wizard to see what you can do. Some of the most useful ones help you manage labels and titles. Click **Next**, instead of **Finish**, after choosing the chart type and sub-type and the Wizard walks you through these steps:

Step 2 of 4: The changes offered here depend on the kind of chart you are making. For example, you may be able to pick up axis labels from somewhere else. This works, even if the labels are numbers. Click on **Next >** when you're done with Step 2 of 4.

Step 3 of 4: Here you find several tabs to help you customize your chart. **Titles** lets you label the axes and the whole chart. **Legend** lets you remove the legend that sits on the right side of the chart; if there's only one row or column of data you don't need it. Click on each of the tabs to see what else they let you do. Click **Next >** when you're finished with Step 3 of 4.

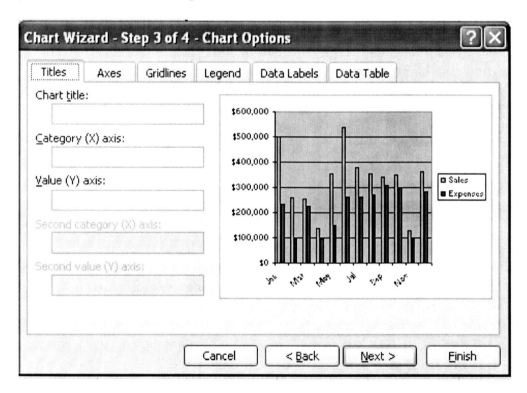

Step 4 of 4: Choose where to put your chart. You can put it on its own new worksheet or in the current worksheet. Click **Finish**.

TRY IT! Say, for example, you would like to visualize your sales and expenses over the past year. Open **sales0.xls**:

	A	B	C
1	Month	Sales	Expenses
2	Jan	$501,035	$233,736
3	Feb	$258,835	$94,390
4	Mar	$253,828	$225,138
5	Apr	$135,894	$94,812
6	May	$355,165	$151,490
7	Jun	$539,222	$262,581
8	Jul	$377,644	$263,001
9	Aug	$353,261	$269,962
10	Sep	$343,598	$307,796
11	Oct	$351,589	$299,937
12	Nov	$131,110	$97,316
13	Dec	$364,158	$283,285

Make a chart to display sales and expenses for each month, using a standard column chart with customized titles. Try it first, and then check what you did against the steps below. First, here they are for pre-2007 Excel:

1. Select the sales and expenses and all labels, A1:C13.

2. Open the Chart Wizard.

3. Select a chart type. For this example, you want a standard labeled chart. Choose the **Column chart type** and the first **Chart sub-type**:

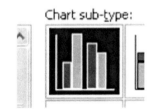

Chart sub-type:

4. Click **Next >** so you can customize the titles. You don't need Step 2 of 4 so click **Next >** again.

5. Enter your titles in Step 3 of 4. Select the **Titles** tab and make the **chart title** Sales and Expenses, the **Category (X) axis** Month, and the **Value (Y) axis** Amount. Click **Finish**.

    A chart appears, floating on top of your spreadsheet:

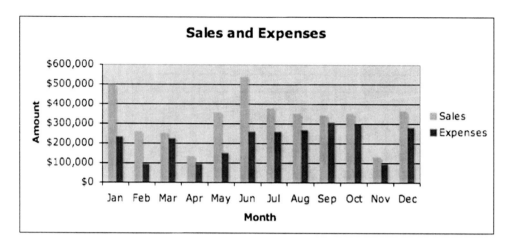

6. Drag the chart where you want it and drag the edges of the chart to resize it if you want.

Here's how to do it in Excel 2007:

1. Select the sales and expenses and all labels, A1:C13.

2. Select **Insert > Charts.**

3. Select a chart type. Choose the **Column chart type** and the first 2-D column sub-type.

4. Select **Chart Tools > Layout > Labels**.

5. Select **Chart Title > Above Chart** and type Sales and Expenses and **Enter**. Select **Axis Titles > Primary Horizontal Axis Title > Title Below Axis** and type Month and **Enter**. Finally, select **Axis Titles > Primary Vertical Axis Title > Rotated Title** and type Amount and **Enter**.

   A chart appears, floating on top of your spreadsheet.

6. Drag the chart where you want it and drag the edges of the chart to resize it if you want.

The completed spreadsheet is **sales.xls.**

Which car is the best value?
Comparing cost and benefit

FOCUS: Balancing multiple criteria, balancing cost and benefit

TOOLKIT: Charts (Chapter 11), weighted totals and normalized scores (Chapter 10), AutoFill (Chapter 4)

Like Woody, Pat is looking for a car, but she has a lot more flexibility as far as price. She wants a sporty convertible and has several options at various prices. Here they are, along with her ratings. This is **sportscar1.xls**:

	A	B	C	D	E	F
1	Factor	Zigzag	Scooter	Luxo	Mastodon	Pocket
2	Price	$35,000	$38,000	$60,000	$91,000	$25,000
3	Warranty	3	4	4	4	4
4	Consumer rating	9.1	9.3	9.4	9.2	9.4
5	Crash test	Excellent	Good	Good	Excellent	Average
6	Engine displacement	3.5	3	4.3	5	1.6
7	Seating capacity	2	2	4	2	4
8	Luggage capacity	7	8	9	10	4
9	Highway mileage	26	29	23	23	32
10	Engine type	V6	Inline 6	V8	V8	Inline 4
11	Parking assist	No	No	No	Front and rear	Rear
12	Driving	3	5	4	4	2
13	Appearance	5	4	4	5	3

While she can afford any of these cars, she wants to be sure she is getting value for her money.

? Pat wants to buy a new convertible. Her options vary greatly in price. Which one provides the best car for the money?

Pulling out cost as a separate consideration

Set aside cost for a while and just evaluate the cars without consideration of price. You can do this the same as before. The difference is that you make the Preference number for Price 0. That makes the result indifferent to price for now. Here's the spreadsheet, built just as before, called **sportscar2.xls**. Note that Pat gave price 0 preference points in G30.

	A	B	C	D	E	F	G	H
1	Factor	Zizgzag	Scooter	Luxo	Mastodon	Pocket		
2	Price	$35,000	$38,000	$60,000	$91,000	$25,000		
3	Warranty	3	4	4	4	4		
4	Consumer rating	9.1	9.3	9.4	9.2	9.4		
5	Crash test	Excellent	Good	Good	Excellent	Average		
6	Engine displacement	3.5	3	4.3	5	1.6		
7	Seating capacity	2	2	4	2	4		
8	Luggage capacity	7	8	9	10	4		
9	Highway mileage	26	29	23	23	32		
10	Engine type	V6	Inline 6	V8	V8	Inline 4		
11	Parking assist	No	No	No	Front and rear	Rear		
12	Driving	3	5	4	4	2		
13	Appearance	5	4	4	5	3		
14								
15	Factor	Zizgzag	Scooter	Luxo	Mastodon	Pocket	Worst	Best
16	Price	$ 35,000	$ 38,000	$ 60,000	$ 91,000	$ 25,000	$ 100,000	$ 20,000
17	Warranty	3	4	4	4	4	3	6
18	Consumer rating	9.1	9.3	9.4	9.2	9.4	1	10
19	Crash test	5	4	4	5	3	1	5
20	Engine displacement	3.5	3	4.3	5	1.6	1.4	6
21	Seating capacity	2	2	4	2	4	2	5
22	Luggage capacity	7	8	9	10	4	4	15
23	Highway mileage	26	29	23	23	32	20	40
24	Engine type	2	2	3	3	1	1	3
25	Parking assist	0	0	0	2	1	0	2
26	Driving	3	5	4	4	4	1	5
27	Appearance	5	4	4	5	3	1	5
28								
29	Factor	Zizgzag	Scooter	Luxo	Mastodon	Pocket	Preference	Weighting
30	Price	0.813	0.775	0.500	0.113	0.938	0	0.000
31	Warranty	0.000	0.333	0.333	0.333	0.333	10	0.095
32	Consumer rating	0.900	0.922	0.933	0.911	0.933	5	0.048
33	Crash test	1.000	0.750	0.750	1.000	0.500	15	0.143
34	Engine displacement	0.457	0.348	0.630	0.783	0.043	10	0.095
35	Seating capacity	0.000	0.000	0.667	0.000	0.667	5	0.048
36	Luggage capacity	0.273	0.364	0.455	0.545	0.000	5	0.048
37	Highway mileage	0.300	0.450	0.150	0.150	0.600	5	0.048
38	Engine type	0.500	0.500	1.000	1.000	0.000	10	0.095
39	Parking assist	0.000	0.000	0.000	1.000	0.500	5	0.048
40	Driving	0.500	1.000	0.750	0.750	0.750	25	0.238
41	Appearance	1.000	0.750	0.750	1.000	0.500	10	0.095
42								
43		0.518	0.612	0.649	0.742	0.462	105	

Now look at the scores at the bottom and what they tell you. So, bottom line, the expensive Mastodon is the best and the cheap Pocket is the worst. No surprise there.

Cost versus benefit

Just looking at best and worst doesn't answer the question. The issue is how much car you get for the money. Make another table in this same sheet to compare cost and value next to each other and calculate the benefit/cost ratio starting in row 45:

1. Label the rows that you group together Car, Price, Score, and Benefit/cost in column A.

2. Fill in the first three rows with values pulled from the tables above.

These formulas do it. Use *AutoFill* to copy them to the right.

B45:   = B29
B46:   = B16
B47:   = B43

		Zizgzag	Scooter	Luxo	Mastodon	Pocket
45	Car					
46	Price	$ 35,000	$ 38,000	$ 60,000	$ 91,000	$ 25,000
47	Score	0.518	0.612	0.649	0.742	0.462

Now you can look at cost and benefit together. The Luxo's score is close behind the Mastodon and at a significantly lower price. But, the Scooter is almost as good for less money. One way to compare these is to take the benefit/cost ratio:

3. Divide the benefit (score) by the cost (price).

Do this on the next line:

B48:   =B47/B46

4. *AutoFill* it across to the other columns.

5. Use the *Increase Decimal* button repeatedly to give you enough decimal places to see the tiny answers.

By the way, you could have multiplied by 1,000,000 or some other big number in the formula. The answers are easier to read and the comparisons come out the same.

		Zizgzag	Scooter	Luxo	Mastodon	Pocket
45	Car					
46	Price	$ 35,000	$ 38,000	$ 60,000	$ 91,000	$ 25,000
47	Score	0.518	0.612	0.649	0.742	0.462
48	Benefit/cost	0.000015	0.000016	0.000011	0.000008	0.000018

Take a look at that last row. These numbers represent the "bang for the buck" for each car. The winner is the Pocket. Very often the least expensive choice comes out the best in benefit for cost. But that doesn't mean that you need to choose it.

Here's an example. A metropolitan area wants to decrease traffic accidents; they have a budget and are examining ways to do it. At one intersection, the stop sign has become obscured by foliage and people are heading dangerously into the intersection without stopping for the cross traffic. Of all the things they could do, the highest benefit/cost ratio is to trim the foliage so that the stop sign is visible. Is that enough? No, they establish a traffic management center that, among other things, responds promptly to remedy hazards of this type. The item with the best benefit/cost was essential, but not enough.

Pat decides that since the Pocket had the lowest score based on her preferences, she'll spring for one of the others. To help her decide, make a scatter plot of benefit versus cost.

Making a cost-benefit chart

Excel has many options for making charts to present your results. You learned about these in the previous chapter. Surprisingly, out of all chart types, only the XY or Scatter plot lets you see the relationship between one quantity and another. You can use these plots to do sensitivity analysis and to see, at once, the outcome of multiple potential futures. Make an XY or Scatter plot to give you a visual image of the prices and scores for the cars:

1. Select only the price and score rows with their row labels (A46 through F47) and make a *chart*.

   Do not select row 45 with the car names or Excel will get confused.

2. Choose **XY (Scatter) {Scatter}** as the **Chart type** and then the first **chart sub-type** (the one with the dots).

3. Click **Finish** in pre-2007 versions.

Here's the chart. Each of the five points represents one of the cars. Read straight down from the point to find its price. Read straight across to the left to find the score.

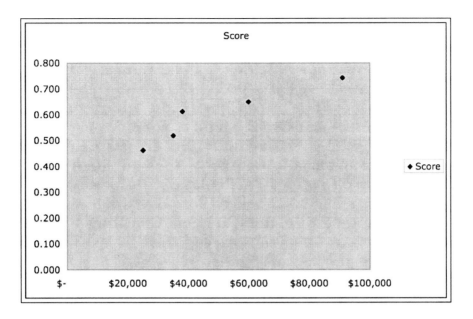

If you want a nicer looking chart, customize it. Unfortunately, there's no automatic way to label these points with the car names, but there are some things you can do to make it easier to interpret by customizing. Here's the result:

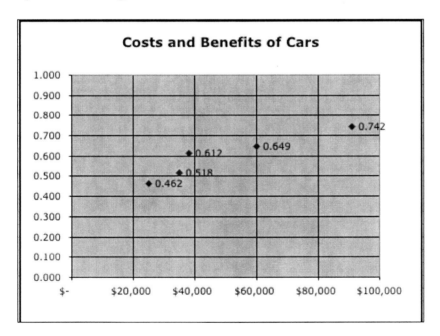

Here's how. For pre-2007 Excel, in Step 3 under **Titles**, add the Chart title, under **Gridlines** choose **Major gridlines**, under

Legend deselect **Show legend**, and set the **Data Label** to **Show Value**. Click **Finish**. Next double click the y-axis (the vertical line on the left, with scores) and set **Scale** to a **Maximum** of 1.0.

In Excel 2007, you can do this using **Chart Tools > Layout** and **Axes**. Choose **Layout > Labels > Legend > None** to remove the legend. To label the points, use **Layout > Data Labels > Right**. To set the scale to a maximum of 1, use **Axes > Axes > Primary Vertical Axis > More Primary Vertical Axis Options... > Maximum > Fixed**, enter 1.0 and click **Close**. For the gridlines, choose **Axes > Gridlines > Primary Vertical Gridlines > Major Gridlines**. For the chart title, you need only select the existing title, Score, type the new one and **Enter**.

Comparing cost and benefit

This chart, in **sportscar.xls**, gives you a visual image of the relative costs and benefits of the choices. You can match the scores on the chart to those on the spreadsheet, and thus to the cars. They are, from left to right, Pocket, Zigzag, Scooter, Luxo, and Mastodon.

The ideal choice would cost nothing, score 1.000 (100%), and show up in the upper left corner. Of course, no such thing exists, but the closer you get to that corner, the better you are. Pat notices that the Scooter (labeled 0.612) is closer to the corner than the others. This looks like a good choice. It is considerably better than the Zigzag, but only slightly more expensive. It is almost as good as the Luxo, but much less expensive. That decides it. She'll buy the Scooter.

Buy or rent?

Comparing annual payments

FOCUS: Annual out-of-pocket costs, mortgage payments, the impact of inflation on expenses

TOOLKIT: Inflation bucket brigade formula and descriptive formulas (Chapter 5), PMT function (Chapter 8 and Case Study 6)

Kristen is trying to decide between buying a house to live in and renting an apartment. She's looked around and found that a suitable apartment runs about $1,500 per month, while an acceptable house is about $500,000. She has enough saved for a down payment. Which should she do? Her big concern is annual out-of-pocket costs. The main difference between the choices, in that regard, is that she expects rent to rise each year, while a fixed mortgage can keep the house payments the same each year.

Comparing annual housing costs

She wants to compare what she will need to pay each month, now and as long as she will live there. As usual in decisions, she needs more information. For the house, she investigates loans. She will need to make a down payment out of her own savings (a percentage of the cost of the house) and pay points, a fee for getting the loan. One "point" is a one-time fee of 1% of the amount of the loan. The big expense will be the monthly payment, which depends on the interest rate and the size and length of the loan. She also investigates rent raises in the area.

? Kristen has a choice between buying a $500,000 house and renting an apartment for $1,500 per month. She can get a fixed, 30-year mortgage at 6% and 1½ points with a 10% down payment. Rents tend to go up 5% a year. Which option has a lower annual payment over the years?

Planning the spreadsheet

Build a spreadsheet to compare buying and renting. Start with what you know. List them as inputs and **create names** for them. It should look something like **house0.xls**:

	A	B	C
1	**Inputs**		
2	Rent	$1,500	per month
3	Rent increase	5%	per year
4			
5	Cost of house	$500,000	
6	Term	30	years
7	Interest rate	6.0%	per year
8	Points	1.50%	of loan amount
9	Percent down	10%	of purchase price

Setting up a table

Now think about what you want to compute. You want the annual cost of each of the two options for each year. Set up a table below the inputs. Make the rows represent years, since there are more years than options. The columns then are Year, Apartment, and House. Number the years from 1 to 20 using *AutoFill*:

	A	B	C
1	**Inputs**		
2	Rent	$1,500	per month
3	Rent increase	5%	per year
4			
5	Cost of house	$500,000	
6	Term	30	years
7	Interest rate	6.0%	per year
8	Points	1.50%	of loan amount
9	Percent down	10%	of purchase price
10			
11	**Annual costs**		
12	**Year**	**Apartment**	**House**
13	1		
14	2		
15	3		

Annual rents

Rents start at some initial amount and grow by a percentage each year. This is just like investments or inflation and there's a simple **bucket brigade formula** to handle it. The starting line is just the initial amount. Here, that's the rent for the first year, which is just the monthly rent multiplied by 12. So, here's the formula for B13:

=12*Rent

The other rows result from multiplying by (1 + *growth rate*):

=*Apartment* previous * (1+Rent_increase)
or
B14:   =B13 * (1+Rent_increase)

Did you get $18,900? **AutoFill** this formula down the column. Avoid copying the first year, since that's a special case and doesn't use the general formula.

As you build this spreadsheet, you may wish to **change column width** or **format cells** to make it clearer.

You see that the rent raise goes up a little more each year (because it's compounded) and, eventually, the rent gets quite pricey.

TRY IT! Try larger and smaller values for the annual rent increase and see what happens. This is one of those quantities that has a big effect on the outcome, but that you can neither control nor predict. The advantage of using Excel is that it helps you look at the full range of realistic numbers and think about how, or whether, you can live with the possible outcomes.

11	Annual costs	
12	Year	Apartment
13	1	$ 18,000
14	2	$ 18,900
15	3	$ 19,845
16	4	$ 20,837
17	5	$ 21,879
18	6	$ 22,973
19	7	$ 24,122
20	8	$ 25,328
21	9	$ 26,594
22	10	$ 27,924
23	11	$ 29,320
24	12	$ 30,786
25	13	$ 32,325
26	14	$ 33,942
27	15	$ 35,639
28	16	$ 37,421
29	17	$ 39,292
30	18	$ 41,256
31	19	$ 43,319
32	20	$ 45,485

Annual house payments

Now look at what the house will cost each year. The big advantage of the house is that, since you have a fixed loan, your monthly payments will never go up.

The loan amount

Remember, you can compute the payment using the built-in function PMT. But first you must compute the size of the loan, which does not include the down payment. For example, the loan amount will be 90% of the cost of the house if you put 10% down.

TRY IT! Write a formula for this loan amount and put it up out of the way in F2. Here's one that works:

=(1- Percent_down) * Cost_of_house

Here the 1 represents 100% and Percent_down is a percentage.

Another way to think of it is to figure the amount of the down payment in dollars by multiplying the cost of the house by the percent down, and then subtracting that from the cost of the house to get the amount of the loan:

=Cost_of_house - Percent_down * Cost_of_house

Either formula works. The computed value is $450,000. That looks right. *Create the name*, Loan, for it so you can use it elsewhere.

=(1-Percent_down) * Cost_of_house					
A	B	C	D	E	F
1 Inputs				Calculated value	
2 Rent	$1,500	per month		Loan	$450,000
3 Rent increase	5%	per year			
4					
5 Cost of house	$500,000				
6 Term	30	years			
7 Interest rate	6%	per year			
8 Points	1.5%	of loan amount			
9 Percent down	10%	of purchase price			

The payment

Recall in Case Study 6 how you used the PMT function to compute monthly car payments. You can do the same thing here to get monthly payments. Remember, since you're looking at the monthly payment, divide the annual interest rate by 12 to get the monthly interest rate, and multiply the term by 12 to get the term in months. Put the calculation in C13.

=PMT(Interest_rate/12, Term*12, Loan)

	=PMT(interest_rate/12, Term*12, Loan)		
	A	B	C
1	**Inputs**		
2	Rent	$1,500	per month
3	Rent increase	5%	per year
4			
5	Cost of house	$500,000	
6	Term	30	years
7	Interest rate	6%	per year
8	Points	1.5%	of loan amount
9	Percent down	10%	of purchase price
10			
11	**Annual costs**		
12	**Year**	**Apartment**	**House**
13	1	$ 18,000	$ (2,698)

Sanity-check time

You get the answer $(2,698). The parentheses indicate a negative number. You can fix this, as before, by putting a - at the beginning of the formula. But even then, $2,698 is suspiciously small for an annual payment on a loan this size. Sure enough, that's monthly. So multiply by 12. **Edit** the formula to get the right one.

=-12*PMT(Interest_rate/12,Term*12,Loan)

Now you should get the more reasonable $32,376.

Payments for all the years

The rest is easy. This is a fixed loan, so every year is the same. You could use the same formula all the way down, but that tends to make it look a lot more complicated than it really is. It's easier to use the Ditto **bucket brigade formula**. This just says, "same as above." Here it is:

=*House* previous

So, for example in C14 you have simply:

=C13

	A	B	C	D	E	F
1	**Inputs**				**Calculated value**	
2	Rent	$1,500	per month		Loan	$450,000
3	Rent increase	5%	per year			
4						
5	Cost of house	$500,000				
6	Term	30	years			
7	Interest rate	6%	per year			
8	Points	1.5%	of loan amount			
9	Percent down	10%	of purchase price			
10						
11	**Annual costs**					
12	**Year**	**Apartment**	**House**			
13	1	$ 18,000	$ 32,376			
14	2	$ 18,900	$ 32,376			
15	3	$ 19,845	$ 32,376			
16	4	$ 20,837	$ 32,376			
17	5	$ 21,879	$ 32,376			
18	6	$ 22,973	$ 32,376			
19	7	$ 24,122	$ 32,376			
20	8	$ 25,328	$ 32,376			
21	9	$ 26,594	$ 32,376			
22	10	$ 27,924	$ 32,376			
23	11	$ 29,320	$ 32,376			
24	12	$ 30,786	$ 32,376			
25	13	$ 32,325	$ 32,376			
26	14	$ 33,942	$ 32,376			
27	15	$ 35,639	$ 32,376			
28	16	$ 37,421	$ 32,376			
29	17	$ 39,292	$ 32,376			
30	18	$ 41,256	$ 32,376			
31	19	$ 43,319	$ 32,376			
32	20	$ 45,485	$ 32,376			

Comparing the costs of rent and mortgage

Take a look at the results. The house costs much more initially, but after 14 years the apartment becomes more expensive.

TRY IT! Change the monthly rent, the cost of the house, the interest rate, or any of the other input values and see how they change the results. This spreadsheet is called **house1.xls**. Keep this open for the next case study.

Buy or rent?

Comparing total costs

FOCUS: Total costs, mortgage payments and remaining loan, home equity build-up, the impact of inflation on rent and house value

TOOLKIT: Inflation bucket brigade formula and descriptive formulas (Chapter 5), **PMT, PPMT** functions (Chapter 8, Case Study 6), **IF** function (Chapter 9), and the Case Study 11 spreadsheet.

Kristen is beginning to think that the apartment makes more sense, based on Case Study 11, since she'll stay there only about five years. But, wait, what about at the end of the five years?

If she buys a house, she can sell it and recover the equity that she has built up from her payments, as well as any appreciation in value. And what about those points...and that big down payment?

Modify the spreadsheet to look at the *total* costs. First, obtain more information: the amount of the deposit on the apartment, how much you expect the house to increase in value each year, and the cost of selling the house (mostly the real estate commission). Kristen investigates and adds these values to the considerations.

? Kristen has a choice between buying a $500,000 house and renting an apartment for $1,500 per month. She can get a fixed, 30-year mortgage at 6% and 1½ points with a 10% down payment. *The house will increase in value 5% a year and cost 6% to sell.* Rents tend to go up 5% a year. *There is a $1,000 deposit.* Which option has lower *total* costs?

Enter the additional inputs. Use **house1.xls** or the spreadsheet you built for the previous case study. Enter these values in F6

through F8 and ***create names*** for them:

	A	B	C	D	E	F	G
1	Inputs				Calculated value		
2	Rent	$1,500	per month		Loan	$ 450,000	
3	Rent increase	5%	per year				
4							
5	Cost of house	$500,000			**More inputs**		
6	Term	30	years		Deposit	$1,000	for apartment
7	Interest rate	6%	per year		House increase	5%	value per year
8	Points	1.5%	of loan amount		Sales cost	6%	of sales price
9	Percent down	10%	of purchase price				

Planning the spreadsheet

Think about how you can modify the previous spreadsheet to answer the new question of total costs. Figuring rent is straightforward: total the expenditures that you've already computed plus any initial costs, like the deposit.

For the house, though, you need to know how much equity has built up, either by paying off the loan or from an increase in value. So, you need to consider the initial costs such as down payment as well as the amount of the loan paid off each year and the appreciation in value. Then, combine these costs and returns from the house and compare them with costs of the apartment to see which looks better.

Computing total costs

For the total costs, you'll want to add the initial cost to the annual costs. A good place to keep track of initial costs is in a new "year 0" line. ***Insert*** this ***row*** in row 13 just above year 1.

TRY IT! Fill out this starting line. Then, check it against this.

A13 and B13 are easy.

Year: 0

Apartment: =Deposit

The deposit is the only initial cost of the apartment.

The initial costs for the House (C13) are a little more complicated. First, there is the amount of the down payment as a percentage of the cost of the house:

Percent_down * Cost_of_house

Then there are the points as a percentage of the loan:

Points * Loan

Add these together to get the formula under House, year 0 (C13).

House: =Percent_down*Cost_of_house + Points*Loan

There are other formulas that work just as well, such as:

=Cost_of_house – Loan + Points*Loan

Did you get $56,750?

Now you're ready to compute the running totals. Add columns labeled Apartment Total and House Total in D12 and E12 to keep track of the total spent on each option over the years. *Wrap text* in the row if you want narrower columns. You saw in Chapter 5 a *bucket brigade formula* for a running total like this. The starting line formula in Apartment Total for year 0 is:

=Apartment
or
D13:   =B13

The rest build on the number just above. The formula in Apartment Total for year 1 and beyond is the usual running total:

=Apartment Total previous + Apartment
or
D14:   =D13+B14

AutoFill year 1 down the column. This takes care of the total cost of renting. You see that renting for 20 years will cost Kristen $596,187. Do the same thing for the house. Because of the way the columns are laid out, you could even *AutoFill* the formulas across.

	A	B	C	D	E
1	**Inputs**				Calculated va
2	Rent	$1,500	per month		Loan
3	Rent increase	5%	per year		
4					
5	Cost of house	$500,000			**More inputs**
6	Term	30	years		Deposit
7	Interest rate	6%	per year		House increase
8	Points	1.50%	of loan amount		Sales cost
9	Down payment	10%	of purchase price		
10					
11	**Annual costs**				
12	**Year**	**Apartment**	**House**	**Apartment Total**	**House Total**
13	0	$ 1,000	$ 56,750	$ 1,000	$ 56,750
14	1	$ 18,000	$ 32,376	$ 19,000	$ 89,126
15	2	$ 18,900	$ 32,376	$ 37,900	$ 121,501
16	3	$ 19,845	$ 32,376	$ 57,745	$ 153,877
17	4	$ 20,837	$ 32,376	$ 78,582	$ 186,253
18	5	$ 21,879	$ 32,376	$ 100,461	$ 218,629
19	6	$ 22,973	$ 32,376	$ 123,434	$ 251,004

You see that the house costs more than the apartment, no matter how long she stays there. But she's building equity in the house that she can get back when she finally sells. There are two ways of building equity—paying off the loan and growth in the house value.

Building equity by paying off the loan

You need more columns to figure the amount of equity that builds up each year. Part of it comes from paying off the loan, so start a new column Remaining Loan in F12 to keep track of how the loan amount decreases each year. In year 0, Kristen has yet to pay anything off. So, you get:

F13:   =Loan

Before you build the rest of this column, think about how you could calculate the amount paid off each year. Then build the formula from partial formulas.

Part of every monthly payment goes to pay off part of the loan. Back in Case Study 6, you saw that PPMT tells you how much goes toward this principal. Here's the form:

=PPMT(Interest_rate/12, *Per*, Term*12, Loan)

That *Per* is the number of the period, in other words, the month.

TRY IT! Enter this in F14 with 1 for *Per*. Kristen will pay off about $448 the first month. Try 12 for *Per*. The twelfth month it will be about $473.

So far, you have a formula for the principal payment for one month. You see that it's different for each of the 12 months of the year. The principal payments for the first year would be the sum of 12 such formulas, with *Per* going from 1 to 12. That's a wicked, long formula! So estimate it. The principal payments over the year are lower in the beginning of the year and higher later. In the middle of the year you get a pretty good estimate for the average over the year. So, compute the principal payment for the sixth month of each year and use it to estimate the whole year.

Here's a formula that turns out to give you the period corresponding to the sixth month of each year:

=*Year**12 - 6

For example, in year 1, you get month 6 and, in year 2, you get month 18. Edit F14 to put this in for *Per* and you get the formula to estimate each principal payment during the year.

=PPMT(Interest_rate/12, *Year**12-6, Term*12,Loan)

You get $(459). That means Kristen will pay off approximately $459 of the loan each month the first year on average.

Computing the amount remaining on the loan

Now you can fill in the Remaining Loan column.

Subsequent years knock off the 12 principal payments that were made during the year. Edit the formula in F14 for the payment.

=*Remaining Loan* previous +
        12*PPMT(Interest_rate/12,*Year**12-6,Term*12,Loan)

Here's what you get in F14:

=F13+12*PPMT(Interest_rate/12,A14*12-6,Term*12,Loan)

You may wonder why you add, rather than subtract this. Remember that PPMT gives a negative value, so this formula does exactly what you want. The amount remaining decreases, as you'd expect. It gives you $444,489, which seems reasonable.

	Year		Apartment	House	Apartment Total		House Total	Remaining Loan
12	Year		Apartment	House	Apartment Total		House Total	Loan
13		0	$ 1,000	$ 56,750	$ 1,000	$	56,750	$ 450,000
14		1	$ 18,000	$ 32,376	$ 19,000	$	89,126	$ 444,489
15		2	$ 18,900	$ 32,376	$ 37,900	$	121,501	$ 438,637
16		3	$ 19,845	$ 32,376	$ 57,745	$	153,877	$ 432,425
17		4	$ 20,837	$ 32,376	$ 78,582	$	186,253	$ 425,829
18		5	$ 21,879	$ 32,376	$ 100,461	$	218,629	$ 418,827
19		6	$ 22,973	$ 32,376	$ 123,434	$	251,004	$ 411,393
20		7	$ 24,122	$ 32,376	$ 147,556	$	283,380	$ 403,500
21		8	$ 25,328	$ 32,376	$ 172,884	$	315,756	$ 395,121
22		9	$ 26,594	$ 32,376	$ 199,478	$	348,132	$ 386,224
23		10	$ 27,924	$ 32,376	$ 227,402	$	380,507	$ 376,779
24		11	$ 29,320	$ 32,376	$ 256,722	$	412,883	$ 366,752
25		12	$ 30,786	$ 32,376	$ 287,508	$	445,259	$ 356,106
26		13	$ 32,325	$ 32,376	$ 319,834	$	477,634	$ 344,803
27		14	$ 33,942	$ 32,376	$ 353,775	$	510,010	$ 332,803
28		15	$ 35,639	$ 32,376	$ 389,414	$	542,386	$ 320,064
29		16	$ 37,421	$ 32,376	$ 426,835	$	574,762	$ 306,538
30		17	$ 39,292	$ 32,376	$ 466,127	$	607,137	$ 292,178
31		18	$ 41,256	$ 32,376	$ 507,383	$	639,513	$ 276,932
32		19	$ 43,319	$ 32,376	$ 550,702	$	671,889	$ 260,746
33		20	$ 45,485	$ 32,376	$ 596,187	$	704,265	$ 243,562

Stop for a moment to see how you built this rather complex formula. You started on the inside with PPMT and worked your way outward. This allowed you to check intermediate values to make sure they made sense. It also reminded you that the result of PPMT is a negative value, so adding it does what you want. Use this technique for building formulas from the inside out whenever you need a complex formula. This formula works when copied. So, *AutoFill* it down to the bottom of the Remaining Loan column.

Building equity through increased house value

Next, look at how much you expect the house to be worth each year, in case she sells it. Add a Value of House column (column G). The initial Value of House for year 0 is exactly what she paid for it:

G13: =Cost_of_house

Each year the value grows by the House_Increase percentage:

=*Value of House* previous * (1+House_Increase)
or
G14: =G13*(1+House_increase)

Use this formula for the remaining years. *AutoFill* it down to the bottom of the Value of House column:

12	Year		Apartment		House		Apartment Total		House Total		Remaining Loan		Value of House	
13	0	$	1,000	$	56,750	$	1,000	$	56,750	$	450,000	$	500,000
14	1	$	18,000	$	32,376	$	19,000	$	89,126	$	444,489	$	525,000
15	2	$	18,900	$	32,376	$	37,900	$	121,501	$	438,637	$	551,250
16	3	$	19,845	$	32,376	$	57,745	$	153,877	$	432,425	$	578,813
17	4	$	20,837	$	32,376	$	78,582	$	186,253	$	425,829	$	607,753
18	5	$	21,879	$	32,376	$	100,461	$	218,629	$	418,827	$	638,141
19	6	$	22,973	$	32,376	$	123,434	$	251,004	$	411,393	$	670,048
20	7	$	24,122	$	32,376	$	147,556	$	283,380	$	403,500	$	703,550
21	8	$	25,328	$	32,376	$	172,884	$	315,756	$	395,121	$	738,728
22	9	$	26,594	$	32,376	$	199,478	$	348,132	$	386,224	$	775,664
23	10	$	27,924	$	32,376	$	227,402	$	380,507	$	376,779	$	814,447
24	11	$	29,320	$	32,376	$	256,722	$	412,883	$	366,752	$	855,170
25	12	$	30,786	$	32,376	$	287,508	$	445,259	$	356,106	$	897,928
26	13	$	32,325	$	32,376	$	319,834	$	477,634	$	344,803	$	942,825
27	14	$	33,942	$	32,376	$	353,775	$	510,010	$	332,803	$	989,966
28	15	$	35,639	$	32,376	$	389,414	$	542,386	$	320,064	$	1,039,464
29	16	$	37,421	$	32,376	$	426,835	$	574,762	$	306,538	$	1,091,437
30	17	$	39,292	$	32,376	$	466,127	$	607,137	$	292,178	$	1,146,009
31	18	$	41,256	$	32,376	$	507,383	$	639,513	$	276,932	$	1,203,310
32	19	$	43,319	$	32,376	$	550,702	$	671,889	$	260,746	$	1,263,475
33	20	$	45,485	$	32,376	$	596,187	$	704,265	$	243,562	$	1,326,649

What happens when she sells the house?

Now, you can figure out the total cost of owning the house. First, compute how much she pockets if she sells the house during any particular year. Use column H, Net if sold. This is the sales proceeds after the costs of sale. Try filling in this column, then check what you did against what follows.

Net if Sold for year 0 represents how much she ends up with (nets) if she sells the house in year 0, i.e., immediately after buying it. Write the formula for H13. Remember, she has to pay off the loan and pay the real estate agent. The sales price of the house is the Value of House. From this she must pay off the Remaining Loan amount. She also has commissions and other costs to sell the house, which are together 6% of the sales price, or

Sales_cost * *Value of House*.

So, here is the formula for Net if Sold for year 0:

=*Value of House* - *Remaining Loan* - Sales_cost*Value of House*
or
H13:   =G13 - F13 - Sales_cost*G13

This says that she gets $20,000. Sanity check time! Why would she come out ahead if she sells the house she just bought? She wouldn't. She had to shell out $56,750 in down payment and points, so she's actually out $36,750 in points and sales commissions. This seems reasonable.

This formula works just as well for the other years. *AutoFill* it down the column. If she lives in the house for 20 years and then sells, she walks away with over a million dollars! Does this make sense? Yes, if you believe that house values will continue to grow at a rate of 5%.

TRY IT! Try different growth rates and see what happens.

Finally, the total net cost of the house

Add a House Net Cost column (I). This is the total cost to own the house if she sells it in a particular year, including everything she's spent from the beginning and over the years, less whatever she makes on the sale.

House Net Cost for any year is:

=House Total - Net if Sold
or
I13:   *=E13-H13*

Taking a look at the costs

Surprisingly, you see that after three years the total costs start dropping with each year and, after 10 years, the costs become negative:

12	Year	Apartment	House	Apartment Total	House Total	Remaining Loan	Value of House	Net if sold	House Net Cost
13	0	$ 1,000	$ 56,750	$ 1,000	$ 56,750	$ 450,000	$ 500,000	$ 20,000	$ 36,750
14	1	$ 18,000	$ 32,376	$ 19,000	$ 89,126	$ 444,489	$ 525,000	$ 49,011	$ 40,114
15	2	$ 18,900	$ 32,376	$ 37,900	$ 121,501	$ 438,637	$ 551,250	$ 79,538	$ 41,964
16	3	$ 19,845	$ 32,376	$ 57,745	$ 153,877	$ 432,425	$ 578,813	$ 111,659	$ 42,218
17	4	$ 20,837	$ 32,376	$ 78,582	$ 186,253	$ 425,829	$ 607,753	$ 145,459	$ 40,794
18	5	$ 21,879	$ 32,376	$ 100,461	$ 218,629	$ 418,827	$ 638,141	$ 181,025	$ 37,603
19	6	$ 22,973	$ 32,376	$ 123,434	$ 251,004	$ 411,393	$ 670,048	$ 218,452	$ 32,552
20	7	$ 24,122	$ 32,376	$ 147,556	$ 283,380	$ 403,500	$ 703,550	$ 257,837	$ 25,543
21	8	$ 25,328	$ 32,376	$ 172,884	$ 315,756	$ 395,121	$ 738,728	$ 299,283	$ 16,473
22	9	$ 26,594	$ 32,376	$ 199,478	$ 348,132	$ 386,224	$ 775,664	$ 342,900	$ 5,232
23	10	$ 27,924	$ 32,376	$ 227,402	$ 380,507	$ 376,779	$ 814,447	$ 388,801	$ (8,294)

What does this mean? Kristen gets more from the sale of the house than the total of all the money she put into it—down payment, points, and payments. She receives money for living in the house! Let's look more closely at this surprising result in the next case study.

Comparing total costs

Now you can compare the costs of the two options, Apartment Total and House Net Cost. You see that renting is less expensive if you stay only a couple years. To make this comparison clearer, use column J to write the preferred option for each year. Label this column Which one? Let Excel make the comparison for you. The function that checks conditions and gives different answers depending on the result is IF. Here's its form:
=IF(*condition, value if true, value if false*).

The condition to check is whether renting is less costly than buying:

Apartment Total < House Net Cost

If this is true, Kristen wants to rent. Otherwise, she wants to buy. So here's the formula. Remember to put text in quotes:

=IF(*Apartment Total < House Net Cost*, "Rent", "Buy")
or
J13:   =IF(D13<I13, "Rent", "Buy")

	A	B	C	D	E	F	G	H	I	J
1	Inputs				Calculated value					
2	Rent	$1,500	per month		Loan	$ 450,000				
3	Rent increase	5%	per year							
4										
5	Cost of house	$ 500,000			More inputs					
6	Term	30	years		Deposit	$1,000	for apartment			
7	Interest rate	6%	per year		House increase	5%	value per year			
8	Points	1.50%	of loan amount		Sales cost	6%	of sales price			
9	Percent down	10%	of purchase price							
10										
11	Annual costs									
12	Year	Apartment	House	Apartment Total	House Total	Remaining Loan	Value of House	Net if sold	House Net Cost	Which one?
13	0	$ 1,000	$ 56,750	$ 1,000	$ 56,750	$ 450,000	$ 500,000	$ 20,000	$ 36,750	Rent
14	1	$ 18,000	$ 32,376	$ 19,000	$ 89,126	$ 444,489	$ 525,000	$ 49,011	$ 40,114	Rent
15	2	$ 18,900	$ 32,376	$ 37,900	$ 121,501	$ 438,637	$ 551,250	$ 79,538	$ 41,964	Rent
16	3	$ 19,845	$ 32,376	$ 57,745	$ 153,877	$ 432,425	$ 578,813	$ 111,659	$ 42,218	Buy
17	4	$ 20,837	$ 32,376	$ 78,582	$ 186,253	$ 425,829	$ 607,753	$ 145,459	$ 40,794	Buy
18	5	$ 21,879	$ 32,376	$ 100,461	$ 218,629	$ 418,827	$ 638,141	$ 181,025	$ 37,603	Buy
19	6	$ 22,973	$ 32,376	$ 123,434	$ 251,004	$ 411,393	$ 670,048	$ 218,452	$ 32,552	Buy
20	7	$ 24,122	$ 32,376	$ 147,556	$ 283,380	$ 403,500	$ 703,550	$ 257,837	$ 25,543	Buy
21	8	$ 25,328	$ 32,376	$ 172,884	$ 315,756	$ 395,121	$ 738,728	$ 299,283	$ 16,473	Buy
22	9	$ 26,594	$ 32,376	$ 199,478	$ 348,132	$ 386,224	$ 775,664	$ 342,900	$ 5,232	Buy
23	10	$ 27,924	$ 32,376	$ 227,402	$ 380,507	$ 376,779	$ 814,447	$ 388,801	$ (8,294)	Buy
24	11	$ 29,320	$ 32,376	$ 256,722	$ 412,883	$ 366,752	$ 855,170	$ 437,108	$ (24,225)	Buy
25	12	$ 30,786	$ 32,376	$ 287,508	$ 445,259	$ 356,106	$ 897,928	$ 487,947	$ (42,688)	Buy
26	13	$ 32,325	$ 32,376	$ 319,834	$ 477,634	$ 344,803	$ 942,825	$ 541,452	$ (63,817)	Buy
27	14	$ 33,942	$ 32,376	$ 353,775	$ 510,010	$ 332,803	$ 989,966	$ 597,764	$ (87,754)	Buy
28	15	$ 35,639	$ 32,376	$ 389,414	$ 542,386	$ 320,064	$ 1,039,464	$ 657,033	$ (114,647)	Buy
29	16	$ 37,421	$ 32,376	$ 426,835	$ 574,762	$ 306,538	$ 1,091,437	$ 719,413	$ (144,652)	Buy
30	17	$ 39,292	$ 32,376	$ 466,127	$ 607,137	$ 292,178	$ 1,146,009	$ 785,071	$ (177,933)	Buy
31	18	$ 41,256	$ 32,376	$ 507,383	$ 639,513	$ 276,932	$ 1,203,310	$ 854,179	$ (214,666)	Buy
32	19	$ 43,319	$ 32,376	$ 550,702	$ 671,889	$ 260,746	$ 1,263,475	$ 926,920	$ (255,031)	Buy
33	20	$ 45,485	$ 32,376	$ 596,187	$ 704,265	$ 243,562	$ 1,326,649	$ 1,003,488	$ (299,223)	Buy

AutoFill it down the column. You see that it is less costly to rent only if she stays two years or less. However, this all depends on the inputs you choose.

TRY IT! What if the house were more expensive? What if its value increased only 2% per year? What if the loan interest rate were 10%? All of these change the answer. Try various reasonable scenarios like this before making a final decision. This is the spreadsheet called **house2.xls**.

Kristen is now leaning toward buying the house. She will probably stay more than two years and, if she stays long enough, it won't cost her anything. If she stays 20 years, she will earn almost $300,000 for living there! Is this possible? Well, not exactly, as you'll see next.

Keep this spreadsheet open for the following case study.

Buy or rent?
Present value

FOCUS: Total out-of-pocket costs, mortgage payments and remaining loan, home equity build-up, the impact of inflation on rent and house value, present value

TOOLKIT: Inflation and present value bucket brigade formulas and descriptive formulas (Chapter 5), **PMT** and **PPMT** functions (Chapter 8 and Case Study 6), **IF** function (Chapter 9), Case Studies 11 and 12.

Kristen calculated, in Case Study 12, that she will be ahead almost $300,000 if she buys a house and holds it for 20 years. That's above and beyond all the costs and payments. This seems much too good to pass up.

Well, the hard fact of the matter is that money now is worth more than money later. It will be 20 years before that windfall hits and those dollars will be worth a lot less than those she shelled out in payments. Modify the spreadsheet to get a better handle on this. Here's your new question:

? Kristen has the choice of buying a $500,000 house or renting an apartment for $1,500 per month. She can get a fixed, 30-year mortgage at 6% and 1½ points with a 10% down payment. The house will increase in value 5% a year and cost 6% to sell. Rents tend to go up 5% a year. There is a $1,000 deposit. Which costs less in total *current* dollars, buying or renting?

Pay me now or pay me later

Key to this is the concept of present value, which is the value of future income relative to current dollars. A dollar now is worth more than a dollar five years from now. You saw in Chapter 5 how to build a ***bucket brigade formula*** that computes present value, and how you can get multipliers by finding present values for $1.

Open your spreadsheet from the last case study (or **house2.xls**). Think about what you need to do to convert all of these numbers to their present value so you can compare them.

First, you need the most important number in any present value calculation, the "cost of money" percentage. This is a measure of how much more a dollar is worth if you get it a year earlier. Add this to your inputs just under Sales cost. Label it "Cost of money" and input 6%. ***Create a name*** for it.

Then you need a column that gives the present value (PV) Multiplier for each year—how much a future dollar is worth in current dollars. This is useful for multiple columns and streams of expenditure. Multiply any amount of money that changes hands by the multiplier for the year in which it changes hands.

TRY IT! Fill in the Multiplier column. ***Insert cells*** for it after House (Select D12:D33). Label it Multiplier. This is the present value of a dollar received in the future year. Use the formulas from Chapter 5. You get the multipliers by starting with $1. So, put $1 for year 0.

From the present value formula in Chapter 5, the Multiplier for each subsequent year is:

=*Multiplier* previous/(1+Cost_of_money).

If you enter this in Multiplier for year 1, you get $0.94. (***Increase decimal*** places in these cells if needed to see these small amounts.) This means that a dollar received a year from now has the present value of about $0.94. That makes sense since, if you invested the $0.94 now at 6% for a year, you would have about $1. Each successive year, a dollar shrinks by the same percentage. So, use the same formula. ***AutoFill*** it down.

	A	B	C	D	E	F
1	**Inputs**				**Calculated value**	
2	Rent	$1,500	per month		Loan	$ 450,000
3	Rent increase	5%	per year			
4						
5	Cost of house	$500,000			**More inputs**	
6	Term	30	years		Deposit	$1,000
7	Interest rate	6%	per year		House increase	5%
8	Points	1.50%	of loan amount		Sales cost	6%
9	Percent down	10%	of purchase price		Cost of money	6%
10						
11	Annual costs				PV	PV
12	**Year**	**Apartment**	**House**	**Multiplier**	**Apartment Total**	**House Total**
13	0	$ 1,000	$ 56,750	$ 1.00	$ 1,000	$ 56,750
14	1	$ 18,000	$ 32,376	$ 0.94	$ 17,981	$ 87,293
15	2	$ 18,900	$ 32,376	$ 0.89	$ 34,802	$ 116,107
16	3	$ 19,845	$ 32,376	$ 0.84	$ 51,464	$ 143,291
17	4	$ 20,837	$ 32,376	$ 0.79	$ 67,969	$ 168,935
18	5	$ 21,879	$ 32,376	$ 0.75	$ 84,319	$ 193,128
19	6	$ 22,973	$ 32,376	$ 0.70	$ 100,514	$ 215,952
20	7	$ 24,122	$ 32,376	$ 0.67	$ 116,556	$ 237,484

You see, for example, that a dollar 20 years from now is worth only about 31 cents now (or more precisely $0.311805). So, if in 20 years, Kristen nets $300,000 on the sale of the house, this would really be only the equivalent of today's $93,541 (0.311805 * 300,000).

Modifying formulas to get present values

Now you can use these present value multipliers to compute the present value of sums you calculated earlier. It turns out that you need convert only a few of the columns to present value.

Think about when money changes hands. Apartment Total and House Total each represent an uneven stream of expenditures year after year. To convert this to present value you need even more help here than the built-in PV function can give you. But, you can compute present value using *bucket brigade formulas* and the multipliers that you already have.

Here's how. Multiply by the PV Multiplier for that year. Then, use a running total bucket brigade formula to get the present value of the whole stream.

There is one final time that money changes hands and that is upon sale of the house. After everyone's been paid, Kristen will be handed the amount under Net if sold for the year of the sale. She gets the whole thing at one time, so its present value is based on the multiplier for that one year alone. Add that present value to the house total (once it's a present value) and you'll get the present value of the House Net Cost. That's all you need.

Write PV over each of Apartment Total, House Total, and House Net Cost to remind yourself that only these columns need to be converted. Take them one at a time.

Total present value of the costs of renting

Convert the Apartment Total column to present values. Let the Multiplier and *bucket brigade formulas* help you.

TRY IT! Modify column E to get the present value of the total costs for renting. Then check your work against the description below.

The initialization row (year 0) is easy. Leave the formula for Apartment Total unchanged, as there's nothing to accumulate yet and it is already present value:

=Apartment

Now, for the first year...accumulated present value for the previous year is stored right above it. You also have rent payments (Apartment) that year and you can get their present value by multiplying by the PV Multiplier for the year in which they were paid. Revise the formula in Apartment Total for year 0 to:

=Apartment Total previous + *Multiplier*Apartment*
or
E14:   =E13+D14*B14

This formula works all the way down, so *AutoFill* the rest of the column. The total is now only $311,841 in current dollars.

Present values of the house

TRY IT! Modify House Total similarly. Check your work against house.xls or the picture on page 162, which has used the *hide* *columns* feature to focus on the columns of interest. Did you get $428,097 at year 20?

Now you're ready to find the present value for House Net Cost. This is total costs less the present value of what you get back when you sell the house.

TRY IT! Convert House Net Cost (column J) to present value.

Remember that this is just House Total minus Net if Sold. You already have the present value of the total costs under House Total. The present value of the sales proceeds is just the present value of the amount under Net if Sold, since that money all changes hands in that one year. You compute that by using the Multiplier for that year.

*=House Total - Net if Sold * Multiplier*
or
J13:   =F13 - I13*D13

This works for all rows, so *AutoFill* it down. No more negatives.

Comparing the options

The Which one? column remains the same. It still compares the two totals, but now compares present values of the totals. This completes the spreadsheet. You'll find this in **house.xls**.

	A	D	E		F	I	J	K
1	**Inputs**		**Calculated value**					
2	Rent		Loan		$ 450,000			
3	Rent increase							
4								
5	Cost of house		More inputs					
6	Term		Deposit		$1,000			
7	Interest rate		House increase		5%			
8	Points		Sales cost		6%			
9	Percent down		Cost of money		6%			
10								
11	**Annual costs**		PV		PV		PV	
12	Year	Multiplier	Apartment Total		House Total	Net if sold	House Net Cost	Which one?
13	0	$ 1.00	$	1,000	$ 56,750	$ 20,000	$ 36,750	Rent
14	1	$ 0.94	$	17,981	$ 87,293	$ 49,011	$ 41,056	Rent
15	2	$ 0.89	$	34,802	$ 116,107	$ 79,538	$ 45,319	Rent
16	3	$ 0.84	$	51,464	$ 143,291	$ 111,659	$ 49,540	Buy
17	4	$ 0.79	$	67,969	$ 168,935	$ 145,459	$ 53,718	Buy
18	5	$ 0.75	$	84,319	$ 193,128	$ 181,025	$ 57,856	Buy
19	6	$ 0.70	$	100,514	$ 215,952	$ 218,452	$ 61,952	Buy
20	7	$ 0.67	$	116,556	$ 237,484	$ 257,837	$ 66,007	Buy
21	8	$ 0.63	$	132,447	$ 257,797	$ 299,283	$ 70,023	Buy
22	9	$ 0.59	$	148,188	$ 276,960	$ 342,900	$ 73,998	Buy
23	10	$ 0.56	$	163,781	$ 295,038	$ 388,801	$ 77,934	Buy
24	11	$ 0.53	$	179,226	$ 312,093	$ 437,108	$ 81,830	Buy
25	12	$ 0.50	$	194,526	$ 328,183	$ 487,947	$ 85,689	Buy
26	13	$ 0.47	$	209,681	$ 343,362	$ 541,452	$ 89,508	Buy
27	14	$ 0.44	$	224,694	$ 357,682	$ 597,764	$ 93,290	Buy
28	15	$ 0.42	$	239,565	$ 371,191	$ 657,033	$ 97,034	Buy
29	16	$ 0.39	$	254,295	$ 383,936	$ 719,413	$ 100,741	Buy
30	17	$ 0.37	$	268,887	$ 395,959	$ 785,071	$ 104,412	Buy
31	18	$ 0.35	$	283,341	$ 407,302	$ 854,179	$ 108,045	Buy
32	19	$ 0.33	$	297,658	$ 418,002	$ 926,920	$ 111,643	Buy
33	20	$ 0.31	$	311,841	$ 428,097	$ 1,003,488	$ 115,205	Buy

Well, which one: buy or rent?

This spreadsheet provides a much more realistic view of the situation. You don't really get paid to live in the house. In fact, the longer you stay the more it costs, as you'd expect. But, the house does cost less than the apartment if you stay there long enough. Coincidently, as before, the house is less expensive if you stay more than two years. So, is that the answer? Not so fast!

Sensitivity to the cost of money

This comparison is very sensitive to the highly subjective "cost of money." It depends on where you get the money, what you could be doing with it other than spending it on housing, and how risky you think the future payoff is. If you have to borrow the money, then this should be at least the interest rate you are charged. If you take it out of savings, it should be the interest rate that you would have earned or more. Businesses generally use a number between 10 and

15%, since they need ready cash for current operations and growth and must cover risk of future outcomes.

TRY IT! Try 15% for the cost of money. Then you get a completely different answer—rent no matter how long you will stay! This is because the proceeds of that future house sale are too distant and too risky to be worth much. Now try 12%. As before, it is better to buy if you will be there a while, but, surprisingly, renting is better if you stay at least 17 years. This reflects the common wisdom in investment real estate—unless you keep the property long enough you lose on the fees, but if you keep it too long you miss opportunities to invest further. (You now have the tools to analyze this issue if you are interested.)

There are many other factors that we could have included in this spreadsheet. The cost of a house includes property taxes, maintenance, and insurance on the structure. It may also include association dues and additional utilities. The apartment may also have added costs such as coin laundry, but you should get back at least some of your deposit. Either option could have higher transportation costs due to location. Any of these cost differences can be added to the Apartment and House columns. Ignore costs that they have in common (e.g., furniture), since the answer will come out the same.

Subjective factors

Every decision has subjective aspects, and choosing your home is full of them. How much are pride of ownership, freedom to modify your dwelling, a yard, and other benefits of owning a house worth to you? How much are community facilities, flexibility, ease of maintenance, and other benefits of renting worth?

Kristen figured the cost of money at 10%, to cover inflation and the risks of the real estate market. Put 10% in for Cost of money to see her calculations. She plans to stay in the neighborhood about five years. Staying in the house that long would cost $67,077 in current dollars and the apartment will cost $75,711. She really prefers the flexibility and freedom of an apartment, valuing it at more than the difference of $8,634. She also knows there will be other costs of home ownership, such as property taxes and insurance. While she doesn't know exactly how much they are, she knows they are considerable. She would need to investigate them if she were leaning toward buying a house.

"What if?"

Finally, she does some "what-if" analysis. Tentatively, she has decided on an apartment. What could possibly happen that would make this a bad decision? What if rents went up faster, say 10%? She tries it and convinces herself that she could afford the annual rent each year and that the total cost is in line with owning a house for five years. If rents went up faster than that, which seems unlikely, she could move.

What if the housing market takes off, say at 15% a year? She tries that on top of the 10% rent increases. After five years in the house she would be $147,442 ahead! Compared with having to spend $82,818 for the apartment, the house is a no-brainer. Or is it? She thinks this is an unlikely situation. She does not want to buy a house solely on the chance that it will zoom up in value. She has decided on the apartment.

Taking a look at what you did

This three-case-study example shows how to build a model in steps. You started with a simple model, examined the results, and asked questions, uncovering considerations out of the model's scope. You grew the spreadsheet to include these aspects. You focused on cash flow, then added total expenditures, then present value. Rather than the spreadsheet giving you the answer, a final decision was possible only after varying input and thinking about the alternative outcomes. The final decision included subjective factors. Let's use these same techniques to build models to address other questions.

Pension or lump sum?
Comparing retirement options

Focus: Using present value to compare courses of action

Toolkit: Building a spreadsheet model (Chapter 6), **IF** function (Chapter 9), **SUMPRODUCT** function (Chapter 7), present value and other bucket brigade formulas and descriptive formulas (Chapter 5).

Jim is thinking about retiring from his job. He's been at the company long enough that he qualifies for a pension. He has a choice of a monthly pension payment for life or a lump sum equivalent to its present value. Which should he choose?

? Jim is 57 years old and qualifies for a pension that pays $3,500 a month until age 62, then $3,000 a month for the rest of his life. Alternatively, he can choose an immediate lump sum payment equivalent to the present value of the pension. The rate used for the present value calculation is 5.2%. Jim's life expectancy is 83 years. How big is the lump sum? Which should he choose?

The first question is the size of the lump sum. Follow the steps from Chapter 6 to plan and build a spreadsheet to compute it.

Planning the spreadsheet
Make these decisions:

1. What the rows should represent

   The lump sum is based on the total present value of what he will get each month until he's 83. This suggests that the rows will represent payments. To keep things short, have each row represent a year, even though he's paid monthly.

2. What the columns should represent

Here's what you need each year to compute the present value:

a. Jim's age each year
b. The monthly pension payment
c. The annual payment
d. The PV multiplier (to compute present value, as you did in the house example in Case Study 13)

In the house example you needed additional columns to find the cumulative cost and the running total to get the final present value. It turns out here you have enough columns if you use SUMPRODUCT instead.

3. Identify the inputs and decide which should be clustered on top.

Everything you need is in the statement of the decision. The model uses each input in multiple rows, so cluster them all on top. *Create names* for the inputs. This is **pension0.xls**.

	A	B	C	D	E
1	**Inputs**				
2	Pre 62	$3,500	per month through age 62		
3	Post 62	$3,000	per month from age 62		
4	Int rate	5.20%	per year, for present value calculations		
5	Life exp	83	years life expectancy		
6	Ret age	57	years old at retirement		

4. Make sure the output you care about shows up.

The final answer comes from a SUMPRODUCT of the big table. Make it easy to find by putting it up near the top. Skip a couple of lines and make a place for the answer. This way it won't get lost at the bottom of the big table that computes it:

5	Life exp	83	years life expectancy	
6	Ret age	57	years old at retirement	
7				
8				
9	**Result**		is the present value of the pension	

Remember, Excel formulas can display answers anywhere in the spreadsheet, rather than only at the bottom.

Building the spreadsheet

First enter the inputs and the column and row headers. You already have the named inputs. Here are the column headings, as they'd appear in row 12:

9	Result		is the present value of the pens
10				
11				
12	Age	Monthly	Annual	PV multiplier

The ages that appear in the **Age** column work perfectly well for the row headers.

Now fill in the starting row and the bucket brigade formulas. Take it one column at a time.

Age

Age starts at the input retirement age, so in line 13 you have,

Age: =Ret_age

after which it increases by one each time, so in subsequent lines,

Age: =*Age* previous + 1

AutoFill all the ages down to 85.

The expected monthly payment based on age

Think about how you would calculate the monthly payment:

Check the age and enter the right amount:

> $3,500 if under 62
> $3,000 if over 62 but not yet 83
> 0 at 83 and beyond

Jim may live beyond 83, but the present value is based on expected amounts, so it's expected to be 0 starting at age 83.

TRY IT! Now think up a single formula that lets Excel do all this for you, rather than do it manually year-by-year.

Yes, this column is easy enough to fill in by hand, but creating a formula gives you practice with nested IF functions. An extra benefit of a formula is that you can vary retirement age and this column changes automatically. In fact, you'll use that feature soon.

To find this formula, first think more carefully about how you could fill in this column. You can do it by asking two questions:

> *Is he younger than 62 this year?*
> If so, the result is $3,500.
> If not, ask another question:
>> *Is he past 83?*
>> If so, the result is 0, since the expected stop is at age 83.
>> If not, the result is $3,000, since he is at least 62.

This looks like a job for **IF**. Remember what this function looks like?

=IF(*condition, result if true, result if false*)

So, here's what you have for the first question, using descriptive formulas and your input values:

=IF(*Age* < 62, Pre_62, *ask another question*)

and here's what you have for the second:

 IF(*Age* > Life_exp, 0, Post_62)

Put them together and you get the formula

=IF(*Age* < 62, Pre_62, IF(*Age* > Life_exp, 0, Post_62))

Check all the commas and parentheses and enter this in B13. Then verify that you got the $3,500 you expected. Copy it down the column. Check that it works past 62 and 83.

Note: Insurance companies do this by using mortality tables to compute the probabilistic expected amount each year, rather than a fixed life expectancy. If you have such a table[1], you can use SUMPRODUCT to calculate the present value of the pension.

The rest of the table

The annual pension payment is now easy. It's the monthly multiplied by 12:

Annual: =*Monthly* * 12

PV multiplier always starts at 1 for the current year. Then, as before, you get each subsequent multiplier from the previous and the interest rate using a ***bucket brigade formula***.

PV multiplier:
     First line: 1
     Subsequent lines: =*PV multiplier* previous/(1+Int_rate)

Computing the present value using SUMPRODUCT

When you figured the cumulative present value cost of the house in the last case study, you multiplied each cost by the PV multiplier and added them. But this is exactly what the function SUMPRODUCT does. So here's a formula to put in B9 to give you the present value of the pension:

=SUMPRODUCT(*PV multiplier* column, *Annual* column)
or
B9:   =SUMPRODUCT(D13:D41, C13:C41)

---

[1] For example, see the death probability in the Period Life Table at www.ssa.gov/OACT/STATS/table4c6.html

Looking at the result

Below is the finished spreadsheet, **pension1.xls**, with formats cleaned up. The present value comes out to $570,179.

	A	B	C	D	E
1	**Inputs**				
2	Pre 62	$3,500	per month through age 62		
3	Post 62	$3,000	per month from age 62		
4	Int rate	5.20%	per year, for present value calculations		
5	Life exp	83	years life expectancy		
6	Ret age	57	years old at retirement		
7					
8					
9	**Result**	$ 570,179	is the present value of the pension		
10					
11					
12	**Age**	**Monthly**	**Annual**	**PV multiplier**	
13	57	$ 3,500	$ 42,000	1.000	
14	58	$ 3,500	$ 42,000	0.951	
15	59	$ 3,500	$ 42,000	0.904	
16	60	$ 3,500	$ 42,000	0.859	
17	61	$ 3,500	$ 42,000	0.816	
18	62	$ 3,000	$ 36,000	0.776	
19	63	$ 3,000	$ 36,000	0.738	
20	64	$ 3,000	$ 36,000	0.701	
21	65	$ 3,000	$ 36,000	0.667	
22	66	$ 3,000	$ 36,000	0.634	
23	67	$ 3,000	$ 36,000	0.602	
24	68	$ 3,000	$ 36,000	0.573	
25	69	$ 3,000	$ 36,000	0.544	
26	70	$ 3,000	$ 36,000	0.517	
27	71	$ 3,000	$ 36,000	0.492	
28	72	$ 3,000	$ 36,000	0.467	
29	73	$ 3,000	$ 36,000	0.444	
30	74	$ 3,000	$ 36,000	0.422	
31	75	$ 3,000	$ 36,000	0.402	
32	76	$ 3,000	$ 36,000	0.382	
33	77	$ 3,000	$ 36,000	0.363	
34	78	$ 3,000	$ 36,000	0.345	
35	79	$ 3,000	$ 36,000	0.328	
36	80	$ 3,000	$ 36,000	0.312	
37	81	$ 3,000	$ 36,000	0.296	
38	82	$ 3,000	$ 36,000	0.282	
39	83	$ 3,000	$ 36,000	0.268	
40	84	$ -	$ -	0.254	
41	85	$ -	$ -	0.242	

So, which is the better deal, the pension or the lump sum? The answer is...neither! The whole idea of present value is that the two things are of exactly the same value. That is, of course, assuming an interest rate of 5.2% and a life expectancy of 83 years. If Jim thinks that he will live well past 83 he should choose the pension. On the other hand, if he thinks he can earn more than 5.2% on his money (and not spend it wildly), he should take the lump sum. In fact, most people given this choice take the lump sum. Jim decides to do just that. But, now he has another decision to make.

Retire now or later?

? Jim can retire now and take the lump sum or he can retire next year, when the interest rate is expected to drop to 4.5%. The monthly payment schedule is the same. How does waiting affect his lump sum payment?

Two things are going to change here: his retirement age and the interest rate. Change them one at a time and see what happens:

TRY IT! First, change his retirement age to 58.

	A	B	C	D	E
1	**Inputs**				
2	Pre 62	$3,500	per month through age 62		
3	Post 62	$3,000	per month from age 62		
4	Int rate	5.20%	per year, for present value calculations		
5	Life exp	83	years life expectancy		
6	Ret age	58	years old at retirement		
7					
8					
9	**Result**	$ 555,644	is the present value of the pension		
10					
11					
12	**Age**	**Monthly**	**Annual**	**PV multiplier**	
13	58	$ 3,500	$ 42,000	1.000	
14	59	$ 3,500	$ 42,000	0.951	
15	60	$ 3,500	$ 42,000	0.904	
16	60	$ 3,500	$ 42,000	0.859	

Waiting a year under these conditions costs him more than $14,000. (Actually, in real life it won't be this bad. His life expectancy will increase slightly and his company may raise his monthly pension based on one more year of service.)

Now see what happens with the new interest rate. Change the interest rate (B4) to 4.5%:

	A	B	C	D	E
1	**Inputs**				
2	Pre 62	$3,500	per month through age 62		
3	Post 62	$3,000	per month from age 62		
4	Int rate	4.50%	per year, for present value calculations		
5	Life exp	83	years life expectancy		
6	Ret age	58	years old at retirement		
7					
8					
9	**Result**	$ 592,309	is the present value of the pension		
10					
11					
12	**Age**	**Monthly**	**Annual**	**PV multiplier**	
13	58	$ 3,500	$ 42,000	1.000	
14	59	$ 3,500	$ 42,000	0.957	
15	60	$ 3,500	$ 42,000	0.916	

The lump sum payment goes up more than $36,000. In fact, this is a bigger lump sum than he would get if he retired this year, despite the fact that the pension pays out for fewer years. As this example shows, the lump sum is quite sensitive to changes in interest rate. The *lower* the interest rate, the *higher* the lump sum is. That's why people nearing retirement are often obsessed with interest rates and hope for a drop in the rate on 30-year bonds or whatever their pension is pegged to. However, this calculation is only part of the decision. Here are some other considerations:

Reasons to wait to retire:
- An extra year of income
- An extra year to build up the pension by contributions
- The satisfaction of the job
- Work-related social relations
- Time to plan retirement activities

Reasons to retire now:
- An extra year to enjoy retirement
- Use of the lump sum for investment or pleasure a year earlier
- Control of potentially shaky pension funds
- Retirement business or leisure activity opportunities

Do I have enough life insurance?
Present value of an income stream

FOCUS: Present value of an uneven stream of money

TOOLKIT: Bucket brigade formulas, present value formula, present value multiplier, and descriptive formulas (all in Chapter 5), SUMPRODUCT function (Chapter 8)

The reason to buy life insurance is to leave your heirs enough to invest to cover the loss of your income. That means that you want the lump sum insurance payment to be equivalent to the present value of the future income stream. Here's a simple example of life insurance to cover alimony and child support payments ordered in a divorce.

Jack and Jill are getting a divorce. Jill has been awarded alimony and child support. Jack has to get life insurance on himself to guarantee the payments. How much life insurance does he need?

? Jack has been ordered to pay Jill $700 a month alimony for five years. In addition, he is to pay $600 a month for child support for each of their children, Dick and Jane, until they complete college. While they are in college the support drops by 1/6 (since the parents will share the college costs). The children are now 7 and 9. The court tells him he needs $500,000 in life insurance to cover future payments should he die. Is this reasonable?

Help Jack build a spreadsheet to compute the actual present value of the support payments. He assumes that both children will attend college from age 18 to 21. He uses present value because the insurance money could be invested to cover the future support payments.

Creating a present value spreadsheet

TRY IT! *Open* a new workbook. Build a model of this decision, using the same techniques as in Case Study 14. Then check your spreadsheet against the steps below.

Spreadsheet plan

You want to know how much he has to pay each year, so the rows represent years. To get the total, you need to know how much he pays each person. This depends on the year and the ages of the children. Finally, you need to figure present values, since he's setting aside current dollars to pay future expenses. All of this suggests your column headings:

Year	Dick's age	Jane's age	Alimony	Support for Dick	Support for Jane	_____ **Annual total**	PV multiplier

Leave a couple rows on top for input and output. Use *bucket brigade* formulas to complete the table, column-by-column.

Columns for year and ages

The year and ages use the same counting or incrementing *bucket brigade formula* you've seen before. You can even fill it across all three columns. They start with 1, 7, and 9, respectively. Fill in these first three columns.

Columns for payments

You could fill in the alimony and child support payments by hand, but it's tedious, so write formulas for them. This also gives you some more practice in using the IF function.

The alimony calculation tests whether it is past year 5. If it is, there is no payment.

=IF(*Year*>5, 0, 700)

The child support payment depends on the child's age relative to 18 and 21. You get a nested IF, similar to one you wrote in the last case study:

=IF(*Dick's age*<18, 600, IF(*Dick's age*>21, 0, 500))

The formula for Jane is similar. In fact, you can AutoFill it from Dick's formula. *AutoFill* all the payment columns down and check that you get what you expected.

Column for annual total

Add the three monthly payments and multiply by 12 to get the annual payment under Annual Total:

=*(Alimony + Support for Dick + Support for Jane)* * 12

Present value multiplier column

The present value multiplier is the same as in the last case study. However, present value needs an interest rate. As often happens, here's a significant quantity that was left out of the original statement of the problem. Make interest rate an input on the first row so you can vary it. *Create a name* Int_rate for it. Jack assumes 5%.

Create a PV multiplier table as before using the present value bucket brigade formula:

First line: 1
Subsequent lines: =*PV multiplier* previous /(1+Int_rate)

The answer is...

As before, you can get the total by applying SUMPRODUCT to the annual total and the PV multiplier. Put this on the first line to make it easy to see.

=SUMPRODUCT(G4:G18, H4:H18)

Taking a look at the spreadsheet

Here is his spreadsheet with the formatting cleaned up, **divorce.xls**:

	A	B	C	D	E	F	G	H
1	Int rate	5%		Present value		$ 182,179		
2								
3	Year	Dick's age	Jane's age	Alimony	Support for Dick	Support for Jane	Annual total	PV multplier
4	1	7	9	$ 700	$ 600	$ 600	$ 22,800	1.000
5	2	8	10	$ 700	$ 600	$ 600	$ 22,800	0.952
6	3	9	11	$ 700	$ 600	$ 600	$ 22,800	0.907
7	4	10	12	$ 700	$ 600	$ 600	$ 22,800	0.864
8	5	11	13	$ 700	$ 600	$ 600	$ 22,800	0.823
9	6	12	14	$ -	$ 600	$ 600	$ 14,400	0.784
10	7	13	15	$ -	$ 600	$ 600	$ 14,400	0.746
11	8	14	16	$ -	$ 600	$ 600	$ 14,400	0.711
12	9	15	17	$ -	$ 600	$ 600	$ 14,400	0.677
13	10	16	18	$ -	$ 600	$ 500	$ 13,200	0.645
14	11	17	19	$ -	$ 600	$ 500	$ 13,200	0.614
15	12	18	20	$ -	$ 500	$ 500	$ 12,000	0.585
16	13	19	21	$ -	$ 500	$ 500	$ 12,000	0.557
17	14	20	22	$ -	$ 500	$ -	$ 6,000	0.530
18	15	21	23	$ -	$ 500	$ -	$ 6,000	0.505
19	16	22	24	$ -	$ -	$ -	$ -	0.481

A couple of things to notice...

The child support payment formulas for Dick in column E can be *AutoFilled* to column F to calculate it for Jane. This works because the ages are in adjacent columns, as are these formulas.

There is only one input, the assumed interest rate. The rest of the numbers (700, 600, 500, 5, 18, 21) are "hard coded" into the formulas. Normally, you would avoid doing this, because it makes them hard to change. In this case, though, they are all a done deal, so the only number in question is the interest rate. Deciding which numbers go in the inputs and which in the formulas is a judgment call. You may have chosen to put the numbers in the inputs so that you could use this spreadsheet for someone else.

Using the spreadsheet

Jack sees that he needs only $182,179 in insurance, assuming a 5% interest rate. As it turns out, the court tells Jack to use 6%.

TRY IT! Change the interest rate to 6%. Did you get $174,264?

The court agrees that $200,000 is plenty of insurance. Jack decides that Excel and this book paid for themselves with this one little exercise.

12

Whatever might happen
Using data tables

Jim found that the interest rate made a big difference in the present value of his pension (Case Study 14). He did this by varying rate values. He'd like to look at a lot of rates at once.

Making a data table

Excel has a feature called a ***data table*** that automatically gives you the outputs for a list of inputs. You can use it to build a table that shows the present value of Jim's pension for a range of interest rates. First set up the table and then tell Excel to fill it.

How to set up a one-variable *data table* in columns:

1. Identify the input and output(s) that interest you. The input must be a cell containing a number, not a formula. Each output may be a formula or a computed cell. Changes to the input should change the outputs.

2. Label columns for the input and output(s). You can have one or multiple output columns.

3. Let the data table know how to calculate or find the outputs. Just below the headers, put a formula for each outputs. If the output is already calculated somewhere in the spreadsheet, just put = and the appropriate cell.

4. Just below the formula row, in the input column, list all the input values you'd like to look at. If they're evenly spaced, enter the first two and then ***AutoFill*** down to enter the rest.

Here's what your data table looks like at this point if you have three outputs:

headers	**input**	**output1**	**output2**	**output3**
formula row		output formula goes here	output formula goes here	output formula goes here
	100			
	101			
	102			
	103			
	104			
	105			
	106			
	107			
	Input values of interest	Excel will fill in these cells for you		

Check your setup. Change the value in the input cell. All of the formulas should change accordingly.

Take a look at the table setup. Notice the formula row between the headers and the table proper. This row breaks up the table, but you need it there to tell Excel how to complete the table. You may want to use *italics* or other formatting to distinguish this row from the others, and remind yourself that it is not part of the table, but only there to define it.

By the way, you may also find it helpful to use formatting on the input and outputs of interest. Usually you will start with a spreadsheet that does some calculation, such as the one for Case Study 14. The input and output are already there before you start. Highlight them to make them easier to find as you build your table.

Now you're ready to let Excel complete the data table for you. But, you haven't yet told it which input cell to vary. Don't worry. Excel will ask you about that when the time comes.

How to fill in a data table:

1. Select the whole area where you want numbers to go. This is the rectangle that includes the formula row and the column of inputs you want it to use. Omit text headers from the selection.

2. Select **Table...** under the **Data** menu {Data > Data Tools > What-If Analysis > Data Table}.

   A dialog box appears.

3. Click in **Column input cell**. Then click on the cell that contains the input. Click **OK**.

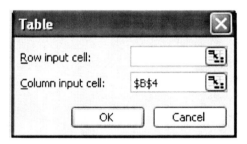

Excel immediately fills in the data table.

TRY IT! Open **pension1.xls**. Make a data table in it to give you the present value of the pension for interest rates from 3.0% to 7.0% in steps of 0.1%. Follow the steps on page 177.

1. Here, the input is the interest rate and the only output is the present value of the pension. Use *italics* to highlight these cells B4 and B9.

2. Start in F1 with the column headings. Make them *bold*.

	A	B	C	D	E	F	G
1	Inputs					Interest rate	Present value
2	Pre 62	$3,500	per month through age 62				
3	Post 62	$3,000	per month from age 62				
4	Int rate	5.2%	per year, for present value calculations				
5	Life exp	83	years life expectancy				
6	Ret age	57	years old at retirement				
7							
8							
9	Result	$ 570,179	is the present value of the pension				

3. The output you want is calculated in B9, so here is G2, the only formula in the formula row:

    =B9

4. Put **3.0%** in F3, **3.1%** in F4, select them both and *AutoFill* down to 7%. (Note: You need to enter 3.0 rather than 3 to keep *AutoFill* from misinterpreting your sequence.)

F	G
Interest rate	**Present value**
	$ 570,179
3.0%	
3.1%	
3.2%	
3.3%	
3.4%	
3.5%	
3.6%	

Now fill it in, by following the steps on the previous page.

1. Select the table except for headers.

    Select F2 through G43.

2. Select Table... under the Data menu {**Data > Data Tools > What-If Analysis > Data Table**}.

    A dialog box appears.

3. Click on **Column input cell** and then click on the input called Int_rate (cell B4).

    This is the number you want the table to change, so that you can see the effect on the output. Click **OK**.

    Excel immediately fills in the data table.

Format column G appropriately.

Taking a look at the data table

Now you should have a spreadsheet like **pension.xls**. If you click on any cell that it filled in automatically, such as G3, you see this formula:

{=TABLE(,B4)}

This tells you that this cell was calculated using a data table with input B4. If you want to see how Excel calculated a data table from the input, look at the formula in the formula row (G2 in this case).

This data table lets you see immediately what the lump sum would be under various interest rates. In this case, a difference of a

F	G
Interest rate	Present value
	$ 570,179
3.0%	$ 707,869
3.1%	$ 700,472
3.2%	$ 693,198
3.3%	$ 686,045
3.4%	$ 679,010
3.5%	$ 672,091
3.6%	$ 665,286
3.7%	$ 658,593
3.8%	$ 652,008
3.9%	$ 645,531
4.0%	$ 639,159
4.1%	$ 632,890
4.2%	$ 626,722
4.3%	$ 620,652
4.4%	$ 614,680
4.5%	$ 608,803
4.6%	$ 603,019

couple of points changes the answer by a hundred thousand dollars or more! This table is useful for someone trying to time retirement by watching fluctuation in interest rates.

Building a stand-alone data table

Usually, as in this example, you have a spreadsheet and you want to run a lot of different cases. Sometimes, though, you just want a table for a formula. You can make a self-contained data table by putting the trial input in the formula row. For example, make a table to see how your car payment varies depending on interest rate. Say the car loan is $30,000 and the loan length is 48 months. Here's the formula (see Case Study 6):

=-PMT(*interest rate*/12, 48, 30000)

TRY IT! Make a data table for this formula with interest rates between 4 and 10% in steps of 0.5%.

First, set up the table. ***Open*** a new workbook.

1. The input can be anything from 4% to 10%. Use, say, 6% as a trial input. The output is the result of the formula. Put the trial input **6.0%** in the formula row in A2. (You can put it wherever you want, but this is convenient and makes the formula row look like the others.)

2. Label columns rate and payment in A1 and B1.

3. Put the formula in B2:

    =-PMT(A2/12, 48, 30000)

4. Put 4.0% in A3, 4.5% in A4 and ***AutoFill*** down to 10% to enter the rest.

Now, let Excel complete the table.

1. Select A2:B15.

2. Select **Table...** under the **Data** menu {**Data > Data Tools > What-If Analysis > Data Table**}.

3. Click in **Column input cell**. Then click on A2. Click **OK**.

Check the table after formatting. Notice that row 7 gives you the same answer for 6% as your formula did. This is **payments.xls**.

	A	B
1	rate	payment
2	6.0%	$704.55
3	4.0%	$677.37
4	4.5%	$684.10
5	5.0%	$690.88
6	5.5%	$697.69
7	6.0%	$704.55
8	6.5%	$711.45
9	7.0%	$718.39
10	7.5%	$725.37
11	8.0%	$732.39
12	8.5%	$739.45
13	9.0%	$746.55
14	9.5%	$753.69
15	10.0%	$760.88

Which medical insurance plan?
What-if analysis

FOCUS: Health insurance, "what-if" analysis, charting the range of possible outcomes

TOOLKIT: MIN function (Chapter 8), data tables (Chapter 12), charts (Chapter 11)

Many decisions depend on future events that you cannot predict. An example is choosing medical insurance. Should you pay extra to get a low deductible? What percentage coverage should you choose? The answer depends on your medical needs in the coming year. The problem is that you don't know what they will be. What if you have few doctor visits? What if you have major, unexpected medical expenses? Excel helps you look at various possibilities.

? Adrienne can buy health insurance through her employer. It's now the one time of year that she can make a selection and that choice will stay in effect until this time next year. There are three plans that vary in terms of deductible, percentage paid, maximum out-of-pocket amount, and cost. All let her go to the doctor she prefers. The table below summarizes them. She could also decline health insurance. Which should she choose?

Choice	Deductible ($)	% to pay after deductible	Maximum out of pocket ($)	Annual cost ($)
A	500.00	90	2,000.00	3,598.00
B	1,000.00	80	5,000.00	2,100.00
C	2,000.00	75	10,000.00	1,100.00

Choosing health insurance

First, let's look at how health insurance works. The insurance pays nothing until her total acceptable expenses reach the deductible.

So, if she were under Choice B and had less than $1,000 in medical costs, she would have to pay them all herself. Anything above the deductible she pays at a percentage. So, if she had $600 of expenses under plan A, she would pay the first $500, the insurance would pay 90% of the remaining $100 ($90), and she'd pay the other 10% of it ($10). So, of the $600, she pays $510 and the insurance pays $90.

Usually, this is all you have to worry about. But if you have major medical expenses during the year, even 10% can add up. Fortunately, a good insurance policy covers you for this. The *maximum out-of-pocket* is the maximum that you need to pay with your percentage share. After that, the insurance pays the whole thing. So, for example, if you had $50,000 of medical expenses in a year under Choice A, you would pay the deductible, $500, and potentially 10% of the remaining $49,500, which comes out to $4,950. But this is more than the maximum of $2,000. So, all you need to pay is the $500 deductible plus the $2,000 maximum. Even if your medical expenses are higher, you pay at most $2,500.

Comparing the options

Choice A is clearly the best, but it's also the most expensive. A reasonable way to compare these options is to look at the total medical costs for the year, including deductible, out-of-pocket expenditures and the cost of the insurance. Of course, this depends on the amount of medical expenses. Build a spreadsheet to compare total costs of each choice for any expense amount you'd like to try.

Planning the spreadsheet

Think about how you can solve this problem. Unlike many of the other spreadsheets, this one looks ahead only one year. Your rows represent the total costs for each of the choices for the next year, computed based on the supposed medical expenses. The columns are the expenses that make up that total cost. You could have chosen to switch rows and columns. It's a personal preference.

Defining the input

The first part of the input is description of the choices. They arrange nicely into a table, as shown below. Add a fourth choice—

do nothing. Remember that doing nothing is one of your options in any decision. In that choice, you buy no insurance, so it pays nothing and the out-of-pocket is unlimited. Represent the maximum out-of-pocket by some huge number. Skip a row and enter typical annual medical expenses. *Create the name* Expenses for B7.

	A	B	C	D	E
1		Deductible	Pays after deductible	Maximum out of pocket	Annual cost
2	Choice A	$500	90%	$2,000	$3,598
3	Choice B	$1,000	80%	$5,000	$2,100
4	Choice C	$2,000	75%	$10,000	$1,100
5	Choice D	$0	0%	$1,000,000,000	$0
6					
7	Expenses	$ 2,000			

This is in **insurance0.xls**. Start with it to build your spreadsheet. When you finish it, try various values for Expenses, since they are unpredictable. Using a reasonable number for Expenses now helps you check your spreadsheet as you develop it.

Setting it up to figure total medical costs

Adrienne's concern is the total amount she will have to pay during the year, which includes the amount paid toward the deductible, her share out-of-pocket, and cost of the insurance itself. The first two depend on the expenses incurred. Set up a table to compute the first two and then add them to the insurance cost. *Copy* row names from the input table or use the Copy *bucket brigade formula.*

	A	B	C	D	E
1		Deductible	Pays after deductible	Maximum out of pocket	Annual cost
2	Choice A	$500	90%	$2,000	$3,598
3	Choice B	$1,000	80%	$5,000	$2,100
4	Choice C	$2,000	75%	$10,000	$1,100
5	Choice D	$0	0%	$1,000,000,000	$0
6					
7	Expenses	$ 2,000			
8					
9		To deductible	Out of pocket	Total medical costs	
10	Choice A				
11	Choice B				
12	Choice C				
13	Choice D				

Since you have some long headers, format the whole spreadsheet to *wrap text*. Now you're ready to write the formulas to complete it.

TRY IT! Write formulas to fill in this table. Then check what you did against the steps that follow.

Amount paid toward the deductible

Write a formula for B10 to calculate the amount that Adrienne must pay toward the deductible. Remember that this is all of her expenses if they are less than the deductible and the amount of deductible if they are more. So, it's either the expenses or the deductible, whichever is less. That suggests the MIN function. Enter the formula using the expenses and deductible (click on them). Here's what you should get:

=MIN(Expenses,B2)

Alternatively, you could have written a formula using the IF function, but the one above is a little simpler.

Try various values for expenses, both above and below the deductible, to check that this does what you want.

Out-of-pocket expenses

Next, write a formula for C10 to calculate the amount that she pays out-of-pocket. This is her portion of the expenses above the deductible, if any, but no more than the maximum out-of-pocket. Click on the cells you want to use as you enter this.

A fairly complex formula like this is easier to build up a little at a time. First, find the amount of the expenses above the amount paid toward the deductible. She must pay a percentage of this portion.

= Expenses - B10

Check that this gives you what you expect. Try expenses both above and below the deductible. Next *edit* this formula to give you the portion that she must pay. The insurance company pays C2 (90%), and Adrienne pays the rest, 1 - C2 (10%). Multiply her percentage by the portion. Put parentheses around each of the two values you're multiplying.

$= (\text{Expenses-B10}) * (1-C2)$

Check that this gives you what you expect. Finally, **edit** this formula to make sure its results stay at or below the maximum out-of-pocket. That means Adrienne pays either the amount you just calculated or the maximum out-of-pocket (D2), whichever is smaller. Sounds like MIN again. Here's the final formula:

$=\text{MIN}((\text{Expenses-B10}) * (1-C2), D2)$

TRY IT! Check this with various values of **Expenses**, above and below the deductible, and big numbers that make you hit the maximum out-of-pocket. If the expenses are less than the deductible, it is 0. However large the expenses, this remains at or below the maximum out-of-pocket, $2,000.

Total medical costs

Finally, in D10, write a formula to add all three costs: deductible, out of pocket, and annual. Click on the numbers and get this:

$=B10+C10+E2$

That takes care of row 10. Check your formulas. You can clone them down the columns for the other three choices using *AutoFill*, because the four choices are laid out in the same order in these calculations as in the inputs above. As long as you maintain relative positions, you can make new tables and still clone the formulas. Check that the results make sense.

What if...?

Now take a look at your completed spreadsheet or **insurance1.xls**.

TRY IT! Enter various expense numbers in B7 and see how the best choice changes.

	A	B	C	D	E
1		Deductible	Pays after deductible	Maximum out of pocket	Annual cost
2	Choice A	$500	90%	$2,000	$3,598
3	Choice B	$1,000	80%	$5,000	$2,100
4	Choice C	$2,000	75%	$10,000	$1,100
5	Choice D	$0	0%	$1,000,000,000	$0
6					
7	Expenses	$ 2,000			
8					
9		To deductible	Out of pocket	Total medical costs	
10	Choice A	$500	$150	$4,248	
11	Choice B	$1,000	$200	$3,300	
12	Choice C	$2,000	$0	$3,100	
13	Choice D	$0	$2,000	$2,000	

...you have normal expenses?

The typical amount of medical expenses for a year for Adrienne is $2,000. The spreadsheet shows that Choice D is the least expensive. This means that, in a typical year, Adrienne would be wasting money to buy insurance. It would cost her less to pay the whole thing herself.

...you have high expenses?

But what if she had high expenses? The highest annual medical expenses she has ever had were $3,000. Try that and see if the answer changes.

7	Expenses	$ 3,000		
8				
9		To deductible	Out of pocket	Total medical costs
10	Choice A	$ 500	$ 250	$ 4,348
11	Choice B	$ 1,000	$ 400	$ 3,500
12	Choice C	$ 2,000	$ 250	$ 3,350
13	Choice D	$ -	$ 3,000	$ 3,000

Same answer. The total costs are a little closer now, but Choice D (no insurance) is still the least expensive. Adrienne is beginning to think she will forgo buying insurance.

...you have a major illness?

Now step back and think about why you buy insurance. Rather than to pay for normal expenses, it's to cover you in the worst case. A major illness or accident hits healthy people unexpectedly. Many people avoid thinking about this, but it's a question to ask before making an insurance decision: How would you pay for major medical expenses?

Try $10,000. One fairly routine surgery could cost this much.

7	Expenses	$ 10,000		
8				
9		To deductible	Out of pocket	Total medical costs
10	Choice A	$ 500	$ 950	$ 5,048
11	Choice B	$ 1,000	$ 1,800	$ 4,900
12	Choice C	$ 2,000	$ 2,000	$ 5,100
13	Choice D	$ -	$ 10,000	$ 10,000

Now choice D looks expensive. But, Adrienne figures this is fairly unlikely and she has savings to cover it. She's still leaning toward going without insurance.

...you experience the worst case?

You must always look at the "worst case scenario" and ask yourself what the worst thing that could happen would be. Though improbable, you want to avoid catastrophe if this happens. Try $100,000, the possible cost of a major illness or accident.

7	Expenses	$ 100,000		
8				
9		To deductible	Out of pocket	Total medical costs
10	Choice A	$500	$2,000	$6,098
11	Choice B	$1,000	$5,000	$8,100
12	Choice C	$2,000	$10,000	$13,100
13	Choice D	$0	$100,000	$100,000

Adrienne could handle this financially for choices A, B or C, but she would have to sell her house to pay the expenses for choice D. She is not willing to take that risk. She decides she'd rather spend a little more each year to get peace of mind.

The big picture

You could try many other cases for annual expenses, but it's easier to let Excel do it for you using a data table. Here, the input is Expenses and the output is total medical costs for the four choices. The table lets you see the total cost of each option for a full range of annual medical expenses, from none to extensive.

A data table to look at all possible expenses

TRY IT! Make a data table starting in A15. First put B7 back to a more typical number, say $5,000. Input is expenses and output is total costs of the four choices. So, here are your headers:

15 Expenses	Total cost of A	Total cost of B	Total cost of C	Total cost of D

Follow the steps from Chapter 12. Enter the output formulas in Row 16. The outputs here are calculated in D10 through D13, so here are the formulas for B16 through E16, respectively,

=D10
=D11
=D12
=D13

		Total cost of A	Total cost of B	Total cost of C	Total cost of D
15	Expenses				
16		$ 4,548	$ 3,900	$ 3,850	$ 5,000

Next, enter the inputs of possible expense levels in Column A. Start with $0 and go up to $50,000 in 1,000-dollar steps. So, put $0 in A17, $1000 in A18, select them both and *AutoFill* down to $50,000.

Now select A16:E67 and make a *data table* with column input cell Expenses (B7). Here is a view of the result:

15	Expenses	Total cost of A	Total cost of B	Total cost of C	Total cost of D
16		$4,548	$3,900	$3,850	$5,000
17	$0	$3,598	$2,100	$1,100	$0
18	$1,000	$4,148	$3,100	$2,100	$1,000
19	$2,000	$4,248	$3,300	$3,100	$2,000
53	$36,000	$6,098	$8,100	$11,600	$36,000
54	$37,000	$6,098	$8,100	$11,850	$37,000
55	$38,000	$6,098	$8,100	$12,100	$38,000
56	$39,000	$6,098	$8,100	$12,350	$39,000
57	$40,000	$6,098	$8,100	$12,600	$40,000
58	$41,000	$6,098	$8,100	$12,850	$41,000
59	$42,000	$6,098	$8,100	$13,100	$42,000
60	$43,000	$6,098	$8,100	$13,100	$43,000
61	$44,000	$6,098	$8,100	$13,100	$44,000
62	$45,000	$6,098	$8,100	$13,100	$45,000
63	$46,000	$6,098	$8,100	$13,100	$46,000
64	$47,000	$6,098	$8,100	$13,100	$47,000
65	$48,000	$6,098	$8,100	$13,100	$48,000
66	$49,000	$6,098	$8,100	$13,100	$49,000
67	$50,000	$6,098	$8,100	$13,100	$50,000

The *split worksheet* lets you see the top and the bottom of the table at the same time. This is **insurance2.xls**. Ignore the first row of the data table. It just holds the formulas. Notice that the first three options "top out" if the expenses are high. They reach a maximum and stay there. This is what insurance should do: protect you from unusually high expenses.

A chart to visualize it

There are a lot of numbers here. A chart makes it easier to visualize. You'd like to get a line for each option that shows how total costs go up as medical expenses go up. You'd also like it labeled to tell which option it represents. The problem is that row 16, which holds the formulas, stands between the results and the labels in row 15. No problem. As long as the input (A16) is blank, Excel ignores the formula row in the type of chart you will make. Just be sure your trial input fits within your list of inputs or you might get a chart that is too big for your data.

It turns out that of all the chart types, only the XY or Scatter plot works well when you have input that is a number. Any other type treats all numbers as output.

Select the entire data table, including headers (A15:E67). Then open the *Chart* feature and click on **XY (Scatter) {Scatter}**. Choices of chart type display.

When you have a lot of data, as you do here, it looks best to use the smooth, connected chart without markers. So, click on the first **Chart sub-type** in the second column {the second one in the first column}. Customize it if you wish.

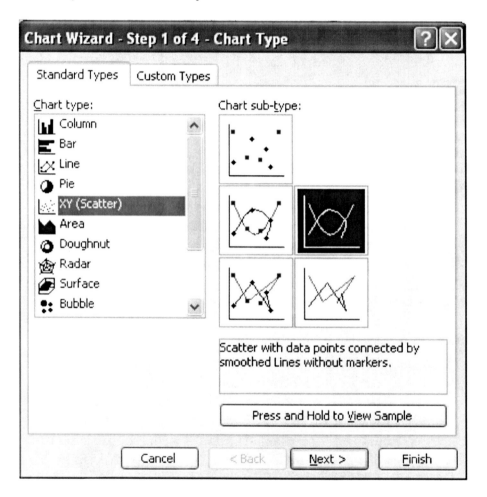

Here's the chart. This is **insurance.xls**.

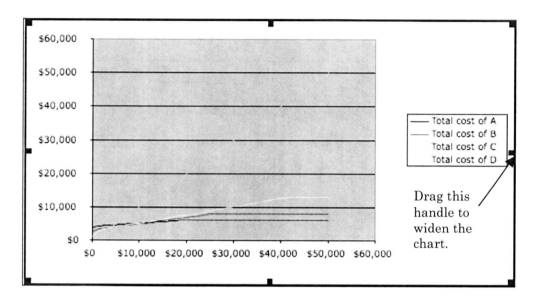

The numbers on the bottom may wrap in a strange way. You can fix that by making the chart a little wider by dragging the handle on the side. Be sure to look at this chart on a color monitor, if you can. The lines display poorly in black and white, as you can see. As usual, Excel works much better on the computer than on paper.

If you really must show the chart in black and white (as we do in this book), you can use chart formatting to fix this. If you're lucky enough to be using Excel 2007, simply choose the black and white **Chart Style** under **Chart Tools > Design > Chart Styles**. Then add the grid lines using **Layout > Axes > Gridlines > Primary Vertical Gridlines > Major Gridlines**.

If you have a Chart toolbar, select each series and **Format Data Series**, then choose **Patterns > Custom**. Otherwise, double click on one of the four plotted lines on the chart. A **Format Data Series** window displays. Choose the tab **Colors and Lines**. In any case, choose a dashed line style (under **Dashed** or **Style**), and black for the **Color**. Unselect **smoothed line**. Then click **OK**. Do this for each of the four, selecting a different dash style for each. You can also add vertical grid lines using **Chart > Chart Options > Gridlines > Value (X) axis > Major gridlines**.

Here's how it might look (**insurance.xls**):

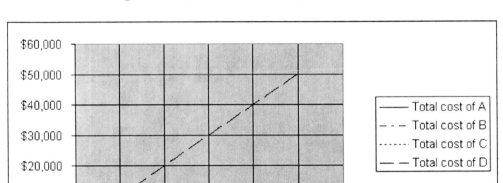

Deciding which plan is best

This chart is only the first step in selecting the best plan. The choice depends on your normal medical expenses and how much you could afford to pay if you had major expenses. In general, the less you have in savings or other "cushion," the more insurance you need.

But the chart and table do give you insight into these choices. If you have low annual medical expenses, D (no insurance) is the least expensive, followed by C, B, and A. At about $3,000, the order turns around, with D becoming more expensive. In fact, D continues to rise while the other choices level out.

Even though it is the least expensive for her typical expenses, Adrienne rules out choice D. She can't afford to risk the cost of a major illness. Choice C, on the other hand, is the next least expensive for typical expenses, but keeps her costs affordable no matter what happens. She chooses Plan C.

13

Working backwards
Goal Seek

You've probably found yourself checking many of the spreadsheets to see whether you will reach a goal. *Will I have enough for my child's education? Will my retirement funds last the rest of my life?* You'll often do trial and error to learn what you need to do to get to your goal. Excel has a feature called Goal Seek that does this for you. It finds the input that gives you a desired output.

First think about your goal. What would success look like? You want some cell, an output of your model, to achieve some value. That is the cell that you want to set.

Next, think about what you want to appear in that cell. This needs to be a number. Sometimes your goal is for two cells to be equal. For example, you want your accumulated savings to equal the cost of college. You can still use Goal Seek in this case. Here's how. Make a new output cell that represents the difference between the two cells. That new cell is now the one you want to set and the value you want it to take is 0.

Finally, identify an input cell that you can change that will affect the outcome. You may have already fiddled with the cell to see what you needed to do to get to the goal. Note that Goal Seek lets you modify only one input. If you want to jiggle multiple inputs at once, you'll need to use Solver and have enough constraints to get an answer. You can explore that on your own.

Now that you've identified which cell you want to set and to what value, and you've picked a cell to change, you're ready to use Goal Seek.

How to use Goal Seek:

1. Identify the input that you want to adjust and the output that you are trying to push toward a goal.

2. Select **Goal Seek...** under the **Tools** menu {**Data > Data Tools > What-If Analysis > Goal Seek**}.

   A dialog box appears.

3. Enter or click on the output cell that you want to set. This is the outcome that you would like to reach some certain value.

4. Press **Tab** to go to the next field. Enter the value that you want the cell to take. This must be a number. It is very often 0.

5. **Tab** to the next field. Enter or click on the input cell that you want to change to get to the goal. This is the answer you seek. This cell must contain a number, not a formula. Click **OK**.

Excel runs through various values for the input, getting successively closer to the goal. It happens so fast on a small spreadsheet that it may look as though the answer appears instantly. When it's done, it gives you the status, usually telling you that it was successful. Click **OK**.

Now, look at the new value of the input. This is your answer.

TRY IT! Use Goal Seek to figure out how much Tiffany, from Case Study 5, can spend each year and have the money last until she's 86. Open **millionaire.xls**.

1. Identify the input that you want to adjust and the output that you are trying to push toward a goal.

   You want the right level of annual spending (cell B2). That's the input you're seeking. You want the funds remaining at age 86 (cell C71) to end up at exactly $0 and no less. That's the output when you reach your goal.

2. Select **Goal Seek**.

3. Click on the output cell of interest, C71, the amount remaining at 86.

4. Press **Tab** to go to the next field. You want the amount remaining to be $0. So enter 0, the value that you want the cell to take.

5. **Tab** to the next field. This is the input you seek. You want to find out what her annual spending should be so that she has exactly $0, and no less, at age 86. That spending amount is in cell B2. Click on it.

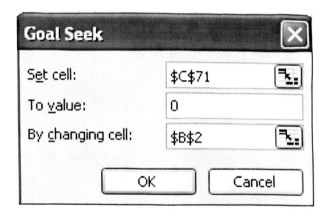

Click **OK**, and Excel tells you that it was successful.

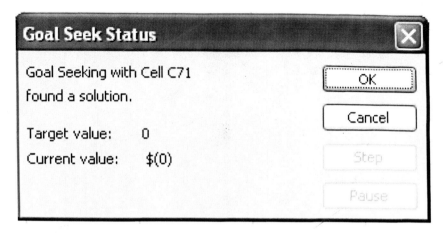

Click **OK**.

Now, look at the new value of the input. This is your answer:

	A	B	C	D	E
1	Start	$1,000,000	Initial amount of money		
2	Annual	$20,618	Annual spending the first year		
3	Inv growth	4%	Annual growth rate of investments		
4	Inflation	3%	Annual inflation rate		
5					
6	Age	Spending	Funds		
7	22	$20,618	$979,382		
8	23	$21,237	$997,320		
9	24	$21,874	$1,015,339		
66	81	$117,936	$572,887		
67	82	$121,474	$474,328		
68	83	$125,118	$368,183		
69	84	$128,872	$254,038		
70	85	$132,738	$131,462		
71	86	$136,720	($0)		

Use a **split worksheet** to see both the inputs and the results at age 86. Sure enough; you see in B2 that, if she spends $20,618 a year, the money will last exactly until age 86.

By the way, depending on your computer, you might get a $0 in C71 in parentheses as above, which indicates a negative number. You can almost never get exactly zero. This is actually a couple millionths of a cent negative. Close enough.

Are we saving enough for college?
Visualizing the future to reach a goal

FOCUS: Visualizing the future through inflation, investment growth, and continued savings; changing savings strategy

TOOLKIT: Bucket brigade formulas, including inflation and investment growth, and descriptive formulas (Chapter 5), Goal Seek (Chapter 13)

Examples in previous case studies showed how to build a model in steps, by examining the results, asking questions, and adding to the spreadsheet. Here, you apply these techniques to build models to address the question, "How much do I need to save for my child's college education?"

Saving for a future event

You probably anticipate an event for which you'd like to save money. Common examples are a retirement fund for yourself or a future college education for your young child. You may want to save for a house, a nice wedding for your daughter, or a big vacation. Whatever it is; the techniques are the same as long as you have a goal and some period of time to reach it. Retirement gets a little more complicated since you first have to figure out what your goal should be. You'll do that in the next case study.

How much will I need?

The first question is, of course, how much you want or need to save. Remember that the cost of your goal goes up with inflation each year. This inflation rate depends on the type of goal. For example, college tuition is increasing faster than the overall cost of living.

You must also ask how long you have to save. With college and retirement, this is pretty clear. But sometimes, such as when saving for a house, you may want to ask, "At this rate, how soon will I reach my goal?"

How annual growth works

In Chapter 5, you learned to calculate annual growth of an investment. Start with the initial amount and, each year, multiply it by 1+ *growth rate*. It's the same technique that you use for inflation. This works, even if you're adding to the account each year. That's the basic technique to use in the models in this case study.

How much do I need to save each year?

Here's a typical example of college planning. You saw this back in Case Study 1. Now, see how to build and extend that model.

? **Example:** Brian and Jaci have a new baby, Zachary. They have already saved $10,000 toward Zachary's college education. The college they would like him to attend currently costs $140,000 for four years, including room and board. They are planning to put aside $15,000 a year in his college fund, which is expected to earn 8% per year. College costs have been going up at a rate of 9% per year. Will they have enough money saved for four years of college by the time he turns 18?

Defining the inputs

Open a new workbook and enter and ***create names*** for the inputs that are given in the question (or just open **college0.xls**).

	A	B	C	D	E	F
1	Start	$10,000	Initial amount in the savings fund			
2	Add	$15,000	Amount added to the fund at the beginning of each year			
3	Inv growth	8%	Annual growth rate of the fund's investments			
4	Cost growth	9%	Annual increase in the cost of college			
5	Current goal	$ 140,000	Cost of 4 years of college			

If you click on B5 (the goal) in **college0.xls**, you see this formula:

=35000*4

There are two reasons for entering a computed input this way. One is to save you the trouble of doing the multiplication. The other, more important, one is to remind you of the number's origin. It's $35,000 per year for four years. This is an easy way of documenting your inputs. You can always see the number, but then click on it and see the calculation.

Setting up the rows and columns

As usual in this sort of decision, each row represents a year. For each year you'd like to keep track of answers to these questions:

- How old will Zachary be?
- How much will be in the fund at the beginning of the year?
- How much will four years of college cost? (This is the goal.)
- How big is the shortfall? (By how much will the amount in the fund fall short of meeting the goal?)

So, here are your column headings:

7	Age	Amount	Cost of college	Shortfall

As in many of the examples you've seen before, most numbers in the columns are of little interest, for example, college costs when Zachary is 10 years old. These are all intermediate values you compute to get you to age 18, when you *do* care. You can use simple *bucket brigade* formulas to step from one year to the next.

TRY IT! Complete the spreadsheet using a starting line and bucket brigade formulas. Then check yourself against the following steps.

The starting line

You can fill in the starting line right away. Zachary is age 0. The starting Amount and Cost of college are straight from the inputs. The Shortfall is just the difference between the Cost of college and the Amount in the fund. So here's the starting line (Row 8):

```
Age:               0
Amount:            =Start
Cost of college:   =Current_goal
```

Shortfall: =*Cost of college - Amount*
        or   =C8 - B8

His age

There's a simple ***bucket brigade formula*** to find Zachary's Age each subsequent year.

Age: =*Age* previous + 1

Enter this in A9 and ***AutoFill*** down to age 18.

Growth of the college fund

There are two reasons the college fund Amount will grow. First, the amount that was in the fund a year ago has had a year to grow through investments. So, you now have the previous amount multiplied by the growth factor:

= *Amount* previous * (1+ Inv_growth)

The fund will also grow when you add some more money to it that year, the amount called Add. This gives you:

= *Amount* previous * (1 + Inv_growth) + Add

Enter this in the Amount column for year 1 (B9) by clicking on the cells:

=B9 * (1 + Inv_growth) + Add

Did you get $25,800? Use ***AutoFill*** to copy it down the column. That takes care of the Amount column.

Keeping your eye on the goal

The goal, the Cost of college, increases by the rate called Cost growth. So, each year, it is the previous year's cost multiplied by the growth factor:

=*Cost of college* previous * (1+ Cost_growth)

Enter this for the Year 1 Cost of college (C9):

=C8 * (1 + Cost_growth)

Did you get $152,600? Copy this down the column using *AutoFill*.

The final column

Shortfall is the difference between the Cost of college and the Amount saved so far, just as it was in the starting line. So, use *AutoFill* to copy D8 down the column.

Taking a look at the spreadsheet

Here's how your spreadsheet looks (**college1.xls**). You might want to *copy a format* to the amounts in this table.

	A	B	C	D	E	F
1	Start	$10,000	Initial amount in the savings fund			
2	Add	$15,000	Amount added to the fund at the beginning of each year			
3	Inv growth	8%	Annual growth rate of the fund's investments			
4	Cost growth	9%	Annual increase in the cost of college			
5	Current goal	$ 140,000	Cost of 4 years of college			
6						
7	Age	Amount	Cost of college	Shortfall		
8	0	$ 10,000	$ 140,000	$ 130,000		
9	1	$ 25,800	$ 152,600	$ 126,800		
10	2	$ 42,864	$ 166,334	$ 123,470		
11	3	$ 61,293	$ 181,304	$ 120,011		
12	4	$ 81,197	$ 197,621	$ 116,425		
13	5	$ 102,692	$ 215,407	$ 112,715		
14	6	$ 125,908	$ 234,794	$ 108,886		
15	7	$ 150,980	$ 255,925	$ 104,945		
16	8	$ 178,059	$ 278,959	$ 100,900		
17	9	$ 207,303	$ 304,065	$ 96,762		
18	10	$ 238,888	$ 331,431	$ 92,543		
19	11	$ 272,999	$ 361,260	$ 88,261		
20	12	$ 309,839	$ 393,773	$ 83,934		
21	13	$ 349,626	$ 429,213	$ 79,587		
22	14	$ 392,596	$ 467,842	$ 75,246		
23	15	$ 439,003	$ 509,948	$ 70,944		
24	16	$ 489,124	$ 555,843	$ 66,719		
25	17	$ 543,254	$ 605,869	$ 62,615		
26	18	$ 601,714	$ 660,397	$ 58,683		

Brian and Jaci see that they will be $58,683 dollars short when Zachary turns 18. The presumed high growth rate of college costs is a killer.

TRY IT! Try various growth rates. If cost growth is only 8% a year (try it) they'll have enough by the time Zachary is 16. The answer is very sensitive to this growth rate. Brian and Jaci decide that they'll assume 9%, but keep tabs on college costs over the years and raise or lower their savings as appropriate.

Using goal seeking to find what it takes

So, if college costs are going up 9% a year, saving $15,000 a year is not going to make it. Try $20,000--that's plenty. You could keep trying various amounts and eventually approach the exact amount you'd need to save to have just enough for college or you could let Excel do it for you using **Goal Seek**.

TRY IT! You seek the amount to add to the fund each year that gives you a shortfall of exactly 0 at age 18. Set cell D26 (shortfall at age 18) to value 0 by changing cell B2 (amount added each year). The answer is $16,567.

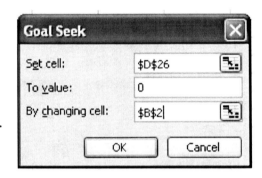

A new saving strategy

At this point, Brian and Jaci are getting a feel for what a big difference cost growth makes. Then they realize that their incomes are going to be going up similarly. They should be able to increase the amount that they save each year. They figure, based on expected raises, that they can increase it by 6% each year.

Letting the added amount grow

Modify the spreadsheet to see where they will be if they use this savings strategy. Think about how you can change the spreadsheet to look at this new strategy. First, you need a new input, Add growth. **Insert a row** for it at the bottom of the inputs. Enter and **create** the **name** Add growth and the value **6%**.

You also need a new column to take care of the amount added to savings each year. **Insert cells** in C8 through C27, between Amount and Cost of college without moving any of the input descriptions above. (Choose **shift cells right**.) Label the new column Added.

TRY IT! Now fill in the Added column. In Year 0, nothing is added beyond the start amount, so enter 0. Year 1 is the original Add amount. After that, it will grow by a factor of 1 + Add_growth. Here are the formulas:

Year 0 (C9):   0

Year 1 (C10):   =Add

Year 2 and beyond: =*Added* previous * (1 + Add_growth)
or for C11:   =C10 * (1 + Add_growth)

Finally, ***edit*** the Amount calculation to use the new column:

=*Amount* previous * (1+Inv_growth) + *Added*
or
B10:   =B9 * (1+Inv_growth) + C10

AutoFill it down the column. Here's the result if they start adding $15,000 a year (**college.xls**):

	A	B	C	D	E	F
1	Start	$10,000	Initial amount in the savings fund			
2	Add	$15,000	Amount added to the fund at the beginning of each year			
3	Inv growth	8%	Annual growth rate of the fund's investments			
4	Cost growth	9%	Annual increase in the cost of college			
5	Current goal	$140,000	Cost of 4 years of college			
6	Add growth	6%	Annual increase in the amount added each year			
7						
8	Age	Amount	Added	Cost of college	Shortfall	
9	0	$ 10,000	$ -	$ 140,000	$ 130,000	
10	1	$ 25,800	$ 15,000	$ 152,600	$ 126,800	
11	2	$ 43,764	$ 15,900	$ 166,334	$ 122,570	
12	3	$ 64,119	$ 16,854	$ 181,304	$ 117,185	
13	4	$ 87,114	$ 17,865	$ 197,621	$ 110,508	
14	5	$ 113,020	$ 18,937	$ 215,407	$ 102,387	
15	6	$ 142,135	$ 20,073	$ 234,794	$ 92,659	
16	7	$ 174,784	$ 21,278	$ 255,925	$ 81,142	
17	8	$ 211,321	$ 22,554	$ 278,959	$ 67,638	
18	9	$ 252,134	$ 23,908	$ 304,065	$ 51,931	
19	10	$ 297,647	$ 25,342	$ 331,431	$ 33,784	
20	11	$ 348,322	$ 26,863	$ 361,260	$ 12,938	
21	12	$ 404,662	$ 28,474	$ 393,773	$ (10,889)	
22	13	$ 467,218	$ 30,183	$ 429,213	$ (38,005)	
23	14	$ 536,589	$ 31,994	$ 467,842	$ (68,747)	
24	15	$ 613,430	$ 33,914	$ 509,948	$ (103,482)	
25	16	$ 698,453	$ 35,948	$ 555,843	$ (142,610)	
26	17	$ 792,434	$ 38,105	$ 605,869	$ (186,565)	
27	18	$ 896,220	$ 40,392	$ 660,397	$ (235,824)	

Taking a look at the result

This made a huge difference! They'll have enough saved by the time Zachary is 12. Inflation can work for you as well as against you. This suggests that they can start out with an even smaller amount. You can figure that amount for them.

TRY IT! Use *Goal Seek* on this spreadsheet to see how much they must add to savings initially to pay for college. You want the Shortfall to go to zero at age 18. You want to find the smallest initial Add amount that will get them there. So, choose *Goal Seek* and enter E27, 0 and B2 in the dialog box.

	A	B	C	D	E	F
1	Start	$10,000	Initial amount in the savings fund			
2	Add	$10,869	Amount added to the fund at the beginning of each year			
3	Inv growth	8%	Annual growth rate of the fund's investments			
4	Cost growth	9%	Annual increase in the cost of college			
5	Current goal	$140,000	Cost of 4 years of college			
6	Add growth	6%	Annual increase in the amount added each year			
7						
8	Age	Amount	Added	Cost of college	Shortfall	
9	0	$ 10,000	$ -	$ 140,000	$ 130,000	
10	1	$ 21,669	$ 10,869	$ 152,600	$ 130,931	
11	2	$ 34,923	$ 11,521	$ 166,334	$ 131,411	
12	3	$ 49,929	$ 12,212	$ 181,304	$ 131,375	
13	4	$ 66,869	$ 12,945	$ 197,621	$ 130,753	
14	5	$ 85,940	$ 13,722	$ 215,407	$ 129,468	
15	6	$ 107,360	$ 14,545	$ 234,794	$ 127,434	
16	7	$ 131,366	$ 15,418	$ 255,925	$ 124,559	
17	8	$ 158,218	$ 16,343	$ 278,959	$ 120,740	
18	9	$ 188,199	$ 17,323	$ 304,065	$ 115,866	
19	10	$ 221,618	$ 18,363	$ 331,431	$ 109,813	
20	11	$ 258,812	$ 19,464	$ 361,260	$ 102,448	
21	12	$ 300,149	$ 20,632	$ 393,773	$ 93,624	
22	13	$ 346,031	$ 21,870	$ 429,213	$ 83,182	
23	14	$ 396,896	$ 23,182	$ 467,842	$ 70,946	
24	15	$ 453,221	$ 24,573	$ 509,948	$ 56,727	
25	16	$ 515,526	$ 26,048	$ 555,843	$ 40,316	
26	17	$ 584,379	$ 27,611	$ 605,869	$ 21,489	
27	18	$ 660,397	$ 29,267	$ 660,397	$ -	

You see that they need to start by saving only $10,869 a year, as long as they increase it by 6% each year. Of course, they should check their progress and current college costs every couple years and adjust accordingly.

Can I afford to retire?

Making your money last a lifetime

FOCUS: Long-term prediction of assets, considering investment growth, inflation, income and spending

TOOLKIT: Growth, inflation, incrementing, copy, and other bucket brigade formulas, and descriptive formulas (all in Chapter 5), SUM function (Chapter 8), IF function (Chapter 9), Goal Seek (Chapter 13)

You may have nearly or just retired and want to know how much you can afford to spend. You can start with the same techniques as for the Millionaire spreadsheet (Case Study 5), though it's more complicated than this, because:

- The savings are spread across various accounts, each with its own growth rate.
- There are other sources of income, such as Social Security.
- Spending needs may vary over the years.

? Steve and Kathey consider retiring when they turn 59 and 57, respectively. They have $500,000 in stocks earning 8%, $500,000 in bonds at 4%, and $10,000 in cash at 1%, all in IRAs. They own rental property that nets $20,000 a year and part-time work for $5,000 a year. At age 68, they will get Social Security of $14,000 and $12,500 a year and quit the part-time work. Major annual expenses are fixed house payments of $20,000 paid off in 11 years, taxes of 15% of their income, and $50,000 in other general expenses. Can they afford to retire?

Visualizing retirement

Amazingly, you could spend more time retired than working. Ever-increasing life expectancy means you could spend 30 years or more in retirement. The object of the game is to make sure your money outlasts you.

Types of money sources during retirement are assets: IRA, 401(k), lump-sum pension, and ordinary savings—funds that you have set aside for retirement—and income: pension, Social Security, annuity, business, and employment—money that arrives during retirement. If you're asking this question, you're probably spending any income in the year you get it, then, having to tap your assets. But, you also want to let assets grow as much as possible.

Many retirees are surprised at their high tax bill because they have been socking their money away, tax-deferred, in IRAs and 401(k)s and it's been growing tax-free. But, in retirement, they have to pay the piper. All the money they take out of their accounts is taxable, placing them in the odd situation of paying taxes on what they spend, rather than what they earn.

There are many strategies for withdrawing living expenses from the various funds. The approach for this spreadsheet is to withdraw proportionately from each fund. This has the advantages of using any tax-free funds to soften the tax blow each year and keeping investments reasonably balanced. In real life you may choose some other strategy, but this is a reasonable assumption to help you think about retirement.

Planning the spreadsheet

First, think about what you will need to answer each year:
- How much income, if any, will they get?
- How much will their expenses be (including taxes)?
- How will their investments grow?
- How much will they need to draw out of each investment to meet expenses?
- How much will they have left in each investment?

Setting up rows and columns for the inputs

In all the previous case studies, there were just a few inputs, which could be clustered at the top. Here, we may have different inputs for each year. Expenses change from year to year. The house gets paid off. Income changes. Businesses are sold. Social Security starts. Employment comes and goes. This suggests a *table* of inputs.

You'll want to follow assets year-by-year as well, as they grow and are tapped. This suggests a table built around years. This couple has a lot of income sources, assets and expenditures to track. A column for each might be more than fits on the screen. So, use the rows for these categories and the columns for the years. Everything you've done to this point has made each year a row. This example shows that you can do it the other way just as well. Putting years in columns makes it easy to see what is going on each year. You can refer to cells in *descriptive formulas* by labels, as before. The only difference now is that the labels are on the rows.

Open a new workbook and lay the columns out with their ages as headers, as shown. Leave the first two columns available. *AutoFill* this out as far as you wish. Here the *split worksheet* shows **retire0.xls** taken out until Kathey's age is 90.

	A	B	C	D	E	AJ	AK
1			His age ->	59	60	91	92
2			Her age ->	57	58	89	90

Hint: Use the counting or incrementing *bucket brigade formula* beginning in column D. Then you can change the starting ages without having to change anything else.

Below this you'll build tables for income, expenditures, assets, and withdrawals.

Predicting income and expenditures

Now fill in the rows to predict income and expenditures for all the years. Isn't this going to be a lot of work to fill in? Not really. Many of these grow steadily at some rate, for example, with inflation. Use column B to hold these rates, and fill them in as shown below. Note the use of keyboard characters, centered using the Formatting Toolbar, to make an arrow to indicate that this Rate label is for a column.

As often happens, statement of the question is incomplete. You've seen the impact of inflation rates. You need to include those as inputs as well. The house payment is the only one that won't go up, since it's a fixed loan. Enter the presumed growth rates for income and expenses in column B (**retire1.xls**):

	A	B	C	D	E	M	N	O
1		Rate	His age ->	59	60	68	69	70
2		|	Her age ->	57	58	66	67	68
3		v						
4	Income	3%	His SS					
5		3%	Her SS					
6		5%	Rental					
7		2%	PT work					
8			Total income					
9								
10	Expenditures	3%	General					
11		0%	House					

Letting 'em grow

TRY IT! Now you can complete each row with a **bucket brigade formula** that you **AutoFill** across the row. For example, put $5,000 in D7 since the part-time work will start the first year. Put the initial value in whatever year the income or expense starts. For example, his social security starts when his age is 68, with a value of $14,000 in M4. Do this for all of the initial income and expenditures except taxes.

Then, apply the usual growth formula to compute each year's amount from the previous value in the row:

$$=previous\ value * (1 + growth\ rate)$$

For example, here is the formula in E7 for the second year of part-time work:

=D7*(1+$B7)

Note the use of the $ in front of the B. That's an **absolute reference**. That means that you want it to stay B (the rate column) when it is cloned. That's all you need to do to make this a formula that you can use for any growth.

Hint: *Copy the cell* E7 and paste it in other cells where you want the formula: E6, E10, E11, N4 and P5. This is a way to clone a formula to cells that are apart from the original.

AutoFill these growth formulas to subsequent years by dragging to the right as far as you need. Bucket brigade formulas work just as well along rows. Check that the cloned formulas make sense and stop when they should. For example, remember that PT work stops when his Social Security starts.

Use the SUM function to get the total income each year. Be sure you sum everything you need, including blank lines (since they might not stay blank). For example, D8 should read, =SUM(D4:D7)

Here's how it looks in **retire2.xls**. Check what you did against it. You may need to scroll or use a *split worksheet* to see the Social Security payments and the end of house payments.

	A	B	C	D	E	M	N	O
1		Rate	His age ->	59	60	68	69	70
2			Her age ->	57	58	66	67	68
3			v					
4	Income	3%	His SS			$ 14,000	$ 14,420	$ 14,853
5		3%	Her SS					$ 12,500
6		5%	Rental	$ 20,000	$ 21,000	$ 31,027	$ 32,578	$ 34,207
7		2%	PT work	$ 5,000	$ 5,100			
8			Total income	$ 25,000	$ 26,100	$ 45,027	$ 46,998	$ 61,559
9								
10	Expenditures	3%	General	$50,000	$51,500	$ 65,239	$ 67,196	$ 69,212
11		0%	House	$20,000	$20,000	$ 20,000	$ 20,000	

You've now completed a spreadsheet that lets them visualize their income and expenses for the rest of their lives. This alone is a valuable first step in planning retirement.

Scroll through the years and compare income and expenses. As usual in retirement, income is not sufficient to cover expenses most years.

Laying out the rest of the spreadsheet

They'll have to dip into savings. In fact, the expenditures above exclude taxes, so the situation will only get worse. Think about the questions you'll need to answer each year in the rest of this spreadsheet.

- How much will they owe in taxes?
- What will their total expenditures be?
- How much will they need from savings to meet expenses?
- How much will be in each fund at the beginning of the year?
- How much will they withdraw from each fund?
- How much will remain in each fund after withdrawal?
- Will they continue to have enough to cover themselves?

Make rows to answer each of these, separated by blank rows. Here's how it might look:

10	Expenditures	3%	General	$	50,000	$	51,500	$	53,045
11		0%	House	$	20,000	$	20,000	$	20,000
12									
13			Taxes						
14									
15			Total expenditures						
16									
17	From savings								
18									
19	Assets	8%	Stock acct						
20		4%	Bond acct						
21		1%	Cash						
22			Total assets						
23									
24	Withdrawals		Stock acct						
25			Bond acct						
26			Cash						
27			Total withdrawals						
28									
29	Amount rem.		Stock acct						
30			Bond acct						
31			Cash						
32			Total remaining						
33									
34			OK?						

Hint: You can save typing the names of the accounts using the copy *bucket brigade formula*. In C24 and C29, just put the formula, =C19, and *AutoFill* it down to the other two accounts. This has the added bonus of allowing you to change the names of the accounts easily.

While you're at it, include the asset growth rates in column B. This is **retire3.xls**.

The first year

This first year (column D) is the starting line for some *bucket brigade formulas*.

TRY IT! Take the questions one at a time and fill in the starting column. Some of these are tricky, so look ahead if you get stuck. Check what you did against the following steps.

Taxes

We pay taxes on the previous year's expenses. Since this is the first year, those expenses are missing from this spreadsheet. This is one more of the missing inputs that you need. Figure the year's taxes that are due on last year's income. It turns out that Steve and Kathey estimate they will owe $10,000. Enter it in D13.

Total expenditures

This is simply the sum of all expenditures, including taxes. So, in D15 you have:

=SUM(D10:D13)

From savings

The amount that they'll need to take out of savings is the shortfall of income relative to expenses, which is:

=Expenditures - Income
or
D17: =D15-D8

Did you get $55,000?

Assets

This is the beginning of the first year. So, the amount in each fund is just what they started with. Fill these in as inputs. Total them using the SUM function. You should get $1,010,000 in D22.

Withdrawals

As is typical in retirement, their income is too small to meet expenditures and they must tap savings to make up the difference of $55,000 (D17). Just to keep things simple, they plan to withdraw all of what they'll need at the beginning of the year and move it into their checking account.

So, there's $55,000 that needs to come out of savings. A reasonable way to do that is tap each account proportionately. That way the assets continue to be invested in all three categories. For example, the stock account comprises 49.5% of all of the investments (computed as 500,000/1,010,000). This means you want to take 49.5% of the needed $55,000 out of that account. So here's how to build that piece of the formula to compute how much to take out of the stock account.

Amount to withdraw from the account:

=Proportion of this account in all accounts * amount from savings
or
=(*Stock acct / Total assets*) * *From savings*
or
D24: =(D19/D$22)*D$17

You get $27,228.

Notice the use of $ in the formula to keep Total assets and From savings on the right rows when you copy it down to the other accounts. By the way, you don't really need the parentheses here, since Excel computes multiplication and division in order from left to right.

Put this formula in D24. ***AutoFill*** it down to the other accounts. Get a total of the withdrawals to check that you withdrew the right amounts to give you the $55,000 you need.

17	From savings			$	55,000
18					
19	Assets	8%	Stock acct	$	500,000
20		4%	Bond acct	$	500,000
21		1%	Cash	$	10,000
22			Total assets	$	1,010,000
23					
24	Withdrawals		Stock acct	$	27,228
25			Bond acct	$	27,228
26			Cash	$	545
27			Total withdrawals	$	55,000

Amount remaining

Find the amount left in each fund after the withdrawal by subtracting the amount withdrawn from the original amount.

D29: =D19-D24

You get $472,772. You can copy this as-is to the other accounts because of the uniform way the table is built.

Total remaining

This is another sum:

D32: =SUM(D29:D31)

Did you get $955,000?

OK?

They're OK so far, unless they've depleted their funds. Use the IF function to check that the total they have remaining is still positive.

D34: =IF(D32>0, "yes", "no")

What you've done so far is **retire4.xls**.

Calculating the rest of the years

You may notice that most of the formulas used in the first year apply just as well to all the rest of the years. The only ones that need new formulas are taxes and assets.

Taxes

Just to keep things simple, Steve and Kathey estimate their taxes at 15% of income. This is not their tax bracket. The tax bracket is the rate at which their *last* dollar gets taxed, and is higher. If you want to estimate this percentage for yourself, divide the total taxes you paid by your income. If you want to estimate future taxes more precisely, estimate your deductions and use a VLOOKUP function and the tax tables. Here, keep things simple by using a percentage.

The rate column is a convenient place to put it, so enter 15% in B13.

So, taxes are based on income. What counts as income when you are retired? Any taxable income, such as wages, plus any withdrawals from tax-deferred accounts. In this case, that's everything they spend. The reason is that all of the savings are in standard IRAs and 401(k)s.

Now you can write a formula to estimate taxes as a percentage of spending in the previous year:

= *Total expenditures* previous * *tax rate*

or for the second year,

E13:   =D15*$B13

This works for all the other years (because you remembered to edit the formula to tie down the B column with a $), so *AutoFill* it across. You may get zeroes, but they'll fill in as you complete the table.

Assets

Check what was left after withdrawal the previous year. This is Amount rem. This asset has had a whole year to grow since the withdrawal at the beginning of the last year. You can use the usual growth formula. So, here's what it's worth now:

= *Amount rem.* previous * (1+ *Rate*)
or
E19:   =D29*(1+$B19)

Again, this works for the rest of the assets, so *AutoFill* it down to the other two, but not the total. It also works for the rest of the years, because of the $, so *AutoFill* all of these across. Fill in everything else in rows 13 through 34 by *AutoFill* across. Pay no attention to error messages until you've filled the whole thing.

Looking at the results

Here is the completed spreadsheet (**retire5.xls**):

	A	B	C	D	E	F		AJ	AK
1		Rate	His age ->	59	60	61		91	92
2		I	Her age ->	57	58	59		89	90
3		v							
4	Income	3%	His SS					$ 27,630	$ 28,459
5		3%	Her SS					$ 23,254	$ 23,951
6		5%	Rental	$ 20,000	$ 21,000	$ 22,050		$ 95,299	$ 100,064
7		2%	PT work	$ 5,000	$ 5,100	$ 5,202			
8			Total income	$ 25,000	$ 26,100	$ 27,252		$ 146,183	$ 152,474
9									
10	Expenditures	3%	General	$ 50,000	$ 51,500	$ 53,045		$ 128,754	$ 132,617
11		0%	House	$ 20,000	$ 20,000	$ 20,000			
12									
13		15%	Taxes	$ 10,000	$ 12,000	$ 12,525		$ 21,947	$ 22,605
14									
15			Total expenditures	$ 80,000	$ 83,500	$ 85,570		$ 150,701	$ 155,222
16									
17	From savings			$ 55,000	$ 57,400	$ 58,318		$ 4,518	$ 2,748
18									
19	Assets	8%	Stock acct	$ 500,000	$ 510,594	$ 520,159		$ 2,426,523	$ 2,616,894
20		4%	Bond acct	$ 500,000	$ 491,683	$ 482,342		$ 725,255	$ 753,186
21		1%	Cash	$ 10,000	$ 9,550	$ 9,098		$ 5,685	$ 5,734
22			Total assets	$ 1,010,000	$ 1,011,827	$ 1,011,599		$ 3,157,463	$ 3,375,815
23									
24	Withdrawals		Stock acct	$ 27,228	$ 28,966	$ 29,987		$ 3,472	$ 2,130
25			Bond acct	$ 27,228	$ 27,893	$ 27,807		$ 1,038	$ 613
26			Cash	$ 545	$ 542	$ 525		$ 8	$ 5
27			Total withdrawals	$ 55,000	$ 57,400	$ 58,318		$ 4,518	$ 2,748
28									
29	Amount rem.		Stock acct	$ 472,772	$ 481,629	$ 490,172		$ 2,423,050	$ 2,614,764
30			Bond acct	$ 472,772	$ 463,790	$ 454,535		$ 724,218	$ 752,573
31			Cash	$ 9,455	$ 9,008	$ 8,574		$ 5,677	$ 5,729
32			Total remaining	$ 955,000	$ 954,427	$ 953,281		$ 3,152,945	$ 3,373,067
33									
34			OK?	yes	yes	yes		yes	yes

Inputs are blue when viewed on the monitor to help them stand out in this big spreadsheet. (Font color on the Formatting Toolbar does this.) You'll notice that the spreadsheet uses a *split worksheet* to show both early and late years. That's what most interests this couple. The early years show how things start out and the later ones show whether their money will last their lifetimes.

What if...?

You see that this retirement plan works for Steve and Kathey. They are left with more than $3,000,000 when she turns 90 (AK34).

TRY IT! Now, answer these questions:

What if he stopped working? (**Hint:** Set D7 to 0. Answer: They are still OK, with more than $3 million remaining.)

What if they didn't have the rental? (**Hint:** Put D7 back to $5,000 and D6 to 0. Answer: They would run out of money when she's 81.)

What's the most they could afford each year in general spending, if they had both the rental and the part-time income, and still have money until she's 90? (**Hint:** First be sure to set D7 back to $5,000 and D6 to $20,000; use *Goal Seek* to set AK32 to 0 by changing D10. The answer, $66,969, should appear in D10.)

Dealing with real-life issues

This is a relatively simple retirement spreadsheet. Real-life retirement is much more complicated. Here are other considerations that may come up in your own retirement. These are all included in the spreadsheet retirecomplex.xls that you can download from www.decisionspreadsheets.com.

- There is a penalty if you draw from IRAs or 401(k)s before 59½.
- There are minimum withdrawals from standard IRAs and 401(k)s starting at age 70½.
- If you happen to have excess income in some years, IRA rules may not allow you to put it into your accounts.
- The government taxes only *some* expenditures. Specifically, you do not pay taxes on money that you hold outside of IRAs and 401(k)s, nor on withdrawals from Roth IRAs.
- Capital gains are taxed at a different rate.
- Some Social Security may be exempt from taxes.
- Actual tax calculations use tax tables, which change over the years, rather than taking a fixed percentage of income.
- You may have discretionary spending that you can eliminate if things get tight.
- The strategy for spreading withdrawals across the accounts breaks down if you run out of money, but then so does everything.

Taxes are a big deal in retirement. For example, using retirecomplex.xls you can see that the amount you can spend in retirement is surprisingly sensitive to how tax brackets will be adjusted in the future.

14

The great unknown
Looking at risks

It's relatively easy to make a decision if you know the consequences of each alternative. But, who has a crystal ball? How can you know what will work, how long tasks will take, how much things will cost, how well your investments will do, how long you will live, and what will go wrong? An approach that has always worked before, may stop working. As they say in the disclaimers for investments, "past performance is no guarantee of future results."

The good news is that, even if you don't know exactly what will happen, you can talk about what might happen and even assign probabilities to it. You can then use random numbers in your models to look at possible outcomes.

You can model uncertainties like this using the function RAND. RAND has no arguments, so you write it =RAND( )

Enter it in an unused cell in a spreadsheet and you get some decimal number between 0 and 1:

=RAND( )			
	A	B	C	D
1	first	1		
2	second	2		0.02976701
3	third	3		

Now, change anything in the spreadsheet and you get a new number:

=RAND( )			
	A	B	C	D
1	first	1		
2	second	2		0.200464641
3	third	4		

The numbers you get are almost certainly different from these because they're, well, random.

Random events

Often, you get different outcomes depending on whether or not some random event occurs. Use RAND to help you think about situations if you can estimate the probability. Probability is just a number between 0 and 1 that tells how often you expect the event to occur. For example, if the probability of rain were 60% you would expect rain during 60% of days like that.

How to generate a representative situation when you have a probability of something happening:

=IF(RAND( ) < *probability, outcome if it happens, outcome if it doesn't*)

TRY IT! Write a formula to model 60% chance of rain:

=IF(RAND( ) < .60, "rain", "clear")

This works because the random number is less than .60 exactly 60% of the time. Try it:

=IF(RAND( ) < .60, "rain", "clear")			
	A	B	C	D
1	first	1		
2	second	2		clear
3	third	4		

Change some number in the spreadsheet and you get another random number and, possibly, another outcome. If you do this long enough you get "rain" about 60% of the time. A little later you'll learn how to get Excel to do these repetitions for you.

Random fluctuation

Though many quantities, such as investment growth and inflation, are uncertain, you often can estimate bounds on numbers like these. Then, you can use RAND to give you random numbers within these bounds to help you think about the possible outcomes.

How to get a random number between a minimum and maximum:

$=minimum + (maximum - minimum)*$RAND( )

TRY IT! Write a formula to get a random amount of time it takes to do a task that you expect to take between 10 and 36 hours. Use 10 and 36 as inputs in B1 and B2, respectively.

=B1 + (B2 – B1)*RAND( )

=B1 + (B2 – B1)*RAND( )		
	A	B	C
1	minimum	10	
2	maximum	36	
3	random	26.01646715	

This is the simplest of many ways to represent random fluctuation. But, real life yields more outcomes in the middle than on the ends. The normal (bell-shaped) curve is often a model for such fluctuation. Here's a formula that gives a random number from a normal distribution:

=NORMINV(RAND( ), *mean, standard deviation*)

Looking at representative outcomes

Random numbers help you think about unknowns. Every time you run your spreadsheet with new random numbers, you see a possible outcome. Each outcome could happen. How would you handle it?

Double click any empty cell and press **Enter** and you see another outcome. If you continue doing this, you see representative outcomes, with more likely outcomes appearing more often. Do the good results justify the risk of the bad results?

Estimating risk with Monte Carlo models

It turns out that you can use Excel's data tables to run hundreds or thousands of cases, one after the other, and list and summarize the results. This technique of running multiple random cases is called Monte Carlo modeling, after the famous gambling center. Investment analysts use it increasingly to understand risk.

Turning any spreadsheet into a Monte Carlo model

Use *data tables* to turn any Excel spreadsheet that uses random numbers into a Monte Carlo model. The trick is to use the run numbers as the input. A Monte Carlo *run* or *iteration* is the outcome of one set of random numbers. Number the runs 1 through 100 and you get 100 unique random outcomes.

How to set up a table for 100 unique outcomes:

1. Use the RAND function to model random outcomes, such as an outcome that occurs with some probability or a random quantity.

2. Identify the outcomes that you want to examine. (The inputs are the run numbers, even though the calculations ignore them.)

3. Find a spot for the table of outcomes. The first column will be called Run. Label a column for each outcome.

4. Enter a formula to report each outcome in the next row.

   =*outcome cell*

5. Below that, list all the run numbers in the first column. Start with 1, 2, and then *AutoFill* down to 100.

Notice that, after the first step, these are the same steps used in Chapter 12 to create a *data table*.

Now you're ready to tell Excel to fill it in with 100 random results. Again, this is just a data table.

How to fill in the table you just set up:

1. Select the table excluding headers.

2. Choose **Data > Table...** {**Data > Data Tools > What-If Analysis > Data Table**}.

   A dialog box appears.

3. Since the table is in columns, leave the **Row input cell** blank. For the **Column input cell** click on any cell that is *not* being used anywhere in the model. Click **OK**.

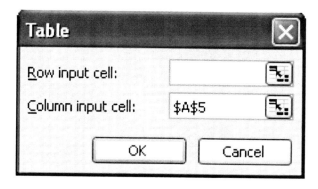

TRY IT! Turn **coins1.xls** into a Monte Carlo model.

First, open **coins1.xls**. Here's what it does. Imagine that you are offered a chance to play a game for even money. Eight fair coins will be tossed. If you get the same number of heads as tails you win. If not, you lose. Should you play? Since heads and tails are equally likely, on average you'd get four of each and win. Sounds good, but look at it in Excel first to be sure.

Click on cells to see the source of random outcomes and the way Excel determines whether you win or lose. You'll see the probability formula from page 220. Enter and change numbers in unused cells to get new outcomes. Do you think you should play? Using the steps above as a guide, turn this into a Monte Carlo model and estimate your chance of winning, as follows:

1. The outcomes of the tosses are already random.

2. Here, there's only one outcome—win or lose—and it's in J2.

3. Find a spot for the table of outcomes. Put Run in A4 and Outcome in B4.

4. In the first cell in the outcome column, enter a formula to tell Excel to get the outcome. There's only one outcome of interest here, and it's in J2. So, in B5 enter

    =J2

5. Below the formula row, list all the run numbers. Enter 1 in A6, 2 in A7, and *AutoFill* down to 100 to get 100 runs.

Now fill it in.

1. Select A5 through B105.

2. Choose **Data > Table…** {**Data > Data Tools > What-If Analysis > Data Table**}.

    A dialog box appears:

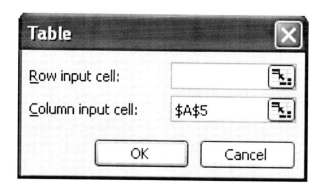

3. Since the table is in columns, leave the Row input cell blank. For the Column input cell, click on any cell that is not being used. Click **OK**.

The table fills with the results of 100 runs:

	A	B	C
1	1st coin	2nd coin	3rd coin
2	H	T	T
3			
4	Run	Outcome	
5		lose	
6	1	lose	
7	2	lose	
8	3	win	
9	4	lose	
10	5	win	
11	6	lose	
12	7	lose	
13	8	win	
14	9	lose	
15	10	lose	

You will almost certainly get results different from those shown here, because it's random. In any case, you'll get the results of 100 random games. If you then double click any blank cell and enter, you'll get a new set of random outcomes.

How does this work? Here's what's going on. Each row has a run number for input into a cell that doesn't do anything with it. Any Excel table automatically picks up the input from each row, substitutes it into the input cell, and gives the resulting output. In this case the inputs, run numbers, don't change anything, but Excel just goes ahead and re-computes the outcome each time. That's all it takes to get a new set of random numbers. This is **coins2.xls**.

Using a Monte Carlo model

Take a look at the results of the 100 runs. It seems that you lose more than you win. To be more precise, count the number of wins in B6 to B105:

=COUNTIF(B6:B105, "win")

Notice you don't count B5 because it's not part of the table.

Divide by 100, the number of runs, to get the percentage:

=COUNTIF(B6:B105, "win") / 100

	A	B	C	D	E	F	G	H	I	J
1	1st coin	2nd coin	3rd coin	4th coin	5th coin	6th coin	7th coin	8th coin	No. heads	Outcome
2	H	T	H	T	T	T	H	H	4	win
3										
4	Run	Outcome		wins	% wins					
5		win		28	28%					
6	1	lose								
7	2	lose								
8	3	win								

This (**coins.xls**) shows that 28% of the time you would win if you played 100 games that turned out the way these did. You may have a different number in your spreadsheet, but it's probably somewhere between 15% and 35%. Though less than precise, this answer tells you what you need to know. You tend to lose a lot more often than you win. As an even-money bet, this game is a bad deal!

As you see from this example, 100 runs are too few to get a precise answer. More runs would give you more consistent answers, though they can never be precise. Rather than an exact answer, the answer you get from a Monte Carlo model is an estimate of the answer you would get if you could run the model forever. Of course, your answer is never any better than your model assumptions.

Tired of the wait?

Even in this simple little model, you have probably been annoyed with the time it takes to recalculate everything any time you change something. It even recalculates when you change some other spreadsheet. This is especially frustrating when you are modifying the model, which you'll often want to do. The best models are created following "build a little, test a little." A good model raises questions that suggest model changes. So, you'll want to be able to make changes to your Monte Carlo model. You don't want Excel to recalculate anything until you've finished the whole package of changes.

Fortunately, you can turn off recalculation of the Monte Carlo runs. Here's how.

Open the Excel options or preferences. Choose **Tools > Options [Excel > Preferences] {Office > Options}**:

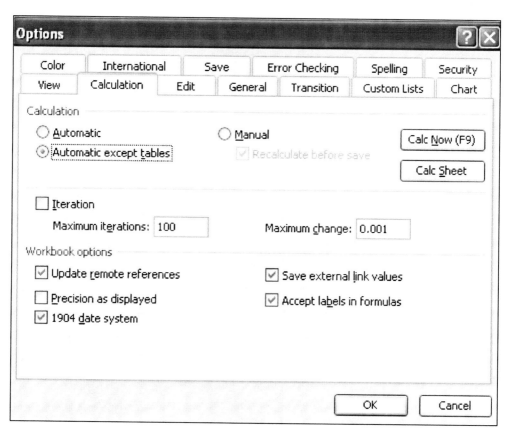

Click on **Calculation**. Choose either **Automatic except tables** or **Manual**. This prevents Excel from recalculating the Monte Carlo tables unless you tell it to. **Automatic except tables** is useful, because your main model will be updated as you make changes, so you can see the effects of what you're doing, but you won't be slowed down by Monte Carlo runs.

Before you click **OK**, notice that in the upper right of the window there is the **Calc Now** button with which you can "calculate now." To be sure that the numbers you see are current, before you examine the results, recalculate: press **F9 [Command and =]**.

Using the Monte Carlo technique

The example here looks at something that happens randomly, the result of a coin toss. This same method could be used to think about other events that you cannot predict if you can estimate their probabilities. Consider the chance that it will rain (and ruin your garden party), an investment will go belly up, you will have a major illness in the next year, a piece of equipment will fail, and so on.

The next case study looks at random fluctuation of investments. This technique can be applied to any quantities that vary randomly, such as the number of daily orders, the time needed to do a job, or the output of a sensor or measuring device.

Can I afford aggressive investment risk?

The chance that your money will last a lifetime

FOCUS: Long-term prediction of assets, random fluctuation, Monte Carlo modeling, the probability of reaching a goal

TOOLKIT: Retirement analysis (Case Study 18), random fluctuation and Monte Carlo models (Chapter 14)

Steve and Kathey found in the last case study they could, in fact, afford to retire, even with general spending of $66,969. But now, they wonder how aggressive their investments should be. They want to maximize asset growth, without risking losing assets and jeopardizing the retirement they have planned. They are especially concerned about the stock account, which tends to be volatile, with past annual returns as high as 21%, and money-losing years.

? Steve and Kathey consider retiring when they will be 59 and 57. They have $500,000 in a stock account that earns *between -5% and 21%* and all other investments, income, and fixed expenses as in Case Study 18. They plan *$66,969* in other general expenses. What is the *probability* they can retire?

The new statement of the problem asks for the probability that their money will last their lifetimes at a general spending rate of $66,969, taking into account the expected fluctuation in performance of the stock account. The average return is the same.

Adding random fluctuation values

Open **retire5.xls**. Change the general expenditures (D10) to $66,969. Make sure the other inputs match the question from Case

Study 18. If so, you see that this couple runs out of money only at the last minute (AK32 is very small).

Think about how you might modify this spreadsheet to model random fluctuation year-to-year in the performance of the stock fund.

First, you need a place for the extra input. You now have a minimum and a maximum rate for the stock fund, instead of a single rate. *Insert* a new *column*, C. Label it Max rate. You can use this later to look at fluctuation of other rates. *Enter* the minimum and maximum rates for the stock fund.

	A	B	C	D
1		Min Rate	Max rate	His age ->
2		|	|	Her age ->
3		v	v	
4	Income	3%		His SS
5		3%		Her SS
6		5%		Rental
7		2%		PT work
8				Total incom
9				
10	Expenditures	3%		General
11		0%		House
12				
13		15%		Taxes
14				
15				Total exper
16				
17	From savings			
18				
19	Assets	-5%	21%	Stock acct
20		4%		Bond acct
21		1%		Cash

Now change any formula that uses the stock fund rate so that it uses a random draw.

Here's how you can find all of the formulas in the whole worksheet that use a particular cell. Click on the cell of interest (B19 in this case). Select **Tools > Formula Auditing > Trace Dependents** **[Tools > Auditing > Trace Dependents] {Formulas > Formula Auditing > Trace Dependents}.** Arrows appear from the cell to all of the other cells that use it:

21	Assets	-5%	21% Stock acct	$ 500,000	$ 441,153	$ (68,900)	$ (68,202)
22		4%	Bond acct	$ 500,000	$ 482,947	$ (1,247,764)	$ (1,352,130)

Above, it points to F19 and all of its clones. So you only need to change this one formula and re-clone:

=E29*(1+$B19)

Before you edit the formula, get that arrow out of your way using **Tools > Formula Auditing > Remove all arrows [Tools > Auditing > Remove all arrows] {Formulas > Formula Auditing > Remove all arrows}**

TRY IT! *Edit* this formula to use a random number between $B19 and $C19, instead of $B19 alone. Here it is:

```
=E29*(1+$B19+($C19-$B19)*RAND( ))
```

This is just the old formula, with the formula for a random fluctuation from Chapter 14 in place of the original rate. Check that this makes sense. Now convince yourself that this is in a form to be cloned to the rest of the row (note the $s to make sure it always uses the right rates). *AutoFill* it across the row.

How did they do?

Take a look at the results. What you see is one possible future. Is there a yes at the bottom of each year's column? If so, they were lucky and had enough money. If there is any no, that means they were unlucky and ran out of money early. Because it's random you may see either situation.

Now build a Monte Carlo model to compute the probability that they get lucky. First, the model must be able to check whether the results are all yeses. Again, exploit the old trick of using 1 for yes and 0 for no. *Edit* the formula in E34, which checks whether they're OK, to read:

```
=IF(E32>0, 1, 0)
```

AutoFill this across. Verify whether they made it by checking that there are no 0s. Here's a formula to do it:

```
=MIN(E34:AL34)
```

Convince yourself that this formula gives you a 1 (yes) if they made it fine through the years and a 0 (no) if they ever came up short. Put this in AM34.

Making a Monte Carlo model

Now you're ready to turn this into a Monte Carlo model. Follow the steps from the last chapter.

1. You already have random numbers in the spreadsheet.

2. The single outcome you want to examine is whether they have enough money, in AM34.

3. Put the data table in columns AN and AO. Label them Run and OK?

4. In the first cell in the outcome column labeled OK?, enter a formula to tell Excel to get the appropriate outcome.

    =AM34

5. Below the formula row, list all the run numbers in the first column. Start with 1, 2, and then *AutoFill* down to 100.

Now you can get Excel to fill in the table for you.

1. Select the table excluding the headers, AN2:AO102.

2. Choose **Data > Table...**

AN	AO
Run	OK?
	0
1	1
2	1
3	0
4	0
5	1
6	0
7	1
8	1
9	0
10	1
11	0

3. Since the table is in columns, leave the **Row input cell** blank. For the **Column input cell**, click on any cell that is *not* being used in the model. Click **OK**.

    The table fills in with the results of 100 runs. You may have to wait for it; there's a lot of computing going on here.

Looking at the results

Both 1s and 0s display in the OK? column. This means that they may or may not be able to spend at this rate.

Write a formula to count the number of times they were OK, and then divide by 100 to get the average. You could use COUNTIF to do this, but this one is even simpler (another example of how using 1 for yes and 0 for no makes things easier):

=SUM(AO3:AO102)/100

Notice that the sum starts with row 3, the first of the table proper, so you get exactly 100 results. Put this in AP2 and give it the % format. This is **retire.xls**:

The number you get for **probability OK** is most likely different from the 46% shown, but it's probably not much more than 50% and most likely much less. This is a very rough estimate, but it's good enough for the decision at hand.

AN	AO	AP
Run	OK?	probability OK
	0	46%
1	1	
2	1	
3	0	
4	0	
5	1	

The spending plan is too aggressive to give them enough assurance that the money will last their lifetimes. Even though, with average performance, they are covered, fluctuation introduces too much risk. Just as in the coin toss game of Chapter 14, averages tell only part of the story.

What are the options?

Steve and Kathey find this spending plan unacceptable. They're looking for at least 90% probability of success.

TRY IT! Does lowering their general spending rate to $60,000 a year do it?

Enter 60000 in E10. Chances are you get a probability of 95 to 100%. That little extra bit of cushion is all they need.

TRY IT! What if they could get a more aggressive stock fund, that averaged a higher 8.5%, but that varied between -15% and 32%?

Enter -15% in B19 and 32% in C19 to see that the probability of success drops, even though the average growth is better.

Always take into account the simplifying assumptions made by any spreadsheet when making a decision such as this. Here are the major ones for this model:

- Assumption: The random draws are independent from one year to the next.

  Fact: In reality, bear or bull markets can last several years. This means that strings of good or bad years are more likely than this spreadsheet indicates. Consequently, the swings will be even more dramatic. So, the probability estimates here are optimistic.

- Assumption: The random draw is just as likely to pick a number near the minimum or maximum as in the middle and always picks a number inside the range.

  Fact: More realistic is a normal distribution, in which numbers in the middle are more likely, but in which there is a small chance of getting numbers far from the middle. The spreadsheet retirecomplex.xls uses normal distributions.

Remember, too, that the answer depends on your goal. If you were trying to amass as much money as possible to leave to your children (while providing for yourself from some other source), you might compute the probability of having at least a million dollars at age 90. This would lead you to choose aggressive investments. If you had a shorter life expectancy there would be less time for fluctuations to average out, so you'd want to be more conservative.

As you see by variation in the results, 100 runs are too few to get a stable answer. This number only keeps the spreadsheet size manageable and the computation time tolerable. A serious Monte Carlo analysis uses thousands of iterations.

15

The bottom line
Summary

You have decisions to make

You've seen examples here of 15 unique decisions in 19 case studies. As you worked through them, you learned techniques that you can apply to your own decisions. Now it's your turn. You have the tools to address some fairly complicated decisions. Practice. Keep Excel open on your computer to make quick calculations, organize your thoughts, and think about possible outcomes. Many useful spreadsheets start just that way. Explore other features of Excel, since this book just scratched the surface. If you'd like to see more examples of decision spreadsheets, check out:

www.decisionspreadsheets.com.

How to think about your decision

First, make sure you understand the question:

What are you trying to decide? Write a clear and complete question that you are trying to answer.

How will you measure success? This could change the answer. For example, are you trying to maximize your expected assets or minimize your risks?

Are there multiple criteria? If so, you must balance them by using weighted normalized scores, even swaps, or simply a list of pros and cons. Be sure you understand all your criteria, especially the subjective ones.

How much risk can you accept? Think about worst-case scenarios. Decide whether you would be comfortable with the outcomes or whether your solution needs to include a way to avoid or soften them. Use a Monte Carlo model to understand the level of risk.

Next, spend some time identifying your alternatives, including doing nothing. Sometimes, rather than distinct alternatives, you seek an amount that meets the goal. An example is the amount to save each month to meet your retirement savings goal. Think about realistic limits on these amounts, such as the maximum you could save each month. You may discover other alternatives as you explore the decision. For example, the initial strategy for saving for college was to set aside the same amount each year. But, the effects of inflation in the spreadsheet suggest an alternative: increase savings each year.

Now list every influence on the outcome. Is anything missing? You may have to do some research to get all the numbers you need. List key characteristics of the alternatives. Make them as numerical as possible. For example, give subjective ratings on a scale of 1 to 5. These are all part of your inputs.

Next, think about what you yet need to know. Unpredictable quantities, such as future inflation or investment growth, affect most difficult decisions. What you don't know *can* hurt you! Make these unknowns inputs to your model, and then vary them to see what happens. Do "what-if" analysis. Look at the worst case and typical cases. Do sensitivity analysis. Randomize inputs and do a Monte Carlo analysis.

Often your input includes numbers that you seek, such as savings level. Vary these to see how they affect the outcome. Use *Goal Seek* to figure out what they should be to reach your goal.

Building a model in Excel

Start with inputs at the top. These include everything you know, the unknowns you want to vary, and first guesses at the quantities you want to find. Fill in reasonable guesses for the unknowns. *Create names* for all of the inputs so you can refer to them in formulas.

Set up the problem in a table so you can build up the answer year-by-year or month-by-month. In most decisions, the rows represent years, months, or items. Think about which quantities you want to track for each row. These are your columns. Make clear, but concise, row and column headings. Often, *AutoFill* simplifies entry of row headings.

Fill in formulas for the first row. Think about how each quantity comes from the inputs. Enter a formula, starting with =, that does the calculation. Click on the numbers you want to use as you build the formula. Then check whether you got the result you expected. Insert intermediate calculations if you need to.

Fill in the next row using similar techniques. Use the previous row as much as possible. Maybe you can use the same formula using *AutoFill*. Maybe you can build on it with a *bucket brigade formula*. Appendix D has formulas you may find useful. Check that your formulas give you the answers that you expected. Now look at the formulas and see whether you can use them in the rest of the rows. Put a $ (*absolute reference*) in front of anything in the formula that you want to stay the same when it's copied. *AutoFill* the formulas down a couple rows and check the results. When you're satisfied, go ahead and AutoFill the whole thing.

Build complicated formulas step-by-step from the inside out. Think about the steps you need to take to get to the answer. Write a simple formula to get to the first step. Check the result to see whether it makes sense. Now think about what you need to do with that answer to get to the next step. Treat the previous formula as you would a single cell reference and build a formula around it. Again, check the answer. Keep going until you have a formula that does the whole thing. Another approach is to add columns to calculate these intermediate answers and use a series of simple formulas. Then, when you're satisfied that this works, *hide the* intermediate *columns*.

Let the built-in functions help you. Chapter 8 describes some of the most useful ones. **Browse the function library** to find appropriate functions and guidance in filling in their arguments.

Using the model

Before you use your model, do some sanity checks. Make sure you believe all the answers. Vary some of the input. Pick values, such as zero, that give you answers you can do in your head. Try very large numbers. Do they affect the answer the way you would expect?

Now you're ready to use your model. Examine it on the monitor, rather than on paper, so you can scroll and change things. Change some of the input under your control and see how the outcome changes. Use **Goal Seek** to find out exactly what you need in order to reach your goal. Change alternatives and see how each one comes out. Change some of the input that is not under your control and see whether you can live with all the possible outcomes. Do sensitivity analysis to find out what really drives the outcome. Chart the results to visualize them. If you have multiple criteria, use normalized, weighted scores or apply the Even Swap method. Compare cost and benefit.

Finally, make your decision based on what you've learned. Think about how you feel about the answer. Are there subjective factors you've forgotten? Are your priorities and goals realistic? Were there any surprises? What do you learn from that? Does it raise additional questions? Are there factors yet to consider? Expand the model to gain better understanding of the problem, through broader, different, or more detailed considerations. This is called, "build a little, test a little."

Remember: Excel is not a spectator sport. It's a tool to help you think.

Appendix A

Excel techniques

Following, in alphabetical order, are short descriptions of the most useful Excel techniques. Any different instructions for Excel 2007 are shown in {braces}. Where instructions differ for Windows and Macintosh versions, Macintosh steps are in [brackets].

There are usually multiple ways to perform any technique. You may discover others that you prefer, such as keyboard shortcuts.

Absolute reference

Why: Keep copied or AutoFilled formulas pointing to the same row, column, or cell.

How: Put $ in front of any part of the cell reference that you want to keep fixed. For example, $A1 in a formula always refers to column A, C$5 always refers to row 5, and G7 always refers to cell G7, even when copied elsewhere in the spreadsheet.

Reference: Introduced in Chapter 4, used in Case Studies 8, 9, 18, and 19

AutoFill a sequence

Why: Save yourself the trouble of entering a sequence like 1, 2, 3, etc. or the same value in successive cells.

How: *Select* the first one or two cells. Move the cursor to the lower right corner of the selection until the fill handle appears. Click and drag the fill handle down or across the cells you want to fill. You may also see an AutoFill Options button icon with choices.

Reference: Introduced in Chapter 4, used in Case Studies 3, 6, 11, 16, and 19, and Chapters 12 and 14

AutoFill to clone a formula

Why: Save yourself the trouble of entering a formula in successive cells. Use bucket brigade formulas.

How: *Select* the cell(s) containing the formula(s). Move the cursor to the lower right corner of the selection until the fill handle appears. Click and drag the fill handle down or across the cells you want to fill.

Reference: Introduced in Chapter 4, used in Case Studies 3 through 15 and 17 through 19

AutoSum

Why: The easiest way to add a column of numbers is to use the **AutoSum** button. Add income, expenditures, future costs, or preference points. Use totals as a step in computing an average.

How: It's on the Standard toolbar {**Home > Editing**} and looks like **Σ**. Click on a cell below the list you want to total. Then click on the **AutoSum** button. Excel shows you which cells it is going to sum, by drawing a box around them. It gives you the summation formula to accept or modify. If it's what you want, press **Enter**.

Note that, if you have any blank cells in the column, AutoSum may not select all the cells you want. Check the formula. While it's displayed just drag over the cells that you want to sum and the formula will fix itself. Then press **Enter**.

Click on the arrow to the right of the button to see and select the other options, such as average.

Reference: Used in Case Study 2, Chapter 3, and elsewhere

Bold and italics

Why: You can highlight column or row headers, major inputs or outputs, or other cells of interest.

How: *Select* the cells you want to format. Click on the **B** icon for bold or the *I* icon for italics on the formatting toolbar {under **Home > Font**}. Click on the icons again to turn them off.

Reference: Used in Case Studies 2 and 11 and Chapter 12

Browse the function library

Why: Explore the functions that Excel makes available for you to use in formulas. Get help entering the arguments of functions.

How: Select the cell where you want the function to calculate. Click on the Insert Function *fx* button on the formula bar or standard toolbar. Select a category from the list or pull-down menu in the dialog box. Click on any of the listed functions and read the description at the bottom. Select the function you want and click **OK**. Another window opens up, telling you exactly what information (arguments) you need to give the function. Fill in the arguments one by one by tabbing through them. Use the descriptions and click on cells you want to use. Click **OK**.

Reference: Introduced in Chapter 7, used in Case Study 6 and Chapters 9 and 15.

Bucket brigade formulas

Why: Build complex calculations line-by-line with simple formulas.

How: Identify rows that take you step-by-step to your outcome. Often these represent years. Fill in the first row. Then write formulas in the second row that take advantage of the calculations in the previous row. Make sure the formula applies as well to any of the subsequent rows. You may need to use *absolute references* to do this. *AutoFill* the formulas down the columns.

Reference: Introduced in Chapter 5, used in Case Studies 4, 5, 6, 8, 9, 11 through 15, 17, and 18

Change column width or row height

Why: Make the column wide enough to display the text or numbers in it. A too-narrow column shows just #s.

How: Hover the cursor over the little line between the column headers until a vertical line crossed by a double-headed arrow appears. Drag it to make the column wider or narrower. Another way is to use **Format > Column > AutoFit Selection {Home > Cells > Format > Cell Size > AutoFit Column Width}**. Make a row taller similarly.

Reference: Used in Chapter 3 and Case Studies 2, 4, 5, and 11

Chart your results

Why: A picture is worth a thousand numbers. Use a chart to display a visual image of your results.

How: First select a table with or without labels. Select **Insert > Chart {Insert > Charts}**. Click on the chart type you want, such as a bar or pie chart, then choose a chart sub-type. Pre-2007 Excel walks you through customization steps, but the defaults generally work well, so you can just click **Finish**, or click on **Next** successively to customize the chart. Excel 2007 makes the chart first; customize a chart by clicking on it, if necessary, to get the **Chart Tools**, and then on the appropriate tab.

Reference: Introduced in Chapter 11, used in Case Studies 10 and 16

Clear an area of the spreadsheet

Why: This erases trial ("scratchpad") calculations or anything else you wish to delete permanently.

How: Clear one rectangular area at a time. *Select* the area. Choose **Edit > Clear > All. {Home > Editing > Clear** (the eraser icon) **> Clear all}**. This removes everything from the cells, including formatting. The cells themselves are still there but are empty.

Reference: Used in Case Study 3

Copy formats

Why: Reuse formats that you like anywhere else in the spreadsheet.

How: Click on any cell that's formatted as you like. Click on the Format Painter on the Standard Toolbar **{Home > Clipboard}** (the paintbrush icon). Then drag over the cells you want to format.

Reference: Used in Case Study 17

Copy a cell or a block of cells

Why: Rearrange a spreadsheet to make it clearer and easier to use. Use copied blocks of cells elsewhere and build new spreadsheets by lifting from old ones.

How: *Select* a block of cells. Choose **Edit > Copy {Home > Clipboard >** Copy icon}. Click on the upper left corner of the new location and choose **Edit > Paste {Home > Clipboard >** Paste icon}. Note that you overwrite whatever is already there. Use *insert* instead, if you want what's there to move to make room.

Reference: Used in Case Studies 9 and16

Create names

Why: Names for inputs or other frequently used cells make formulas easier to read. You can then copy the formulas and they always refer to the same cells. This is particularly convenient if you've already labeled the cells.

How: Enter the names you want next to the cells that you want to name and select both names and cells. You may even already have labels that you can use for names. Use **Insert > Name > Create {Formulas > Defined Names > Create from Selection}**. A dialog box asks you where the names are relative to the cells.

Reference: Introduced in Chapter 3, used in Case Studies 5, 6, 11, 12, 13, 14, 16, and 17

Currency and percent format

Why: Make numbers that represent currency look like it with a dollar sign ($) and two decimal places. Make percentages look like percentages.

How: *Select* the cells. Click on the currency button, $, or the percent button, %, in the formatting toolbar {**Home > Number**}.

Here's another way to do it: Excel automatically formats for you if you include the $ or % while entering data.

Note that Excel stores percentages as decimals. For example, 5% is stored as .05. If you enter 5 and then format as a percentage, you'll get 500%. To prevent this problem, format before entering, or use the % in the entered number.

Reference: Used in Chapter 3 and Case Studies 3 and 4

Data table

Why: Look at outcomes over a large number of situations, do sensitivity analysis, or make a Monte Carlo model.

How: Find a place to put the table and label columns for the input and outputs. Just below the output headers, put a formula for each of the outputs. Just below this formula row, list in a column all the input values you'd like to look at. *Select* the rectangle that includes the formulas that you've just entered and the column of inputs you want it to use. Select **Data > Table...** {**Data > Data Tools > What-If Analysis > Data Table**}. Click in **Column input cell**. Then click on the cell that contains the input for your main spreadsheet. Click **OK**.

Reference: Introduced in Chapter 12, used in Case Studies 16 and 19

Decrease decimal

See *Increase or decrease decimal*.

Delete rows, columns, or cells

Why: As your spreadsheets evolve, you may find you have data and calculations that you no longer need.

How: *Select* the rows, columns, or cells. Choose **Edit > Delete**. If you are removing cells, reply to the prompt that asks which way you want to move the adjacent cells to fill the gap. {For Excel 2007, choose **Home > Cells > Delete**. This deletes without a prompt. If you want to choose, click on **Delete > Delete Cells...**}.

Formulas automatically adjust for the new cell locations. By the way, though you might expect to delete large areas of your file using the **Backspace [Delete]** key, it is dedicated to editing only within cells. If you want to delete the contents of cells without moving any other cells use *Clear*.

Descriptive formula

Why: Write a formula in an easily readable form to guide entry, document the spreadsheet, and reuse the formula elsewhere.

How: Identify each cell by its column header (in italics), possibly followed by "previous." This tells you whether the cell is in this row or the previous one. Use these descriptors to represent cell references in a formula. The formula may be preceded by the name of the row. For example,

Running total: = *Running total* previous + *Net*

adds the contents of the cell in the previous row under the Running total column to the contents of the cell in this row under the Net column and puts the answer in this row under Running total. Enter it by clicking on the referenced cells and typing the rest (e.g., = and +). You may sometimes see descriptive formulas that reference columns, depending on how the spreadsheet is organized, as in Case Study 18.

Descriptive formulas that use functions may use italics and the normal font to represent generic arguments. Italics are also used to represent general inputs, as in Appendix D.

Reference: Introduced in Appendix B, Chapter 5, and Case Study 4, used in Chapter 4, Case Studies 4 through 7, 11 through 15, 17, and 18

Edit the contents of cells

Why: Fix mistakes or expand formulas. Add $ to formulas to get absolute references.

How: Double click on the cell. Click on the entry or the formula bar. Use the mouse to move the cursor. Insert by typing. Delete characters with the **Backspace [Delete]** key. Select with the mouse. If the cell you're editing contains a formula, click on other cells to include them in the formula. Press **Enter** when you're done or **Esc** to put it back the way it was. Be sure to finish editing a formula and enter it before using the arrow keys or clicking on other cells, unless you want those cells to appear in the formula.

Reference: Used in Case Studies 6, 9, 11, 12, 16, 17, and 19

Enter information in cells

Why: Cells are where you put information in the form of numbers, dates, currency, text, formulas, etc. See also **Write formulas**.

How: Click on the cell and start typing. Excel goes into entry mode. Text appears in the cell and in the formula bar as if by a tiny word processor that works only for that cell. Edit your entry in the cell or formula bar by using **Backspace [delete]** or moving the cursor. (Warning: Using arrow keys for this in a formula may cause unwanted change.) Press **Enter** or **Tab**. What you typed is now stored in the cell, where other cells can refer to it. Use **Enter** for entering data in columns and **Tab** for filling rows. Note that, even if you *select* several cells, your entry appears only in the first cell. Note that AutoComplete may fill in if you start typing something it has seen above. Accept it or keep typing.

Reference: Used in all Case Studies

Format cells

Why: Highlight cells of special interest or put them in an appropriate form, such as for money, percentages, dates or times.

How: The most common formats are on the Formatting Toolbar. (To show this, select **View** > **Toolbars** > **Formatting**). {The most common formats are in **Home** > **Font** and **Home** > **Number**.}

Hover the cursor over each tool to explore what it does. In pre-2007 Excel, open Toolbar Options [More buttons] at the end of the toolbar. Some of the buttons you need may be there.

To apply formatting, **select** the cells that you wish to format and click on the desired features. See **Bold and italics**, **Currency and percent**, **Increase or decrease decimal**, **Copy a format**, **Special format for numbers**, or **Wrap text**.

Reference: Used in Chapter 3 and Case Studies 2 through 5, 9 through 11, 13, 16, and 17

Formula

See **Write formulas**.

Functions

Why: Excel has a library of functions to use in formulas to do a wide variety of calculations. For example, SUM totals a column.

How: Enter the formula in the form =*function name (function arguments)*. Separate the arguments with commas. The arguments for the SUM function, for example, are the values to be totaled. See Chapter 8 or **browse the function library** to see what the particular arguments are for each function.

Reference: Introduced in Chapters 7 through 10, used in Chapters 10 and 14, Case Studies 7, 9, 12, 14, 15, 16, and 18

Goal Seek

Why: Work the problem backwards to find an input that gives you the desired output. Find out what you need to reach a goal.

How: Identify the input cell that you want to find and the output cell that you need to reach a numerical goal. Select **Tools > Goal Seek {Data > Data Tools > What-If Analysis > Goal Seek}**. In the dialog box, enter or click on the cell in which you want to reach a number, type the number that you want it to reach, and click on the input cell that you want to change. Excel puts the answer in the input cell.

Reference: Introduced in Chapter 13, used in Case Studies 17 and 18

Hide rows or columns

Why: Focus on results, rather than on intermediate calculations.

How: *Select* the rows or columns to hide. For columns, choose **Format > Column > Hide {Home > Cells > Format > Hide & Unhide > Hide Columns}**. To make it all reappear, choose **Format > Column > Unhide {Home > Cells > Format > Hide & Unhide > Unhide Columns}**. The technique for rows is similar.

Reference: Used in Case Study 13 and Chapter 15

Increase or decrease decimal

Why: Show currency rounded to the nearest dollar or cent and make the number of decimals shown in a column consistent. Show enough significant digits for very small numbers.

How: *Select* the cells. Click on the increase decimal or decrease decimal button on the Formatting Toolbar {under **Home > Number**}.

This changes only the displayed number. The one used in the calculations keeps all its accuracy.

Reference: Used in Case Studies 9, 10, and 13

Insert rows, columns, or cells

Why: You often build new spreadsheets from old ones. This means moving things around to make room for new data or calculations.

How: *Select* the rows, columns, or an area in which you want to insert new cells. It's OK if there's already something there; Excel moves it to make room. Select **Insert > Row, Insert > Column**, or **Insert > Cells**. If it's cells, reply to the prompt that asks which way you want the original cells moved. {Select **Home > Cells > Insert**. This inserts without a prompt. If you want to choose, click on **Insert > Insert Cells...**}. Blank cells appear and everything else moves out of the way. Excel automatically adjusts all formulas for the new cell numbers.

Reference: Used in Chapter 5 and Case Studies 9, 12, 13, 17, 18, and 19

Italics
See *Bold and italics*.

Name cells
See *Create names*

Open a workbook
Why: Start a new spreadsheet from scratch or use an existing one.

How: Start Excel. Select **File > New... > Blank workbook [File > New Workbook]** {Office button > **New**} to start from scratch or **File > Open...**, {Office button > **Open**} which prompts you to find a file to open. Excel may open automatically with a blank worksheet to save you the trouble. Excel files end in .xls {.xlsx}.

Reference: Used in all Case Studies

Percent
See *Currency and percent formats*.

Reference cells
Why: Refer to cells in formulas so you can use them in the calculation. The references are also useful when you are talking about spreadsheets.

How: Excel refers to a cell by its column and row. For example, the upper left cell is 'A1'. It refers to a rectangular area by its upper left and lower right corners. See the area B2:C4, below:

	A	B	C	D
1				
2				
3				
4				
5				

Rows and columns use a similar notation. For example, row 3 is 3:3, and column D is D:D.

Reference: Used in all Case Studies

Relative references

Why: Automatically change cell references in formulas when copied; construct bucket brigade formulas.

How: Click on unnamed cells when entering formulas to get the standard "A1" relative reference. See *Absolute references*.

Select cells

Why: Select a single cell to enter something in it. Select single or multiple cells to format them or use them in a formula.

How: Select a cell by clicking on it. Use this guide to select multiple cells:

To select	Click
Multiple cells in a rectangle	...and drag upper left to lower right
A column	its letter
A row	its number
The whole sheet	the box in the upper left corner, right above the column of row numbers

Reference: Used in all Case Studies

Sort and filter

Why: Focus on rows of special interest. Put lists or data in order.

How: Click somewhere in the rows. Select **Data > Filter > AutoFilter {Home > Editing > Sort & Filter > Filter}**. Then open the menu attached to any header to see all values in the column. Pick one and see only the rows with that value. For example, look just at incomplete or assigned tasks. You can sort rows, but first check that you can get back to the original order if you need to.

Special format for numbers

Why: Make dates, times, or other numbers look like what they are.

How: *Select* cells. Choose **Format > Cells**. Click the **Number** tab. Select a **Category**. Make a selection. {**Home > Number >** number format pull-down menu. Click on the desired format or find categories for more choices under **More Number Formats.**}

Reference: Used in Case Studies 3 and 4

Split the worksheet

Why: Look at two parts of a large spreadsheet at once.

How: Drag the slider on the right or top end of either scroll bar to get two panes that scroll independently. Split in both directions to get four panes. Drag the slider back to un-split.

To keep the left and/or topmost panes (usually your headers) from scrolling, freeze them by choosing **Window > Freeze panes {View > Windows > Freeze Panes > Freeze Panes}**. To put it back, choose **Window > Unfreeze panes {View > Freeze Panes > Unfreeze Panes}**.

Reference: Used in Chapter 13 and Case Studies 6, 16 and 18

Undo an action

Why: Everybody makes misteaks.

How: Choose **Edit > Undo**, {**Quick Access >** Undo icon} as many times as you want to back out of the last things you did. The **Edit** menu {Undo icon} shows what it's going to undo before you choose.

Wrap text within a cell

Why: Sometimes, a cell contains long, descriptive text. Make the text visible while keeping the columns a reasonable size by wrapping it to multiple lines within the cell.

How: *Select* the cell or cells. Select **Format > Cells**. Click the **Alignment** tab. Under **Text Control**, check the **Wrap text** checkbox. {**Home > Cells > Format > Format Cells > Alignment > Wrap text.**} Click **OK**.

Reference: Used in Case Studies 2, 4, and 16

Write formulas

Why: Formulas do calculations based on everything else in the spreadsheet. Without them, Excel is nothing but a list manager.

How: Click on the desired cell and type = to tell Excel you are entering a formula. Until you **Enter** the formula, you are in formula entry mode and everything you do goes into the formula. When you click on cells, they become part of your formula. This is the easiest way to enter formulas. You can also type numbers, arithmetical operators (+, -, *, /, ^), parentheses, and Excel functions with their arguments.

Reference: Introduced in Chapter 3, used in Case Studies 3 through 19

See Appendix D for some of the most useful formulas.

Appendix B

Notation

This book uses formatting conventions to clarify the descriptions.

Excel techniques

The name of an Excel technique is in **_Bold Italics_**. For example, "Use **_Goal Seek_** to find how much they need to save each year." Anything in bold italics you can look up in Appendix A.

Commands and files

A prompt, keyboard key, or selectable word or phrase that appears in a menu, toolbar, palette, or dialog window is **Bold**. Names of example Excel files are also bold.

For a sequence of commands, the symbol **>** separates successive selections, such as menu options. For example, "**Format > Cells > Alignment > Wrap text**" means to pull down the **Format** menu at the top of the screen, select **Cells**, click on the **Alignment** tab, and check the **Wrap text** box. First in the sequence is always a menu name or a tab on the Excel ribbon. This shorthand is quicker to follow than an instruction such as, "Select Copy under the Edit menu."

Formulas

A formula or anything that could be part of a formula, such as a function, text, numbers, or labels, is in a sans serif font, such as this. An Excel function is in ALL CAPS.

Sometimes a formula includes phrases that describe what appears in general, rather than actual, text. These phrases are in _italics_. For example, here is the function that computes loan payments:

PMT(_interest rate, number of periods, present value, future value, type_)

Descriptive formulas

Descriptive notation expresses a formula. This tells you which cells to click when entering the formula, making the formula easier to understand and use elsewhere. Consider the following cells of a spreadsheet, for example:

	A	B	C	D
1		income	expense	balance
2	start			$10,000
3	Jan	$ 1,000	$ 2,000	$ 9,000
4	Feb	$ 3,000	$ 1,000	$ 11,000
5	Mar	$ 5,000	$ 4,000	$ 12,000
6	Apr	$ 6,000	$ 2,000	$ 16,000
7	May	$ 5,000	$ 6,000	$ 15,000
8	Jun	$ 10,000	$ 3,000	$ 22,000

The formula for the balance each month starts with the previous balance, adds the income, and subtracts the expense. Here is its descriptive notation:

balance: =*balance* previous + *income* - *expense*

This tells you to enter the formula for the balance by clicking on the balance in the previous row, and the income and expense in this row. Column or row names are italicized. Everything else, except the word "previous," is entered as written. Here is what the entered formula will look like in D3:

=D2 + B3 - C3

Excel versions

Most of the techniques are standard across recent versions of Excel. In the few exceptions, the book gives Windows instructions for Excel 2003 or earlier, followed by the Macintosh instructions in [brackets] or Excel 2007 in {braces}.

Appendix C

Decision questionnaire

This questionnaire walks you through some of the questions you need to ask yourself when you start thinking about your decision. The blank form is in Chapter 1. You can also download it (MS Word format) from:

www.decisionspreadsheets.com/simplespreadsheets.html,

so that you can print out as many copies as you need.

Following are several examples of completed questionnaires from the case studies.

What are you trying to decide? Write a question you are trying to answer.
Which apartment should I choose? (Case Study 8)

How will you measure success? List all of the criteria as quantitatively as possible, but remember the subjective considerations as well.
Minimize rent, maximize square footage, have at least two bedrooms plus a room to use as an office, and have exercise facilities (prefer a pool); more is better.

What are the alternatives? This might be a list of options or a quantity.
Vista de Nada, Clark Gables, Stilted Manor

What do you know? List only items that affect your measure of success.
Rent, square footage, number of bedrooms and dens, types of exercise facilities (Note: Other considerations are equivalent for these alternatives and so are not listed.)

What don't you know, but can learn. You'll need to do some research.
Relative preference among the criteria; must decide this case-by-case while working through the decision

What don't you know, but can control. Vary to see how they change your success.
Nothing

What don't you know and can't control. Vary these to see how well you can adapt.
Nothing

What are you trying to decide? Write a question you are trying to answer.
Which car is the best value? (Case Study 10)

How will you measure success? List all of the criteria as quantitatively as possible, but remember the subjective considerations as well.
Maximize value while minimizing cost. Value is based on the following considerations: warranty, consumer rating, crash test, engine displacement, seating capacity, luggage capacity, highway mileage, engine type, parking assist, driving pleasure, and appearance.

What are the alternatives? This might be a list of options or a quantity.
Zigzag, Scooter, Luxo, Mastodon, and Pocket

What do you know? List only items that affect your measure of success.
Quantities for all of the considerations that go into the value, including the subjective ones, for each of the cars

What don't you know, but can learn? You'll need to do some research.
Must think about and weight the various considerations

What don't you know, but can control? Vary to see how they change success.
Nothing

What don't you know and can't control? Vary to see how well you can adapt.
Nothing

What are you trying to decide? Write a question you are trying to answer.
Should I buy a house or rent an apartment? (Case Study 13)

How will you measure success? List all of the criteria as quantitatively as possible, but remember the subjective considerations as well.
Compare the present value of the total net costs over five years. I want to minimize this, but balance the difference against subjective considerations.

What are the alternatives? This might be a list of options, or a quantity.
Buy a house with a fixed rate mortgage, and sell after five years. Rent an apartment for five years.

What do you know? List only items that affect your measure of success.
Cost of the house Monthly rent of the apartment Loan rates and terms Typical rent increases

What don't you know, but can learn? You'll need to do some research.
Cost to sell the house Apartment deposit amount Percentage value to use for present value

What don't you know, but can control? Vary to see how they change success.
Years spent living in the house or apartment

What don't you know and can't control? Vary to see how well you can adapt.
Annual increase in the value of the house Actual future rent increases

What are you trying to decide? Write a question you are trying to answer.
Pension or lump sum? (Case Study 14)
How will you measure success? List all of the criteria as quantitatively as possible, but remember the subjective considerations as well.
Whichever produces the most income over a lifetime (present value)
What are the alternatives? This might be a list of options or a quantity.
Take a lifetime monthly pension or a lump sum immediately upon retirement.
What do you know? List only items that affect your measure of success.
Payment schedule for the pension
What don't you know, but can learn? You'll need to do some research.
Lump sum amount (can calculate)
What don't you know, but can control? Vary to see how they change success.
Retirement age
What don't you know and can't control? Vary to see how well you can adapt.
How long I'll live

| **What are you trying to decide?** Write a question you are trying to answer. |
| Which medical insurance plan? (Case Study 16) |

| **How will you measure success?** List all of the criteria as quantitatively as possible, but remember the subjective considerations as well. |
| Minimum total cost of insurance plus out-of-pocket costs for typical, expected, or potential annual medical expenses |

| **What are the alternatives?** This might be a list of options or a quantity. |
| Choice A, Choice B, Choice C, or no insurance |

| **What do you know?** List only items that affect your measure of success. |
| The deductible amount, the percentage paid after the deductible is met, the maximum out-of-pocket, and the annual cost of each plan |

| **What don't you know, but can learn?** You'll need to do some research. |
| Typical medical expenses each year |

| **What don't you know, but can control?** Vary to see how they change success. |
| Nothing |

| **What don't you know and can't control?** Vary to see how well you can adapt. |
| Medical expenditures required in future years |

What are you trying to decide? Write a question you are trying to answer.
Are we saving enough for our child's college education? (Case Studies 1 and 17)

How will you measure success? List all of the criteria as quantitatively as possible, but remember the subjective considerations as well.
The amount saved equals at least the future cost of four years of college when the child turns 18.

What are the alternatives? This might be a list of options or a quantity.
The amount to put into the college fund each year

What do you know? List only items that affect your measure of success.
Current cost of four years at the college of choice

What don't you know, but can learn? You'll need to do some research.
Nothing

What don't you know, but can control? Vary to see how they change success.
Amount added to the fund each year How this amount increases over the years

What don't you know and can't control? Vary to see how well you can adapt.
Increase in the cost of college Investment returns

What are you trying to decide? Write a question you are trying to answer.
Can I afford to retire? (Case Studies 18, 19)

How will you measure success? List all of the criteria as quantitatively as possible, but remember the subjective considerations as well.
Taking into account all future income, assets, and spending, the money will not run out during our lifetimes.

What are the alternatives? This might be a list of options, or a quantity.
Retire later. Retire now, but adjust spending or income to ensure the money lasts.

What do you know? List only items that affect your measure of success.
Current ages, assets, future expected income and mortgage expenses

What don't you know, but can learn? You'll need to do some research.
Future taxes (can estimate; remember money taken from IRAs or 401(k)s is taxable)

What don't you know, but can control? Vary to see how they change success.
Annual spending apart from mortgage and taxes Post-retirement income (to some extent)

What don't you know and can't control? Vary to see how well you can adapt.
Inflation, investment returns, fluctuation in returns, how long we will live

Appendix D

Useful formulas

Annual growth or inflation

Uses	Model investment growth, inflation, and price or wage increases.
Inputs	*growth rate* (per year), *starting amount*
Each row is	a year
Output	new *amount* for each year in the future
First row	=*starting amount*
Other rows	=*amount* previous * (1+*growth rate*)
Introduced	Chapter 5
Used	Case Studies 5, 11, 12, 13, 17, 19

Current assets from income and expenditures

Uses	Keep a running total of assets with deposits and withdrawals, such as a bank account, retirement savings, or business proceeds.
Inputs	*initial amount*, all *deposit*s and *withdrawal*s in chronological order
Each row is	a deposit, withdrawal, or both
Output	new *amount* following each deposit and/or withdrawal
First row	=*initial amount*
Other rows	=*amount* previous + *deposit* - *withdrawal*
Introduced	Chapter 5
Used	Chapter 5, Case Study 4

Ditto or "same as above"

Uses	Copy cells down a column or across a row so that any changes to the original are reflected in the copy.
Inputs	*original amount*
Output	copied *amount*
First row	*original amount*
Other rows	=*amount* previous
Introduced	Chapter 5
Used	Case Study 11

Counting or incrementing

Uses	Make a sequential list, such as year or age, that changes if you change the starting value.
Inputs	*first number*
Each row is	an incremental increase, such as another year
Output	incremented *amount*
First row	*first number*
Other rows	=*amount* previous + 1
Introduced	Chapter 5
Used	Case Studies 5, 11, 14, 15, 17, and 18

Running Total

Uses	Accumulate totals over time, for example, costs, sales, income, or time expended.
Inputs	a list of *amounts*, such as monthly profit
Each row is	an accumulated item or a year, month, or other period of time
Output	cumulative *total* for each row
First row	=starting *amount*
Other rows	*total* previous + *amount*
Introduced	Chapter 5
Used	Chapter 5, Case Studies 12 and 13

Copy of a column (or row)

Uses	Copy row (or column) headers so that they change with changes in the original.
Inputs	the original *column*
Output	the *copied column*
All cells	=*column*
Introduced	Chapter 5
Used	Case Studies 8, 9, 16, and 18
Note	Rows are similar, but AutoFill across

Present value of a future amount

Uses	Compare the value of money to be spent or received in the future (such as the sale of your house) with money to be spent or received now.
Inputs	the future *amount*, assumed *interest rate*
Each row is	a year in the future
Output	*present value* of the *amount* for each future year
First row	*amount*
Other rows	=*present value* previous/(1+*interest rate*)
Introduced	Chapter 5

Present value multiplier

Uses	Compute the present value of an income or expenditure stream (see below); convert multiple amounts to present value simply by multiplying.
Inputs	assumed *interest rate*
Each row is	a year in the future
Output	the *present value* of a future dollar for each year in the future
First row	$1.00
Other rows	=*present value* previous/(1+*interest rate*)
Introduced	Chapter 5
Used	Case Study 13, Case Studies 14 and 15 (see below)

Present value of a future stream of money

Uses	Compute the present value of a future income or expenditure stream.
Inputs	*amount* for each year, *present value multiplier* (see above) for each year
Each row is	a year in the future
Output	the total present value of the stream
Formula	=SUMPRODUCT(*amount* column, *present value multiplier* column)
Used	Case Studies 14 and 15

Loan payments

Uses	Compute monthly payments on house, car, or other loans.
Inputs	annual *interest rate*, *loan length* in years, *amount* of loan
Output	the monthly payment on the loan
Formula	=-PMT(*interest rate*/12, *loan length**12, *amount*)
Introduced	Chapters 7 and 8
Used	Case Studies 6, 11, 12, and 13

Loan interest payments

Uses	Compute home mortgage interest payments for tax deduction.
Inputs	annual *interest rate*, *loan length* in years, *amount* of loan
Each row is	a *month* since inception of the loan
Output	the portion of the payment credited to interest, for each *month*
Formula	=-IPMT(*interest rate*/12, *month*, *loan length**12, *amount*)
Introduced	Chapter 8
Used	Case Study 6

Loan principal payments

Uses	Compute the amount of the loan paid off each month.
Inputs	annual *interest rate, loan length* in years, *amount* of loan
Each row is	a *month* since inception of the loan
Output	the portion of the payment credited to principal, for each *month*
First row	=-PPMT(*interest rate*/12, *month, loan length**12, *amount*)
Introduced	Chapter 8
Used	Case Studies 6, 12 13

Loan payoff

Uses	Compute amount remaining on a loan, for example, to compute home equity.
Inputs	annual *interest rate, loan length* in years, *amount* of loan
Each row is	a *month* since inception of the loan
Output	*amount* owing for each *month*
First row	=*amount of loan*
Other rows	=*amount* previous + PPMT(*interest rate*/12, *month, loan length**12, *amount of loan*)
Introduced	Chapter 8
Used	Case Studies 12 and 13

Random outcome based on a probability

Uses	Randomly assign a value based on a probability, to look at representative possible outcomes under uncertainty.
Inputs	*probability* (between 0 and 1 inclusive) that an event will occur, values representing the *outcome if the event occurs* and the *outcome if it does not*
Output	one or the other of the two outcomes
Formula	=IF(RAND( ) < *probability, outcome if the event occurs, outcome if it does not*)
Introduced	Chapter 14
Used	Chapter 14

Random normal outcome

Uses	Randomly generate a representative outcome of some value that is normally distributed. For example, this could approximate representative investment growth.
Inputs	*Mean* (average), *standard deviation*
Output	representative outcome
Formula	=NORMINV(RAND( ), *mean*, *standard deviation*)
Introduced	Chapter 14

Random outcome between minimum and maximum

Uses	Randomly generate a representative outcome of some value that is uniformly distributed between the smallest and largest possible values.
Inputs	*minimum*, *maximum*
Output	random number between minimum and maximum
Formula	=*minimum* + (*maximum* - *minimum*)*RAND( )
Introduced	Chapter 14
Used	Case Study 19

Multiple criteria, normalize scores

Uses	Compare alternatives when there are multiple criteria. Put each criterion on a common scale so that the scores can be compared across criteria.
Inputs	*scores* for each alternative for each criterion, arranged in a table with rows being criteria and columns being alternatives; *best* and *worst* possible scores for each criterion
Each row is	one of the criteria
Output	normalized scores (from 0 to 1, with 1 being best) for each alternative for each criterion, arranged in a table with rows being criteria and columns being alternatives
Formula	=(*score* - *worst*)/(*best* - *worst*)
Introduced	Chapter 10
Used	Case Studies 9 and 10

Multiple criteria, weighted total

Uses	Compare alternatives when there are multiple criteria. Get a single score for each alternative, taking into account the relative importance of each criterion.
Inputs	*normalized scores* arranged in a table with rows being criteria and columns being alternatives (see above); relative *weights* for each criterion, totaling 100%
Each row is	one of the criteria
Output	weighted score for each alternative
Formula	=SUMPRODUCT(*weights* column, *normalized scores* column)
Introduced	Chapter 10
Used	Case Studies 9 and 10

Proportional allocation

Uses	Withdraw money from various funds in proportion to the money in each fund.
Inputs	*Amount* to be withdrawn, amount in the *fund*, *total* amount in all funds.
Formula	=(*fund*/*total*)*amount
Introduced	Case Study 18
Used	Case Study 18

Bonus formulas

These were not covered in the book, but you may wish to explore them on your own if you need to look up values in tables, especially if you want to find intermediate values between the ones in the table. You can use them, for example, to estimate future income taxes using the tax tables.

Look up rate of change

Uses	Estimate in-between values from a two-column table (see below).
Inputs	a table array consisting of two columns with the first column in increasing order
Output	a third column containing rates of change
All rows but the last	= (*value in second column* next - *value in second column*)/(*value in first column* next - *value in first column*)
Last row	not used

Look up in-between values (interpolate)

Uses	Estimate in-between values from a two-column table.
Inputs	*value to look up* (no larger than the last value in the first column), a *table* array consisting of the original two columns with the first column in increasing order and a third column containing the rates of change (see above), such as a tax table
Output	estimated result
Formula	=VLOOKUP(*value to look up*, *table*, 2) + (*value to look up* -VLOOKUP(*value to look up*, *table*, 1)) * VLOOKUP(*value to look up*, *table*, 3)

Appendix E

Recommended books

There are many books that cover the mechanics of using Excel. Consider having one as a reference, to clarify the basics in more depth and to introduce you to the many features of Excel that are beyond the scope of this book. Check to see that it's written for your version and that it has a good, meaty discussion of formulas and functions. There are several thorough, popular series from which to choose. The choice is just a personal preference for style.

The books listed below help you make decisions.

Smart Choices:
A Practical Guide to Making Better Life Decisions
John S. Hammond, Ralph L. Keeney and Howard Raiffa
Broadway Books
1999
242 pages

Smart Choices is a very helpful, easy-to-read, and non-technical guide to the decision process. It includes many examples that help you think through your decisions before you analyze them. There is emphasis on the subjective aspects of decision-making, including psychological traps and risk tolerance. The Even Swap method (used in Chapter 10 and Case Study 8) was developed by the authors and is described in their book. Although the book uses no spreadsheets, I highly recommend it for its guidance on defining the problem, objectives, alternatives, and consequences.

Microsoft Excel Data Analysis and Business Modeling

Wayne L. Winston
Microsoft Press
2004
602 pages

Learn about the full range of Excel features and techniques for making decisions, with examples on applying them. You find many of these techniques only here. There are many exercises with practice files on an included CD. The examples are interesting, many related to baseball. The emphasis is on data analysis, so it is most useful if you have collected a lot of data and want to understand what it all means. There are a lot of statistics, but they are all presented in a clear manner with examples. There is also a version of this book for Excel 2007.

Strategic Decision Making: Multiobjective Decision Analysis with Spreadsheets

Craig W. Kirkwood
Duxbury Press
1997
345 pages

Learn more about comparing apples and oranges. This book starts with normalized scores and weighted totals and takes it from there, taking into account uncertainty, constraints, risk aversion, and dependencies, with emphasis on understanding and mathematically describing preferences. It includes many business decision examples and exercises. This is the most technical/mathematical of the recommended books, but well worth the effort.

Index

HEY, WHERE'S THE CD?

You just saved $5.00. You can get all of the example spreadsheets free from:

www.decisionspreadsheets.com/simplespreadsheets.html

If you *really* want a CD, you can get one for the cost of shipping and handling. Send $5 cash, check, or money order to:

City Shore Press
3646 Long Beach Blvd., Suite 222
Long Beach, CA 90807

Printed in the United States
123088LV00003B/17/P